The FOUNDATIONS Companion Workbook

From Theory to Application:
Scales, Chords, Intervals & Rhythmic Fluency

The FOUNDATIONS Companion Workbook

From Theory to Application:
Scales, Chords, Intervals & Rhythmic Fluency

by Rick Alexander
Edited by Tara Alexander

3T Publishing, LLC
2026

3T PUBLISHING

ISBN: 978-1-971161-02-0

First Edition: 01-10-2026
Cover Design by Trinity Alexander
Edited by Tara Alexander

For permissions, licensing inquiries, or bulk educational use, please contact:
contact@3tpublishing.com

3T Publishing
Kenosha, Wi 53142

LEGAL DISCLAIMER

This publication is intended solely for educational and informational purposes. The material presented in this book is based on the author's personal experience, study, and understanding of the subject matter. The author is not a certified instructor, licensed professional, medical provider, therapist, or formally trained expert in this field. All explanations, recommendations, exercises, methods, and examples reflect the author's own interpretation and are provided in good faith with the hope that they may support the reader's learning.

While every effort has been made to ensure the accuracy and completeness of the information contained herein, the author and publisher make no representations, guarantees, or warranties, express or implied, regarding the accuracy, reliability, applicability, or suitability of the content. Information may contain unintentional errors, omissions, or variations in interpretation. Readers are encouraged to verify information independently and to seek guidance from a qualified instructor, music professional, or relevant specialist when appropriate.

Physical and Vocal Activities

Certain sections of this book include optional exercises involving singing, humming, vocalization, or placing a hand on the throat to feel vibrations while producing sound. These activities are intended only as simple, introductory learning tools. Users should perform them gently, within personal comfort levels, and discontinue immediately if any discomfort, strain, dizziness, or pain occurs. Individuals with medical, vocal, or physical conditions, or any concerns regarding these activities, should consult a qualified professional before attempting them.

Instrument Use and Practice Sheets

The included practice sheets, ear-training exercises, and instrumental activities are intended for general skill development and are not a substitute for formal instruction. The author and publisher are not responsible for any injury, strain, hearing discomfort, equipment damage, or negative outcomes arising from instrument use, practice routines, or technique. Users should follow safe practice habits, proper posture, and appropriate volume levels and should seek professional instruction for personalized guidance.

Ear Training and Emotional/Interpretive Content

Descriptions of interval qualities, emotional associations, or subjective listening responses represent the author's personal understanding and artistic interpretation. Individual perception may vary. No guarantee is made that readers will experience identical results or interpretations.

Assumption of Risk and Limitation of Liability

By using this publication, the reader acknowledges and accepts that all activities, including but not limited to vocal exercises, physical sensations (such as touching the throat), instrumental practice, written exercises, and interpretive listening, are voluntary and undertaken at their own risk. The author and publisher shall not be held liable for any losses, injuries, damages, or adverse outcomes arising directly or indirectly from the use, misuse, or interpretation of the material in this publication.

All content is provided "as is," without warranty of any kind.

3T Publishing
Kenosha, Wi 53142

Preface / About This Workbook

Congratulations on taking the next step in your musical journey. This companion workbook was designed to build upon the concepts introduced in FOUNDATIONS: The Building Blocks of Understanding Music Theory, Practicing & Playing.

While the main FOUNDATIONS book develops understanding through explanation and guided examples, this workbook transforms that knowledge into skill through repetition, structure, and active engagement. It's more than review, it's a hands-on training manual designed for both classroom and individual study.

Each section focuses on applying what you've learned, reinforcing both visual and auditory memory through reading, writing, and playing. The content is structured for gradual skill-building, with multiple copies of each worksheet to allow consistent, repeated practice, the key to true musical mastery.

Whether you're a student, teacher, or self-taught musician, this workbook offers a system that connects theory to practice, knowledge to performance, and understanding to creativity.

How to Use This Workbook

This workbook is designed to be used alongside, and is organized to reflect the same learning sequence as *FOUNDATIONS: The Building Blocks of Understanding Music Theory, Practicing & Playing*.

If you do not already have the instructional text, it is available at: 3TPublishing.com/foundations

Scan the code above to access the instructional text and related learning resources.

Each section may be studied in sequence or used independently as a focused skill module.

Here's how to get the most from it:

1. **Read, Write, Play:**
   Begin each section by reviewing the concepts in your textbook or notes, then move immediately to writing and playing exercises. The act of writing reinforces retention, while playing transforms knowledge into intuition.

2. **Repeat for Mastery:**
   Each worksheet is provided in ten identical copies to encourage repetition. True fluency comes from doing the same skill multiple times in varied contexts.

3. **Use Both Instruments:**
   Exercises include notation, piano, and guitar visualizations. Work through both, seeing how theory appears across instruments builds multi-dimensional understanding.

4. **Track Your Progress:**
   Use the Practice Planner and Weekly Goals pages to plan and reflect on your sessions. Small, consistent practice leads to steady growth.

5. **Teachers & Instructors:**
   These pages are classroom-ready. Instructors can assign specific worksheet sets as weekly practice material, group study, or assessment tools.

Practice Planner & Weekly Goals

To help structure your learning, this workbook includes a Practice Planner Worksheet (adapted from Chapter 7 of FOUNDATIONS) and Weekly Goal Pages.

How to Use the Practice Planner

- Set Focus Areas: Choose the sections you'll practice (e.g., Key Signatures, Intervals, Rhythm).
- Schedule Time Blocks: Plan consistent sessions rather than long, infrequent marathons.
- Reflect Weekly: Write short notes about what improved and what needs more attention.

How to Use the Weekly Goals Pages

- Identify three achievable targets per week (for example: memorize all sharp key signatures, master perfect intervals, or improve metronome timing at 80 BPM).
- At the end of the week, rate your progress and set new goals.
- Use these as checkpoints to measure your consistency and improvement.

Structured Study Plans for 3, 6, and 12 Months of Growth

These guided schedules are designed for learners who prefer a structured, step-by-step approach to mastering the material in The FOUNDATIONS Companion Workbook.

Each plan outlines suggested goals, timelines, and focus areas, offering a flexible path that can be followed as written or customized to your own pace.

Whether you're dedicating a few minutes a day or several hours a week, consistency and reflection are key to long-term progress

3-Month Intensive Plan (Foundational Skills Focus)
Goal: Establish a solid foundation in music reading, key signatures, intervals, and rhythm.

Recommended Schedule:
Practice 5–6 days per week, 20–40 minutes per session.
Use one Weekly Goal Page per week and one Practice Planner page per day.

Month	Focus Area	Weekly Objectives
Month 1	Staff Notation & Basic Reading	Review clefs, note placement, and simple rhythms. Practice reading & writing one octave of major scale notes daily.
Month 2	Key Signatures & Scales	Memorize all sharp and flat key signatures. Write out each major scale and its corresponding notes. Begin identifying chords by formula (I–IV–V).
Month 3	Intervals & Timing	Practice intervals on staff, guitar, and piano. Develop rhythmic control with metronome work at 60–100 BPM. Conclude with short written compositions using learned keys.

End-of-Plan Milestone:
You should be able to identify and write all major key signatures, construct diatonic chords, and play them cleanly on guitar or piano at a slow, steady tempo.

Tips for Staying on Track:

Keep a Practice Journal: Briefly note your accomplishments and struggles after each session

Record Monthly Check-Ins: Use your phone or notebook to log how your playing feels, not just how it sounds.

Celebrate Milestones: Small wins (like memorizing all keys) are major progress markers.

Adjust as Needed: These schedules are flexible. Progress at your pace, not your pressure.

6-Month Development Plan (Expanding Skills & Application)
Goal: Build fluency in applying theory concepts to playing, improvising, and writing.

Recommended Schedule:
4–5 practice days per week, 30–45 minutes each.
Alternate between review and creative application days.

Month	Focus Area	Weekly Objectives
Month 1-2	Notation & Keys	Reinforce clefs, time signatures, and scales. Add natural minor scales and relative majors.
Month 3-4	Intervals & Chords	Expand to compound intervals and seventh chords. Map them on both piano and guitar.
Month 5	Timing & Rhythm	Work on rhythm reading and subdivisions. Play with a metronome and practice switching between 4/4, 3/4, and 6/8 time.
Month 6	Application& Composition	Create 4–8 bar progressions using multiple keys. Write and play short melodies, focusing on connecting theory to creative output.

End-of-Plan Milestone:
You'll have the ability to read and write in all major and minor keys, recognize intervals by sound and sight, and perform with reliable rhythmic accuracy.

12-Month Mastery Plan (Comprehensive Year of Musicianship)
Goal: Achieve complete fluency across theory, application, and performance.

Recommended Schedule:
3–5 sessions per week, 45–60 minutes each.
Divide the year into four quarters of focused development.

Quarter	Focus Area	Weekly Objectives
Quarter 1	Core Theory Foundations	Review notation, intervals, and major scales. Learn circle of fifths by memory. Begin creating chord charts.
Quarter 2	Advanced Keys & Harmony	Study minor keys, modes, and diatonic harmony. Build chord progressions and analyze familiar songs.
Quarter 3	Application & Performance	Apply theory to your instrument. Record yourself playing scales, arpeggios, and progressions in all keys. Begin improvisation exercises.
Quarter 4	Creativity & Integration	Compose a short piece or arrangement demonstrating multiple key changes, rhythmic variation, and expressive dynamics. Reflect on growth and set new goals.

End-of-Plan Milestone:
You'll demonstrate confident musicianship — fluent in notation, keys, chords, intervals, and rhythm , and be capable of composing or performing independently with theoretical accuracy and musical expressiveness.

Table of Contents

Practice Planners

Practice Planner Worksheet
Use this sheet to structure your daily practice sessions.

Date: _____

Goal for Today: (What are you focusing on? A specific scale? Chord shape? Song section?)

_____

_____

_____

1. Review (5 Minutes)
What did you learn last session? Write it, say it aloud, and refresh your memory.
Example: C Major scale formula (W-W-H-W-W-W-H), or review yesterday's riff.

Review Topic(s):

_____

_____

_____

2. Declarative Practice (10 Minutes)
Mental learning, away from your instrument. Study theory, notes, scale shapes, chord formulas, etc.
Write it out, say it aloud, and make sure you understand the "why."

Focus Concept:_____

Write what you learned below

_____

_____

_____

3. Procedural Practice (10 Minutes)
Muscle memory, with your instrument. Practice finger placement, accuracy, technique, and clarity.
Play it slowly and cleanly until you get it right 3x in a row, then speed up.

Skill / Exercise:_____

Did you play it clean 3x?   Yes   No (Try again tomorrow)

4. Free Play / Exploration (As Long As You Like)
Let loose! Improvise, write, or play a favorite song. Apply what you've learned.
What did you explore or enjoy today?_____

Reflections (Optional) What clicked today? What still needs work?_____

Cross out when complete: Review   Declarative   Procedural   Free Play

Practice Planner Worksheet
Use this sheet to structure your daily practice sessions.

Date: _____

Goal for Today: (What are you focusing on? A specific scale? Chord shape? Song section?)

_____

_____

_____

1. Review (5 Minutes)
What did you learn last session? Write it, say it aloud, and refresh your memory.
Example: C Major scale formula (W-W-H-W-W-W-H), or review yesterday's riff.

Review Topic(s):

_____

_____

_____

2. Declarative Practice (10 Minutes)
Mental learning, away from your instrument. Study theory, notes, scale shapes, chord formulas, etc.
Write it out, say it aloud, and make sure you understand the "why."

Focus Concept:_____

Write what you learned below

_____

_____

_____

3. Procedural Practice (10 Minutes)
Muscle memory, with your instrument. Practice finger placement, accuracy, technique, and clarity.
Play it slowly and cleanly until you get it right 3x in a row, then speed up.

Skill / Exercise:_____

Did you play it clean 3x?   Yes   No (Try again tomorrow)

4. Free Play / Exploration (As Long As You Like)
Let loose! Improvise, write, or play a favorite song. Apply what you've learned.
What did you explore or enjoy today?_____

Reflections (Optional) What clicked today? What still needs work?_____

Cross out when complete: Review   Declarative   Procedural   Free Play

Practice Planner Worksheet

Use this sheet to structure your daily practice sessions.

Date: _____

Goal for Today: (What are you focusing on? A specific scale? Chord shape? Song section?)

_____

_____

_____

1. Review (5 Minutes)

What did you learn last session? Write it, say it aloud, and refresh your memory.
Example: C Major scale formula (W-W-H-W-W-W-H), or review yesterday's riff.

Review Topic(s):

_____

_____

_____

2. Declarative Practice (10 Minutes)

Mental learning, away from your instrument. Study theory, notes, scale shapes, chord formulas, etc.
Write it out, say it aloud, and make sure you understand the "why."

Focus Concept:_____

Write what you learned below

_____

_____

_____

3. Procedural Practice (10 Minutes)

Muscle memory, with your instrument. Practice finger placement, accuracy, technique, and clarity.
Play it slowly and cleanly until you get it right 3x in a row, then speed up.

Skill / Exercise:_____

Did you play it clean 3x?   Yes   No (Try again tomorrow)

4. Free Play / Exploration (As Long As You Like)

Let loose! Improvise, write, or play a favorite song. Apply what you've learned.
What did you explore or enjoy today?_____

Reflections (Optional) What clicked today? What still needs work?_____

Cross out when complete: Review   Declarative   Procedural   Free Play

Practice Planner Worksheet
Use this sheet to structure your daily practice sessions.

Date: _____

Goal for Today: (What are you focusing on? A specific scale? Chord shape? Song section?)

_____

_____

_____

1. Review (5 Minutes)
What did you learn last session? Write it, say it aloud, and refresh your memory.
Example: C Major scale formula (W-W-H-W-W-W-H), or review yesterday's riff.

Review Topic(s):

_____

_____

_____

2. Declarative Practice (10 Minutes)
Mental learning, away from your instrument. Study theory, notes, scale shapes, chord formulas, etc.
Write it out, say it aloud, and make sure you understand the "why."

Focus Concept:_____

Write what you learned below

_____

_____

_____

3. Procedural Practice (10 Minutes)
Muscle memory, with your instrument. Practice finger placement, accuracy, technique, and clarity.
Play it slowly and cleanly until you get it right 3x in a row, then speed up.

Skill / Exercise:_____

Did you play it clean 3x?   Yes   No (Try again tomorrow)

4. Free Play / Exploration (As Long As You Like)
Let loose! Improvise, write, or play a favorite song. Apply what you've learned.
What did you explore or enjoy today?_____

Reflections (Optional) What clicked today? What still needs work?_____

Cross out when complete: Review   Declarative   Procedural   Free Play

Practice Planner Worksheet

Use this sheet to structure your daily practice sessions.

Date: _____

Goal for Today: (What are you focusing on? A specific scale? Chord shape? Song section?)

_____

_____

_____

1. Review (5 Minutes)

What did you learn last session? Write it, say it aloud, and refresh your memory.
Example: C Major scale formula (W-W-H-W-W-W-H), or review yesterday's riff.

Review Topic(s):

_____

_____

_____

2. Declarative Practice (10 Minutes)

Mental learning, away from your instrument. Study theory, notes, scale shapes, chord formulas, etc.
Write it out, say it aloud, and make sure you understand the "why."

Focus Concept:_____

Write what you learned below

_____

_____

_____

3. Procedural Practice (10 Minutes)

Muscle memory, with your instrument. Practice finger placement, accuracy, technique, and clarity.
Play it slowly and cleanly until you get it right 3x in a row, then speed up.

Skill / Exercise:_____

Did you play it clean 3x?   Yes   No (Try again tomorrow)

4. Free Play / Exploration (As Long As You Like)

Let loose! Improvise, write, or play a favorite song. Apply what you've learned.
What did you explore or enjoy today?_____

Reflections (Optional) What clicked today? What still needs work?_____

Cross out when complete: Review   Declarative   Procedural   Free Play

Practice Planner Worksheet

Use this sheet to structure your daily practice sessions.

Date: _____

Goal for Today: (What are you focusing on? A specific scale? Chord shape? Song section?)

_____

_____

_____

1. Review (5 Minutes)

What did you learn last session? Write it, say it aloud, and refresh your memory.
Example: C Major scale formula (W-W-H-W-W-W-H), or review yesterday's riff.

Review Topic(s):

_____

_____

_____

2. Declarative Practice (10 Minutes)

Mental learning, away from your instrument. Study theory, notes, scale shapes, chord formulas, etc.
Write it out, say it aloud, and make sure you understand the "why."

Focus Concept:_____

Write what you learned below

_____

_____

_____

3. Procedural Practice (10 Minutes)

Muscle memory, with your instrument. Practice finger placement, accuracy, technique, and clarity.
Play it slowly and cleanly until you get it right 3x in a row, then speed up.

Skill / Exercise:_____

Did you play it clean 3x?   Yes   No (Try again tomorrow)

4. Free Play / Exploration (As Long As You Like)

Let loose! Improvise, write, or play a favorite song. Apply what you've learned.
What did you explore or enjoy today?_____

Reflections (Optional) What clicked today? What still needs work?_____

Cross out when complete: Review   Declarative   Procedural   Free Play

Practice Planner Worksheet
Use this sheet to structure your daily practice sessions.

Date: _____

Goal for Today: (What are you focusing on? A specific scale? Chord shape? Song section?)

_____

_____

_____

1. Review (5 Minutes)
What did you learn last session? Write it, say it aloud, and refresh your memory.
Example: C Major scale formula (W-W-H-W-W-W-H), or review yesterday's riff.

Review Topic(s):

_____

_____

_____

2. Declarative Practice (10 Minutes)
Mental learning, away from your instrument. Study theory, notes, scale shapes, chord formulas, etc.
Write it out, say it aloud, and make sure you understand the "why."

Focus Concept:_____

Write what you learned below

_____

_____

_____

3. Procedural Practice (10 Minutes)
Muscle memory, with your instrument. Practice finger placement, accuracy, technique, and clarity.
Play it slowly and cleanly until you get it right 3x in a row, then speed up.

Skill / Exercise:_____

Did you play it clean 3x?   Yes   No (Try again tomorrow)

4. Free Play / Exploration (As Long As You Like)
Let loose! Improvise, write, or play a favorite song. Apply what you've learned.
What did you explore or enjoy today?_____

Reflections (Optional) What clicked today? What still needs work?_____

Cross out when complete: Review   Declarative   Procedural   Free Play

Practice Planner Worksheet

Use this sheet to structure your daily practice sessions.

Date: _____

Goal for Today: (What are you focusing on? A specific scale? Chord shape? Song section?)

_____

_____

_____

1. Review (5 Minutes)

What did you learn last session? Write it, say it aloud, and refresh your memory.
Example: C Major scale formula (W-W-H-W-W-W-H), or review yesterday's riff.

Review Topic(s):

_____

_____

_____

2. Declarative Practice (10 Minutes)

Mental learning, away from your instrument. Study theory, notes, scale shapes, chord formulas, etc.
Write it out, say it aloud, and make sure you understand the "why."

Focus Concept:_____

Write what you learned below

_____

_____

_____

3. Procedural Practice (10 Minutes)

Muscle memory, with your instrument. Practice finger placement, accuracy, technique, and clarity.
Play it slowly and cleanly until you get it right 3x in a row, then speed up.

Skill / Exercise:_____

Did you play it clean 3x?   Yes   No (Try again tomorrow)

4. Free Play / Exploration (As Long As You Like)

Let loose! Improvise, write, or play a favorite song. Apply what you've learned.
What did you explore or enjoy today?_____

Reflections (Optional) What clicked today? What still needs work?_____

Cross out when complete: Review   Declarative   Procedural   Free Play

10

Practice Planner Worksheet

Use this sheet to structure your daily practice sessions.

Date: _____

Goal for Today: (What are you focusing on? A specific scale? Chord shape? Song section?)

_____

_____

_____

1. Review (5 Minutes)

What did you learn last session? Write it, say it aloud, and refresh your memory.
Example: C Major scale formula (W-W-H-W-W-W-H), or review yesterday's riff.

Review Topic(s):

_____

_____

_____

2. Declarative Practice (10 Minutes)

Mental learning, away from your instrument. Study theory, notes, scale shapes, chord formulas, etc. Write it out, say it aloud, and make sure you understand the "why."

Focus Concept:_____

Write what you learned below

_____

_____

_____

3. Procedural Practice (10 Minutes)

Muscle memory, with your instrument. Practice finger placement, accuracy, technique, and clarity. Play it slowly and cleanly until you get it right 3x in a row, then speed up.

Skill / Exercise:_____

Did you play it clean 3x?   Yes   No (Try again tomorrow)

4. Free Play / Exploration (As Long As You Like)

Let loose! Improvise, write, or play a favorite song. Apply what you've learned.
What did you explore or enjoy today?_____

Reflections (Optional) What clicked today? What still needs work?_____

Cross out when complete: Review   Declarative   Procedural   Free Play

Practice Planner Worksheet
Use this sheet to structure your daily practice sessions.

Date: _____

Goal for Today: (What are you focusing on? A specific scale? Chord shape? Song section?)

_____

_____

_____

1. Review (5 Minutes)
What did you learn last session? Write it, say it aloud, and refresh your memory.
Example: C Major scale formula (W-W-H-W-W-W-H), or review yesterday's riff.

Review Topic(s):

_____

_____

_____

2. Declarative Practice (10 Minutes)
Mental learning, away from your instrument. Study theory, notes, scale shapes, chord formulas, etc.
Write it out, say it aloud, and make sure you understand the "why."

Focus Concept:_____

Write what you learned below

_____

_____

_____

3. Procedural Practice (10 Minutes)
Muscle memory, with your instrument. Practice finger placement, accuracy, technique, and clarity.
Play it slowly and cleanly until you get it right 3x in a row, then speed up.

Skill / Exercise:_____

Did you play it clean 3x?   Yes   No (Try again tomorrow)

4. Free Play / Exploration (As Long As You Like)
Let loose! Improvise, write, or play a favorite song. Apply what you've learned.
What did you explore or enjoy today?_____

Reflections (Optional) What clicked today? What still needs work?_____

Cross out when complete: Review   Declarative   Procedural   Free Play

Weekly Planners

From Planning to Progress: Turning Intent into Improvement

Use this page at the beginning of each week to set focused, achievable goals.

Your weekly targets should align with your daily practice sessions and the broader topics from FOUNDATIONS. Setting clear, realistic goals helps you track progress and celebrate improvement, both in understanding and performance.

WEEKLY GOAL PLANNER

Week of: _____

Instructor (if applicable): _____

Primary Focus for the Week:
(Examples: Sharps/Flats memorization, Major scale fluency, 16th-note timing, interval ear training)

_____

_____

Goal 1: Theory & Understanding
What concept or rule will you master this week?
(Example: Memorize circle of fifths, learn diatonic triads in minor keys.)

Goal: _____

Why it matters: _____

How will you measure success? _____

Progress Notes (End of Week):

☐ Achieved   ☐ Needs Review   ☐ Carry Forward

Goal 2: Technique & Application
What practical or instrument-based skill will you refine?
(Example: Play all major chords cleanly, practice scales at 80 BPM, smooth chord transitions.)

Goal: _____

Practice Focus: _____

How many days did you practice this skill? ☐ 1 ☐ 2 ☐ 3 ☐ 4 ☐ 5+

Progress Notes (End of Week):

☐ Achieved   ☐ Needs Review   ☐ Carry Forward

Goal 3: Creativity & Expression
How will you apply your learning creatively?
(Example: Write an 8-bar melody in G major, improvise using a pentatonic scale, record a rhythm pattern.)

Goal: _____

Activity or Project: _____

Progress Notes (End of Week):

☐ Achieved   ☐ Needs Review   ☐ Carry Forward

WEEKLY REFLECTION
Take a few minutes at the end of the week to think about your progress.

- What did you improve most?
- What was challenging?
- What new question or curiosity did this week spark?

Reflections:

_____

_____

_____

LOOKING AHEAD
Set an intention for next week.
(Example: "Next week, I'll focus on minor scales and new chord voicings.")

_____

_____

_____

From Planning to Progress: Turning Intent into Improvement

Use this page at the beginning of each week to set focused, achievable goals.

Your weekly targets should align with your daily practice sessions and the broader topics from FOUNDATIONS. Setting clear, realistic goals helps you track progress and celebrate improvement, both in understanding and performance.

WEEKLY GOAL PLANNER

Week of: _____

Instructor (if applicable): _____

Primary Focus for the Week:
(Examples: Sharps/Flats memorization, Major scale fluency, 16th-note timing, interval ear training)

_____

_____

Goal 1: Theory & Understanding
What concept or rule will you master this week?
(Example: Memorize circle of fifths, learn diatonic triads in minor keys.)

Goal: _____

Why it matters: _____

How will you measure success? _____

Progress Notes (End of Week):

☐ Achieved   ☐ Needs Review   ☐ Carry Forward

Goal 2: Technique & Application
What practical or instrument-based skill will you refine?
(Example: Play all major chords cleanly, practice scales at 80 BPM, smooth chord transitions.)

Goal: _____

Practice Focus: _____

How many days did you practice this skill? ☐ 1 ☐ 2 ☐ 3 ☐ 4 ☐ 5+

Progress Notes (End of Week):

☐ Achieved   ☐ Needs Review   ☐ Carry Forward

Goal 3: Creativity & Expression
How will you apply your learning creatively?
(Example: Write an 8-bar melody in G major, improvise using a pentatonic scale, record a rhythm pattern.)

Goal: _____

Activity or Project: _____

Progress Notes (End of Week):

☐ Achieved   ☐ Needs Review   ☐ Carry Forward

WEEKLY REFLECTION
Take a few minutes at the end of the week to think about your progress.

- What did you improve most?
- What was challenging?
- What new question or curiosity did this week spark?

Reflections:

_____

_____

_____

_____

LOOKING AHEAD
Set an intention for next week.
(Example: "Next week, I'll focus on minor scales and new chord voicings.")

_____

_____

_____

From Planning to Progress: Turning Intent into Improvement

Use this page at the beginning of each week to set focused, achievable goals.

Your weekly targets should align with your daily practice sessions and the broader topics from FOUNDATIONS. Setting clear, realistic goals helps you track progress and celebrate improvement, both in understanding and performance.

WEEKLY GOAL PLANNER

Week of: _____

Instructor (if applicable): _____

Primary Focus for the Week:
(Examples: Sharps/Flats memorization, Major scale fluency, 16th-note timing, interval ear training)

_____

_____

Goal 1: Theory & Understanding
What concept or rule will you master this week?
(Example: Memorize circle of fifths, learn diatonic triads in minor keys.)

Goal: _____

Why it matters: _____

How will you measure success? _____

Progress Notes (End of Week):

☐ Achieved   ☐ Needs Review   ☐ Carry Forward

Goal 2: Technique & Application
What practical or instrument-based skill will you refine?
(Example: Play all major chords cleanly, practice scales at 80 BPM, smooth chord transitions.)

Goal: _____

Practice Focus: _____

How many days did you practice this skill? ☐ 1 ☐ 2 ☐ 3 ☐ 4 ☐ 5+

Progress Notes (End of Week):

☐ Achieved   ☐ Needs Review   ☐ Carry Forward

Goal 3: Creativity & Expression
How will you apply your learning creatively?
(Example: Write an 8-bar melody in G major, improvise using a pentatonic scale, record a rhythm pattern.)

Goal: _____

Activity or Project: _____

Progress Notes (End of Week):

☐ Achieved   ☐ Needs Review   ☐ Carry Forward

WEEKLY REFLECTION
Take a few minutes at the end of the week to think about your progress.

- What did you improve most?
- What was challenging?
- What new question or curiosity did this week spark?

Reflections:

_____

_____

_____

_____

LOOKING AHEAD
Set an intention for next week.
(Example: "Next week, I'll focus on minor scales and new chord voicings.")

_____

_____

_____

From Planning to Progress: Turning Intent into Improvement

Use this page at the beginning of each week to set focused, achievable goals.

Your weekly targets should align with your daily practice sessions and the broader topics from FOUNDATIONS. Setting clear, realistic goals helps you track progress and celebrate improvement, both in understanding and performance.

WEEKLY GOAL PLANNER

Week of: _____

Instructor (if applicable): _____

Primary Focus for the Week:
(Examples: Sharps/Flats memorization, Major scale fluency, 16th-note timing, interval ear training)

_____

_____

Goal 1: Theory & Understanding
What concept or rule will you master this week?
(Example: Memorize circle of fifths, learn diatonic triads in minor keys.)

Goal: _____

Why it matters: _____

How will you measure success? _____

Progress Notes (End of Week):

☐ Achieved   ☐ Needs Review   ☐ Carry Forward

Goal 2: Technique & Application
What practical or instrument-based skill will you refine?
(Example: Play all major chords cleanly, practice scales at 80 BPM, smooth chord transitions.)

Goal: _____

Practice Focus: _____

How many days did you practice this skill? ☐ 1 ☐ 2 ☐ 3 ☐ 4 ☐ 5+

Progress Notes (End of Week):

☐ Achieved   ☐ Needs Review   ☐ Carry Forward

Goal 3: Creativity & Expression
How will you apply your learning creatively?
(Example: Write an 8-bar melody in G major, improvise using a pentatonic scale, record a rhythm pattern.)

Goal: _____

Activity or Project: _____

Progress Notes (End of Week):

☐ Achieved   ☐ Needs Review   ☐ Carry Forward

WEEKLY REFLECTION
Take a few minutes at the end of the week to think about your progress.

- What did you improve most?
- What was challenging?
- What new question or curiosity did this week spark?

Reflections:

_____

_____

_____

_____

LOOKING AHEAD
Set an intention for next week.
(Example: "Next week, I'll focus on minor scales and new chord voicings.")

_____

_____

_____

From Planning to Progress: Turning Intent into Improvement

Use this page at the beginning of each week to set focused, achievable goals.

Your weekly targets should align with your daily practice sessions and the broader topics from FOUNDATIONS. Setting clear, realistic goals helps you track progress and celebrate improvement, both in understanding and performance.

WEEKLY GOAL PLANNER

Week of: _____

Instructor (if applicable): _____

Primary Focus for the Week:
(Examples: Sharps/Flats memorization, Major scale fluency, 16th-note timing, interval ear training)

_____

_____

Goal 1: Theory & Understanding
What concept or rule will you master this week?
(Example: Memorize circle of fifths, learn diatonic triads in minor keys.)

Goal: _____

Why it matters: _____

How will you measure success? _____

Progress Notes (End of Week):

☐ Achieved   ☐ Needs Review   ☐ Carry Forward

Goal 2: Technique & Application
What practical or instrument-based skill will you refine?
(Example: Play all major chords cleanly, practice scales at 80 BPM, smooth chord transitions.)

Goal: _____

Practice Focus: _____

How many days did you practice this skill? ☐ 1 ☐ 2 ☐ 3 ☐ 4 ☐ 5+

Progress Notes (End of Week):

☐ Achieved ☐ Needs Review ☐ Carry Forward

Goal 3: Creativity & Expression
How will you apply your learning creatively?
(Example: Write an 8-bar melody in G major, improvise using a pentatonic scale, record a rhythm pattern.)

Goal: _____

Activity or Project: _____

Progress Notes (End of Week):

☐ Achieved ☐ Needs Review ☐ Carry Forward

WEEKLY REFLECTION
Take a few minutes at the end of the week to think about your progress.

- What did you improve most?
- What was challenging?
- What new question or curiosity did this week spark?

Reflections:

_____

_____

_____

LOOKING AHEAD
Set an intention for next week.
(Example: "Next week, I'll focus on minor scales and new chord voicings.")

_____

_____

_____

From Planning to Progress: Turning Intent into Improvement

Use this page at the beginning of each week to set focused, achievable goals.

Your weekly targets should align with your daily practice sessions and the broader topics from FOUNDATIONS. Setting clear, realistic goals helps you track progress and celebrate improvement, both in understanding and performance.

WEEKLY GOAL PLANNER

Week of: _____

Instructor (if applicable): _____

Primary Focus for the Week:
(Examples: Sharps/Flats memorization, Major scale fluency, 16th-note timing, interval ear training)

_____

_____

Goal 1: Theory & Understanding
What concept or rule will you master this week?
(Example: Memorize circle of fifths, learn diatonic triads in minor keys.)

Goal: _____

Why it matters: _____

How will you measure success? _____

Progress Notes (End of Week):

☐ Achieved ☐ Needs Review ☐ Carry Forward

Goal 2: Technique & Application
What practical or instrument-based skill will you refine?
(Example: Play all major chords cleanly, practice scales at 80 BPM, smooth chord transitions.)

Goal: _____

Practice Focus: _____

How many days did you practice this skill? ☐ 1 ☐ 2 ☐ 3 ☐ 4 ☐ 5+

Progress Notes (End of Week):

☐ Achieved   ☐ Needs Review   ☐ Carry Forward

Goal 3: Creativity & Expression
How will you apply your learning creatively?
(Example: Write an 8-bar melody in G major, improvise using a pentatonic scale, record a rhythm pattern.)

Goal: _____

Activity or Project: _____

Progress Notes (End of Week):

☐ Achieved   ☐ Needs Review   ☐ Carry Forward

WEEKLY REFLECTION
Take a few minutes at the end of the week to think about your progress.

- What did you improve most?
- What was challenging?
- What new question or curiosity did this week spark?

Reflections:

_____

_____

_____

_____

LOOKING AHEAD
Set an intention for next week.
(Example: "Next week, I'll focus on minor scales and new chord voicings.")

_____

_____

_____

From Planning to Progress: Turning Intent into Improvement

Use this page at the beginning of each week to set focused, achievable goals.

Your weekly targets should align with your daily practice sessions and the broader topics from FOUNDATIONS. Setting clear, realistic goals helps you track progress and celebrate improvement, both in understanding and performance.

WEEKLY GOAL PLANNER

Week of: _____

Instructor (if applicable): _____

Primary Focus for the Week:
(Examples: Sharps/Flats memorization, Major scale fluency, 16th-note timing, interval ear training)

_____

_____

Goal 1: Theory & Understanding
What concept or rule will you master this week?
(Example: Memorize circle of fifths, learn diatonic triads in minor keys.)

Goal: _____

Why it matters: _____

How will you measure success? _____

Progress Notes (End of Week):

☐ Achieved   ☐ Needs Review   ☐ Carry Forward

Goal 2: Technique & Application
What practical or instrument-based skill will you refine?
(Example: Play all major chords cleanly, practice scales at 80 BPM, smooth chord transitions.)

Goal: _____

Practice Focus: _____

How many days did you practice this skill? ☐ 1 ☐ 2 ☐ 3 ☐ 4 ☐ 5+

Progress Notes (End of Week):

☐ Achieved ☐ Needs Review ☐ Carry Forward

Goal 3: Creativity & Expression
How will you apply your learning creatively?
(Example: Write an 8-bar melody in G major, improvise using a pentatonic scale, record a rhythm pattern.)

Goal: _____

Activity or Project: _____

Progress Notes (End of Week):

☐ Achieved ☐ Needs Review ☐ Carry Forward

WEEKLY REFLECTION
Take a few minutes at the end of the week to think about your progress.

- What did you improve most?
- What was challenging?
- What new question or curiosity did this week spark?

Reflections:

_____

_____

_____

_____

LOOKING AHEAD
Set an intention for next week.
(Example: "Next week, I'll focus on minor scales and new chord voicings.")

_____

_____

_____

From Planning to Progress: Turning Intent into Improvement

Use this page at the beginning of each week to set focused, achievable goals.

Your weekly targets should align with your daily practice sessions and the broader topics from FOUNDATIONS. Setting clear, realistic goals helps you track progress and celebrate improvement, both in understanding and performance.

WEEKLY GOAL PLANNER

Week of: _____

Instructor (if applicable): _____

Primary Focus for the Week:
(Examples: Sharps/Flats memorization, Major scale fluency, 16th-note timing, interval ear training)

_____

_____

Goal 1: Theory & Understanding
What concept or rule will you master this week?
(Example: Memorize circle of fifths, learn diatonic triads in minor keys.)

Goal: _____

Why it matters: _____

How will you measure success? _____

Progress Notes (End of Week):

☐ Achieved   ☐ Needs Review   ☐ Carry Forward

Goal 2: Technique & Application
What practical or instrument-based skill will you refine?
(Example: Play all major chords cleanly, practice scales at 80 BPM, smooth chord transitions.)

Goal: _____

Practice Focus: _____

How many days did you practice this skill? ☐ 1 ☐ 2 ☐ 3 ☐ 4 ☐ 5+

Progress Notes (End of Week):

☐ Achieved   ☐ Needs Review   ☐ Carry Forward

Goal 3: Creativity & Expression
How will you apply your learning creatively?
(Example: Write an 8-bar melody in G major, improvise using a pentatonic scale, record a rhythm pattern.)

Goal: _____

Activity or Project: _____

Progress Notes (End of Week):

☐ Achieved   ☐ Needs Review   ☐ Carry Forward

WEEKLY REFLECTION
Take a few minutes at the end of the week to think about your progress.

•   What did you improve most?
•   What was challenging?
•   What new question or curiosity did this week spark?

Reflections:

_____

_____

_____

_____

LOOKING AHEAD
Set an intention for next week.
(Example: "Next week, I'll focus on minor scales and new chord voicings.")

_____

_____

_____

From Planning to Progress: Turning Intent into Improvement

Use this page at the beginning of each week to set focused, achievable goals.

Your weekly targets should align with your daily practice sessions and the broader topics from FOUNDATIONS. Setting clear, realistic goals helps you track progress and celebrate improvement, both in understanding and performance.

WEEKLY GOAL PLANNER

Week of: _____

Instructor (if applicable): _____

Primary Focus for the Week:
(Examples: Sharps/Flats memorization, Major scale fluency, 16th-note timing, interval ear training)

_____

_____

Goal 1: Theory & Understanding
What concept or rule will you master this week?
(Example: Memorize circle of fifths, learn diatonic triads in minor keys.)

Goal: _____

Why it matters: _____

How will you measure success? _____

Progress Notes (End of Week):

☐ Achieved   ☐ Needs Review   ☐ Carry Forward

Goal 2: Technique & Application
What practical or instrument-based skill will you refine?
(Example: Play all major chords cleanly, practice scales at 80 BPM, smooth chord transitions.)

Goal: _____

Practice Focus: _____

How many days did you practice this skill? ☐ 1 ☐ 2 ☐ 3 ☐ 4 ☐ 5+

Progress Notes (End of Week):

☐ Achieved   ☐ Needs Review   ☐ Carry Forward

Goal 3: Creativity & Expression
How will you apply your learning creatively?
(Example: Write an 8-bar melody in G major, improvise using a pentatonic scale, record a rhythm pattern.)

Goal: _____

Activity or Project: _____

Progress Notes (End of Week):

☐ Achieved   ☐ Needs Review   ☐ Carry Forward

WEEKLY REFLECTION
Take a few minutes at the end of the week to think about your progress.

- What did you improve most?
- What was challenging?
- What new question or curiosity did this week spark?

Reflections:

_____

_____

_____

_____

LOOKING AHEAD
Set an intention for next week.
(Example: "Next week, I'll focus on minor scales and new chord voicings.")

_____

_____

_____

From Planning to Progress: Turning Intent into Improvement

Use this page at the beginning of each week to set focused, achievable goals.

Your weekly targets should align with your daily practice sessions and the broader topics from FOUNDATIONS. Setting clear, realistic goals helps you track progress and celebrate improvement, both in understanding and performance.

WEEKLY GOAL PLANNER

Week of: _____

Instructor (if applicable): _____

Primary Focus for the Week:
(Examples: Sharps/Flats memorization, Major scale fluency, 16th-note timing, interval ear training)

_____

_____

Goal 1: Theory & Understanding
What concept or rule will you master this week?
(Example: Memorize circle of fifths, learn diatonic triads in minor keys.)

Goal: _____

Why it matters: _____

How will you measure success? _____

Progress Notes (End of Week):

☐ Achieved   ☐ Needs Review   ☐ Carry Forward

Goal 2: Technique & Application
What practical or instrument-based skill will you refine?
(Example: Play all major chords cleanly, practice scales at 80 BPM, smooth chord transitions.)

Goal: _____

Practice Focus: _____

How many days did you practice this skill? ☐ 1 ☐ 2 ☐ 3 ☐ 4 ☐ 5+

Progress Notes (End of Week):

☐ Achieved   ☐ Needs Review   ☐ Carry Forward

Goal 3: Creativity & Expression

How will you apply your learning creatively?

(Example: Write an 8-bar melody in G major, improvise using a pentatonic scale, record a rhythm pattern.)

Goal: _____

Activity or Project: _____

Progress Notes (End of Week):

☐ Achieved   ☐ Needs Review   ☐ Carry Forward

WEEKLY REFLECTION

Take a few minutes at the end of the week to think about your progress.

- What did you improve most?
- What was challenging?
- What new question or curiosity did this week spark?

Reflections:

_____

_____

_____

_____

LOOKING AHEAD

Set an intention for next week.

(Example: "Next week, I'll focus on minor scales and new chord voicings.")

_____

_____

_____

From Planning to Progress: Turning Intent into Improvement

Use this page at the beginning of each week to set focused, achievable goals.

Your weekly targets should align with your daily practice sessions and the broader topics from FOUNDATIONS. Setting clear, realistic goals helps you track progress and celebrate improvement, both in understanding and performance.

WEEKLY GOAL PLANNER

Week of: _____

Instructor (if applicable): _____

Primary Focus for the Week:
(Examples: Sharps/Flats memorization, Major scale fluency, 16th-note timing, interval ear training)

_____

_____

Goal 1: Theory & Understanding
What concept or rule will you master this week?
(Example: Memorize circle of fifths, learn diatonic triads in minor keys.)

Goal: _____

Why it matters: _____

How will you measure success? _____

Progress Notes (End of Week):

☐ Achieved   ☐ Needs Review   ☐ Carry Forward

Goal 2: Technique & Application
What practical or instrument-based skill will you refine?
(Example: Play all major chords cleanly, practice scales at 80 BPM, smooth chord transitions.)

Goal: _____

Practice Focus: _____

How many days did you practice this skill? ☐ 1 ☐ 2 ☐ 3 ☐ 4 ☐ 5+

Progress Notes (End of Week):

☐ Achieved   ☐ Needs Review   ☐ Carry Forward

Goal 3: Creativity & Expression
How will you apply your learning creatively?
(Example: Write an 8-bar melody in G major, improvise using a pentatonic scale, record a rhythm pattern.)

Goal: _____

Activity or Project: _____

Progress Notes (End of Week):

☐ Achieved   ☐ Needs Review   ☐ Carry Forward

WEEKLY REFLECTION
Take a few minutes at the end of the week to think about your progress.

- What did you improve most?
- What was challenging?
- What new question or curiosity did this week spark?

Reflections:

_____

_____

_____

_____

LOOKING AHEAD
Set an intention for next week.
(Example: "Next week, I'll focus on minor scales and new chord voicings.")

_____

_____

_____

Section 1: Staff Notation Practice

SECTION 1: Staff Notation Practice

This section strengthens your fluency in reading and writing standard music notation. Each set of worksheets focuses on the building blocks of written music, clefs, time signatures, notes, and rests. Write directly on the staff to reinforce pitch placement and rhythmic accuracy.

Goal: To confidently read, write, and identify musical symbols, connecting theory to written sound.

Begin by using the staves below to practice drawing both the Treble and Bass clefs accurately. Start by copying the examples provided, then challenge yourself to draw them freehand. Continue practicing across the staff until each clef feels natural and easy to reproduce.

Focus on correct placement:
The Treble Clef (G Clef) circles around the G line, the second line from the bottom of the staff.
The Bass Clef (F Clef) uses two dots that frame the F line, the second line from the top of the staff.

Notes on the Lines and Spaces

Write the names of the notes on the lines of the treble clef staff (from bottom to top):
E – G – B – D – F ("Every Good Boy Does Fine")

Write the names of the notes in the spaces of the treble clef (bottom to top):
F – A – C – E (spells "FACE")

Write the names of the notes on the lines of the bass clef staff (bottom to top):
G – B – D – F – A ("Good Boys Do Fine Always")

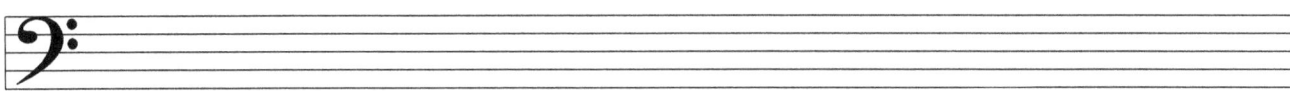

Write the names of the notes in the spaces of the bass clef (bottom to top):
A – C – E – G ("All Cows Eat Grass")

Time Signatures

A time signature tells you how many beats are in each measure and which note value receives one beat. On the staff below, write each of the following time signatures and label what each one means. Example: 4/4 = Four beats per measure; the quarter note gets one beat.

After writing each time signature, create one measure that correctly fits that rhythm. Use any combination of notes and rests as long as the total value matches the number of beats in the time signature.

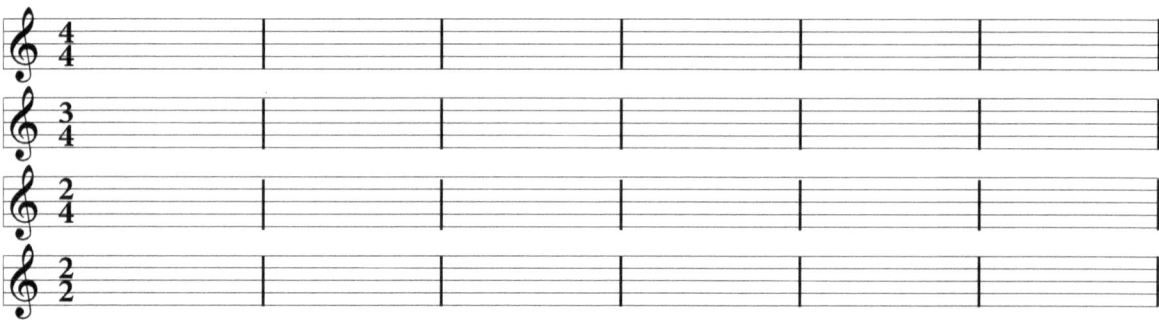

Notating Note Values

On the staff below, draw and label each of the following note types, then write how many beats each note receives in 4/4 time.

Notating Rest Values

Rests represent silence in music, just as important as the notes themselves. On the blank staff below, draw each of the following rest symbols, then write how many beats each rest receives in 4/4 time.

Staff Notation Practice Worksheet

Treble Clef Practice

Bass Clef Practice

Notes on the Lines and Spaces

Staff Notation Practice Worksheet

Treble Clef Practice

Bass Clef Practice

Notes on the Lines and Spaces

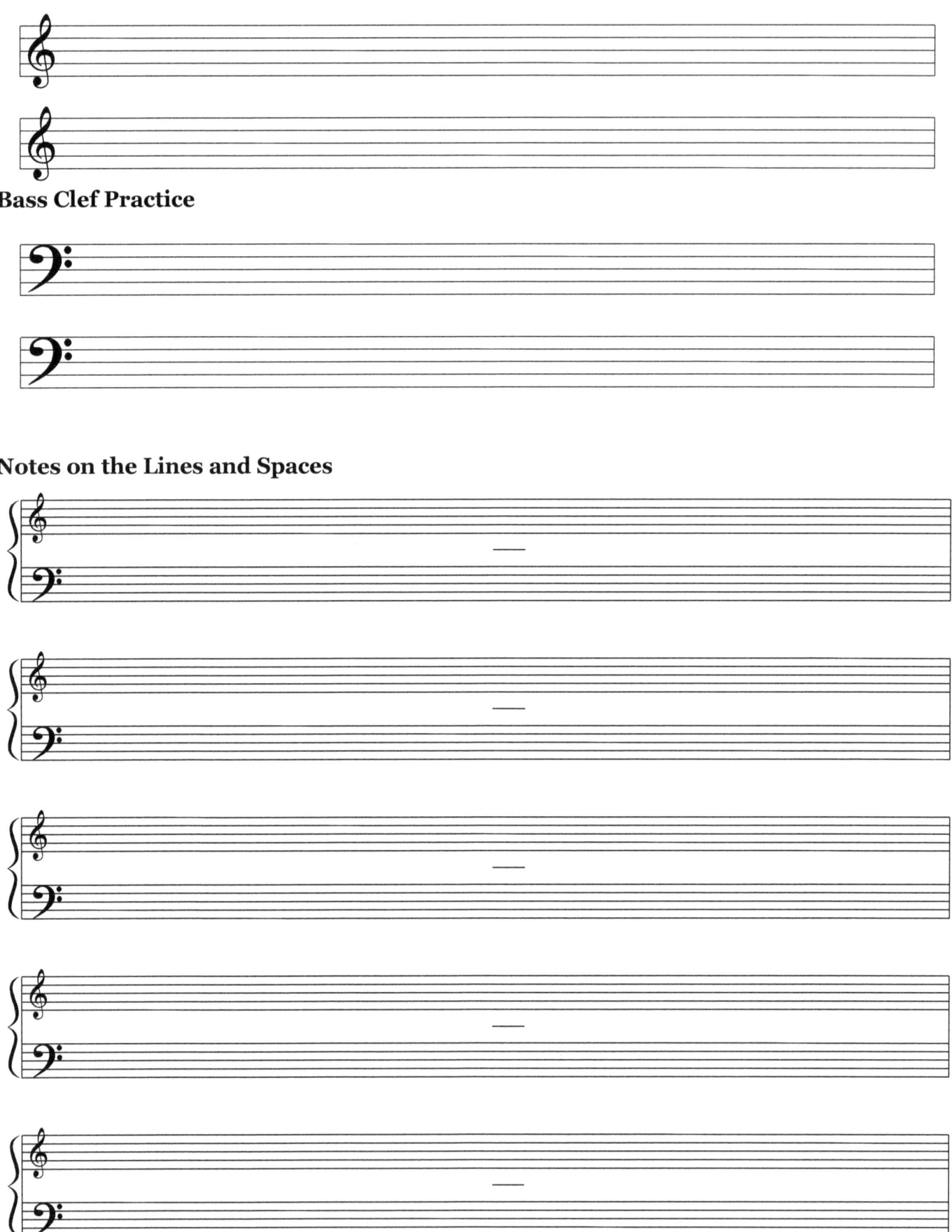

Staff Notation Practice Worksheet

Treble Clef Practice

Bass Clef Practice

Notes on the Lines and Spaces

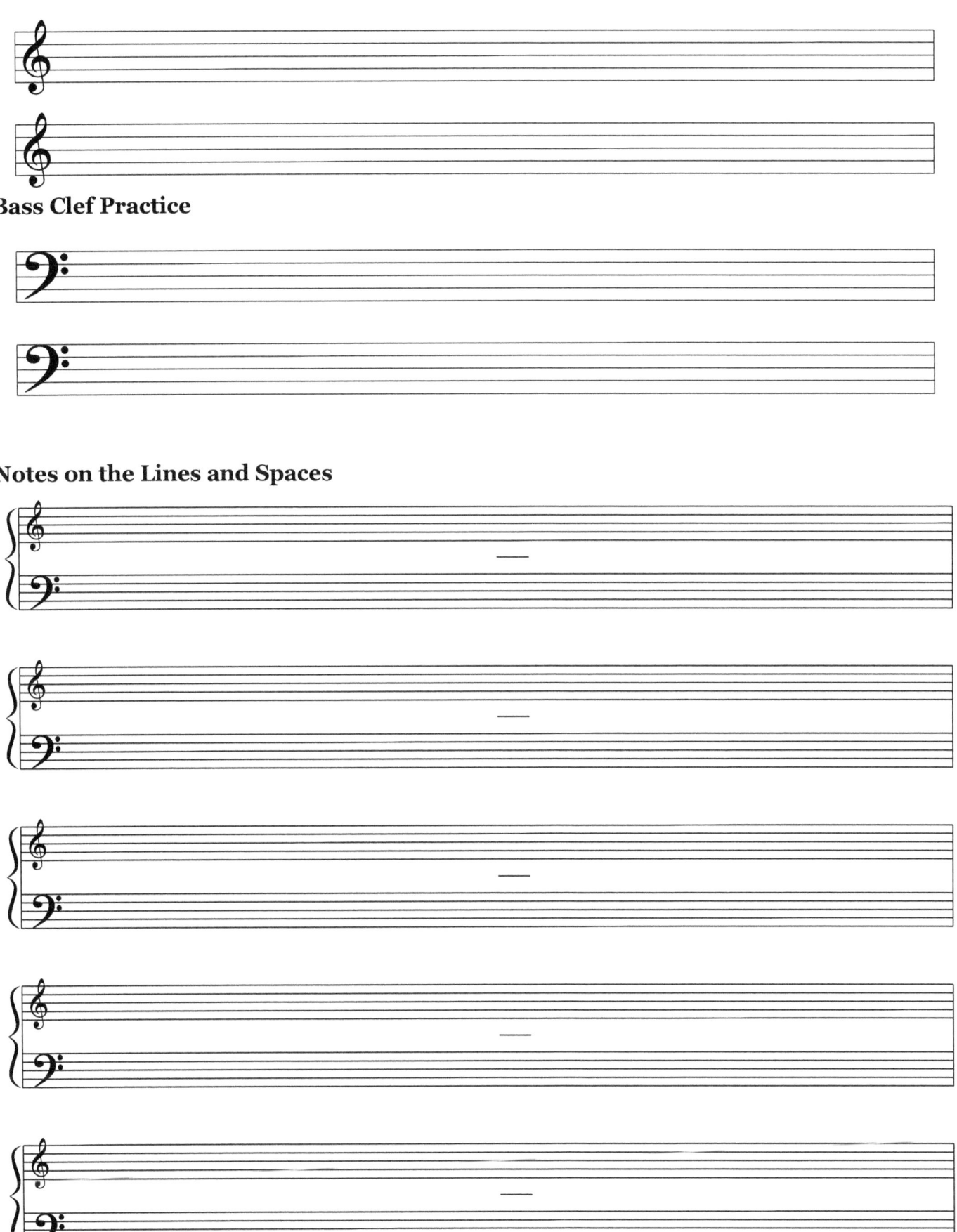

Staff Notation Practice Worksheet

Treble Clef Practice

Bass Clef Practice

Notes on the Lines and Spaces

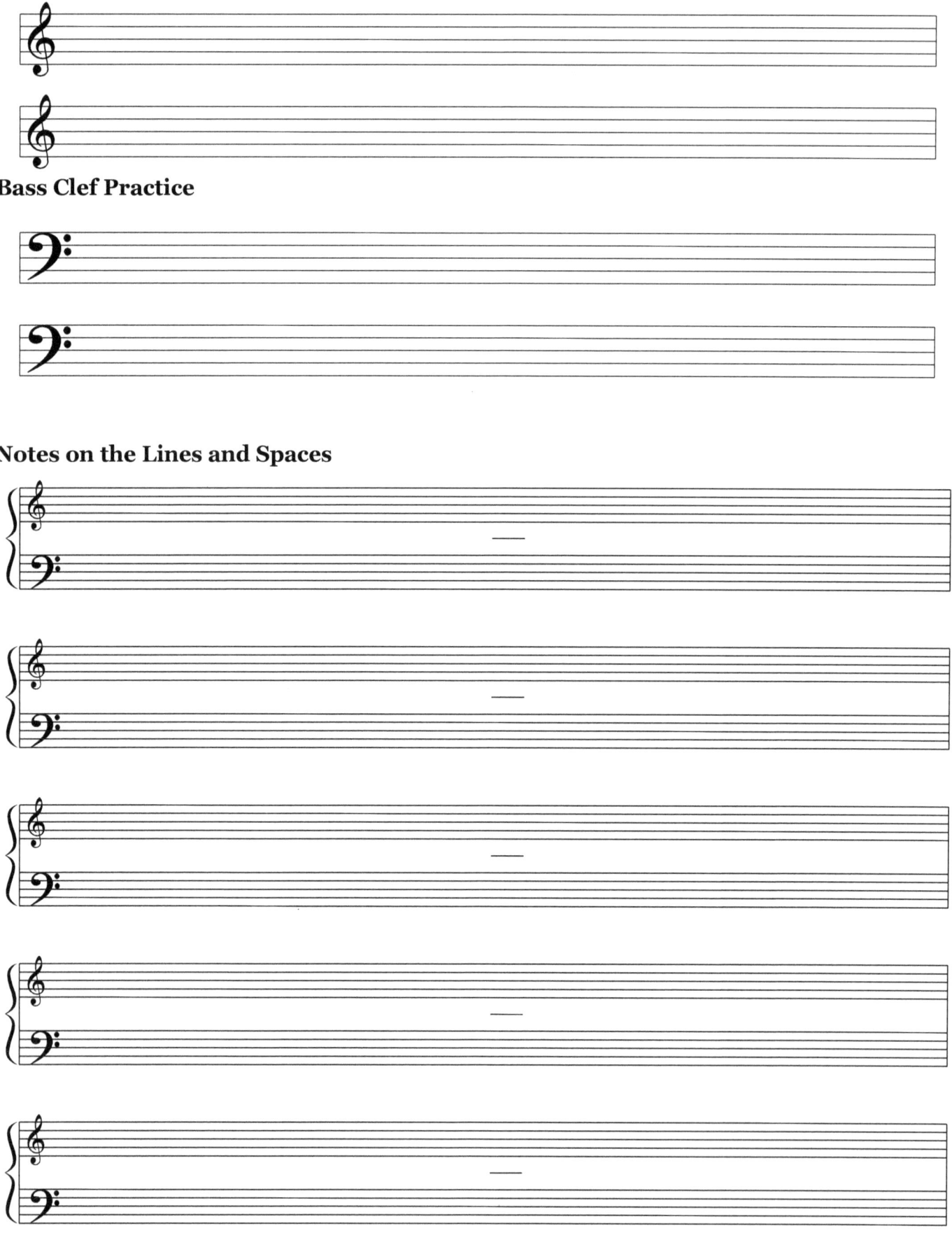

Staff Notation Practice Worksheet

Treble Clef Practice

Bass Clef Practice

Notes on the Lines and Spaces

Staff Notation Practice Worksheet

Treble Clef Practice

Bass Clef Practice

Notes on the Lines and Spaces

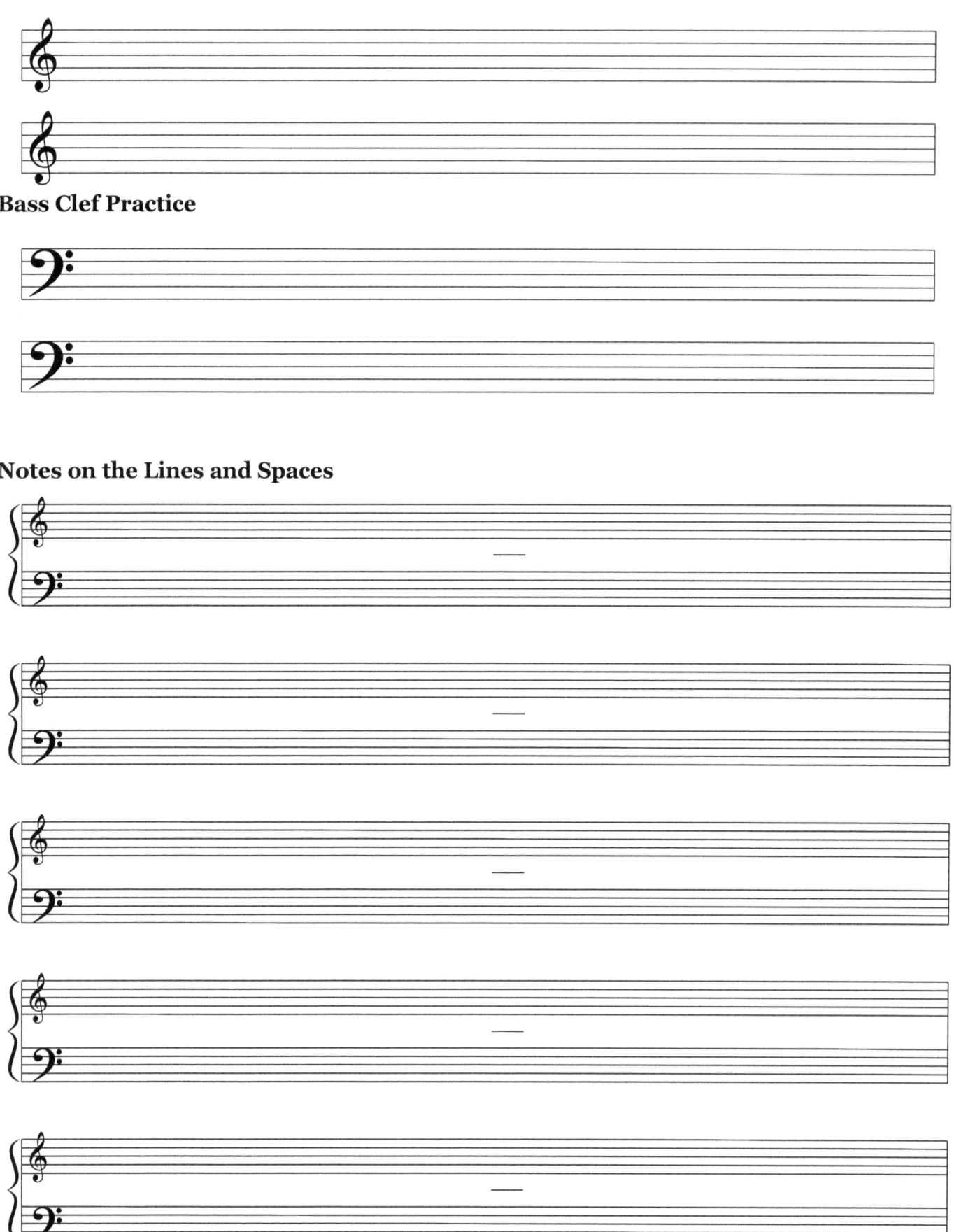

Staff Notation Practice Worksheet

Treble Clef Practice

Bass Clef Practice

Notes on the Lines and Spaces

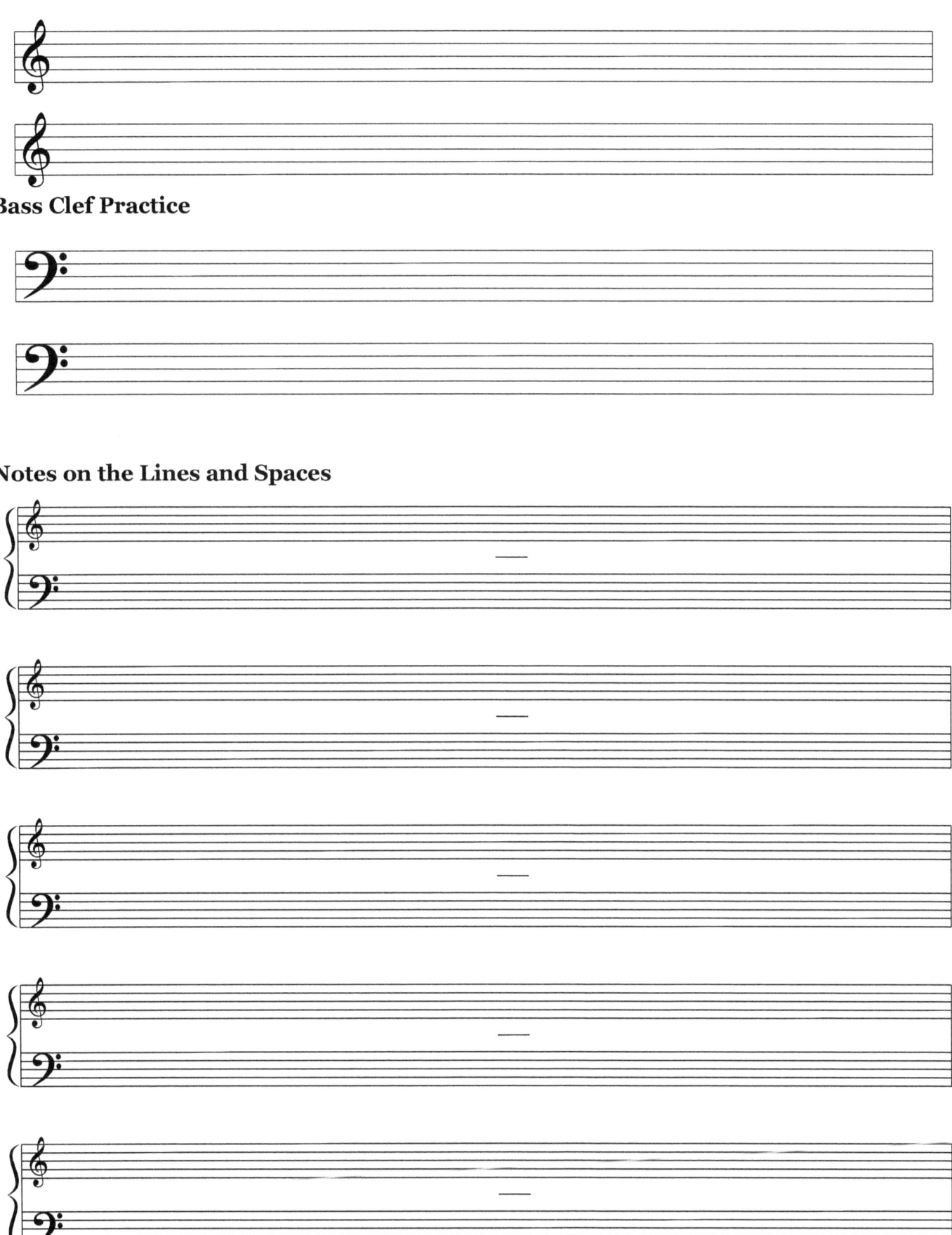

Staff Notation Practice Worksheet

Treble Clef Practice

Bass Clef Practice

Notes on the Lines and Spaces

Staff Notation Practice Worksheet

Treble Clef Practice

Bass Clef Practice

Notes on the Lines and Spaces

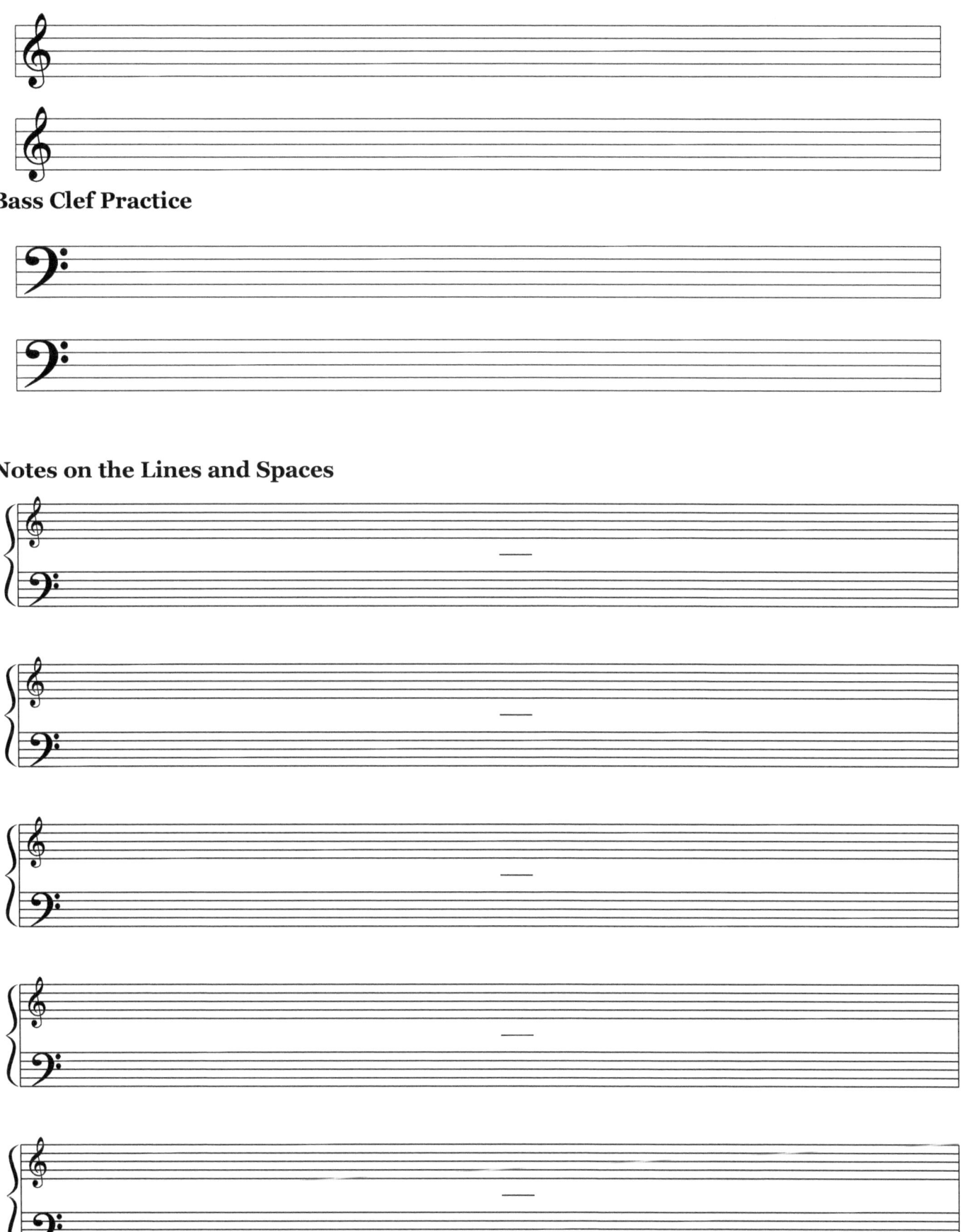

Staff Notation Practice Worksheet

Treble Clef Practice

Bass Clef Practice

Notes on the Lines and Spaces

Time Signatures

A time signature tells you how many beats are in each measure and which note value receives one beat. On the staff below, write each of the following time signatures and label what each one means. Example: 4/4 = Four beats per measure; the quarter note gets one beat.

After writing each time signature, create one measure that correctly fits that rhythm. Use any combination of notes and rests as long as the total value matches the number of beats in the time signature.

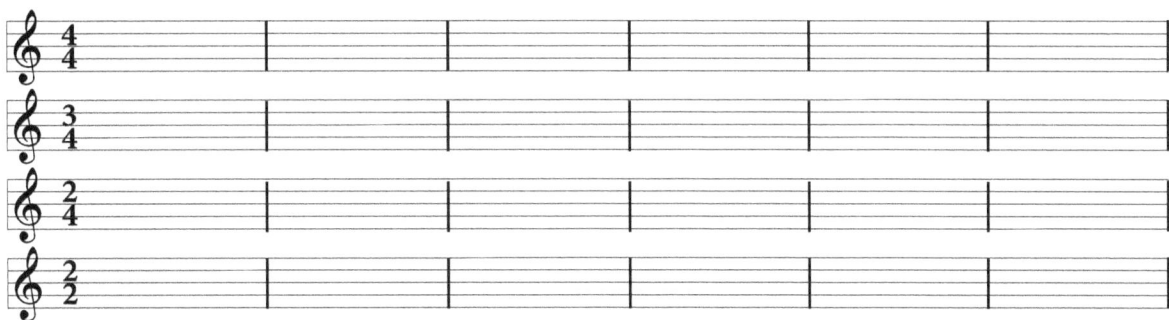

Notating Note Values

On the staff below, draw and label each of the following note types, then write how many beats each note receives in 4/4 time.

Notating Rest Values

Rests represent silence in music, just as important as the notes themselves. On the blank staff below, draw each of the following rest symbols, then write how many beats each rest receives in 4/4 time.

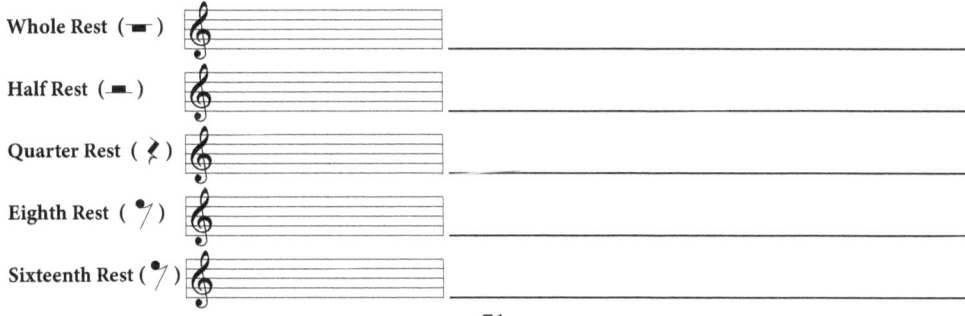

Time Signatures

A time signature tells you how many beats are in each measure and which note value receives one beat. On the staff below, write each of the following time signatures and label what each one means. Example: 4/4 = Four beats per measure; the quarter note gets one beat.

After writing each time signature, create one measure that correctly fits that rhythm. Use any combination of notes and rests as long as the total value matches the number of beats in the time signature.

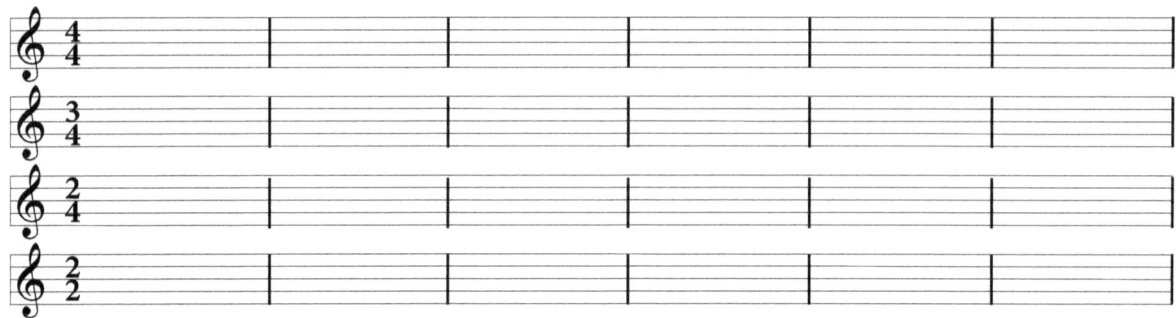

Notating Note Values

On the staff below, draw and label each of the following note types, then write how many beats each note receives in 4/4 time.

Notating Rest Values

Rests represent silence in music, just as important as the notes themselves. On the blank staff below, draw each of the following rest symbols, then write how many beats each rest receives in 4/4 time.

Time Signatures

A time signature tells you how many beats are in each measure and which note value receives one beat. On the staff below, write each of the following time signatures and label what each one means. Example: 4/4 = Four beats per measure; the quarter note gets one beat.

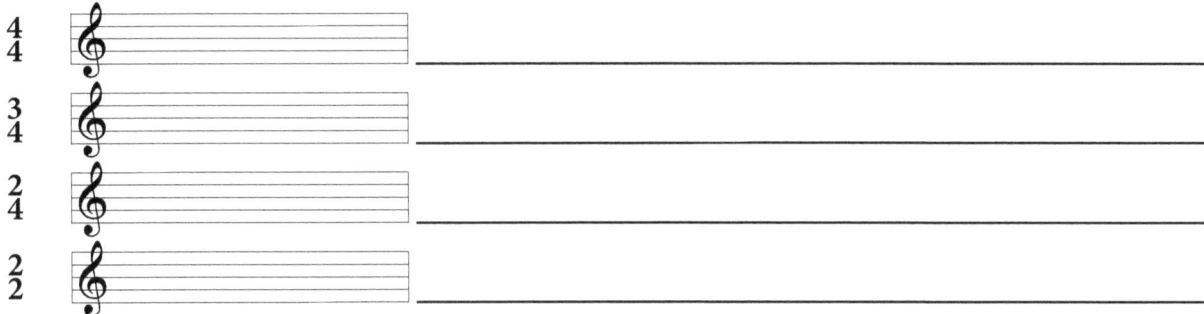

After writing each time signature, create one measure that correctly fits that rhythm. Use any combination of notes and rests as long as the total value matches the number of beats in the time signature.

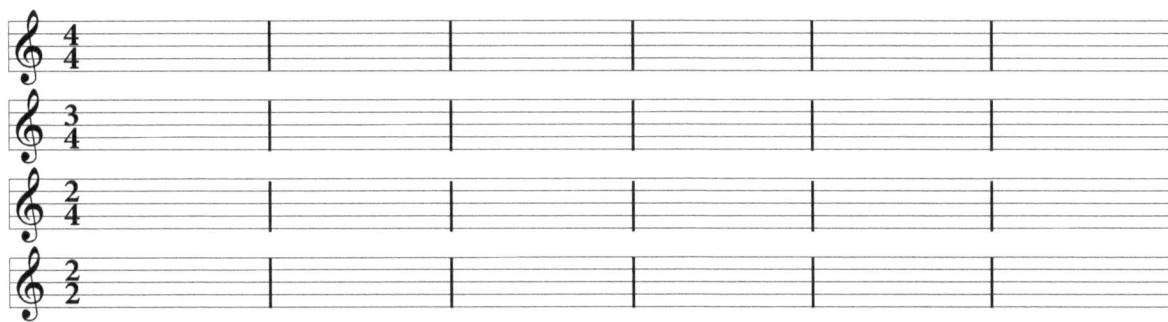

Notating Note Values

On the staff below, draw and label each of the following note types, then write how many beats each note receives in 4/4 time.

Notating Rest Values

Rests represent silence in music, just as important as the notes themselves. On the blank staff below, draw each of the following rest symbols, then write how many beats each rest receives in 4/4 time.

Time Signatures

A time signature tells you how many beats are in each measure and which note value receives one beat. On the staff below, write each of the following time signatures and label what each one means. Example: 4/4 = Four beats per measure; the quarter note gets one beat.

After writing each time signature, create one measure that correctly fits that rhythm. Use any combination of notes and rests as long as the total value matches the number of beats in the time signature.

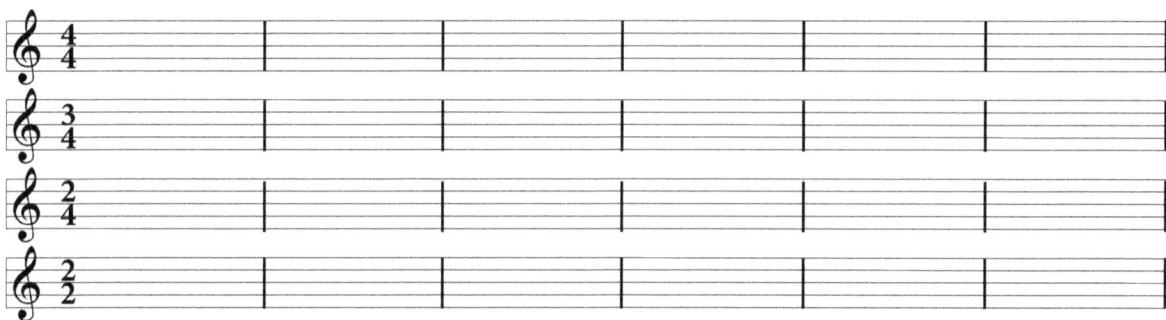

Notating Note Values

On the staff below, draw and label each of the following note types, then write how many beats each note receives in 4/4 time.

Notating Rest Values

Rests represent silence in music, just as important as the notes themselves. On the blank staff below, draw each of the following rest symbols, then write how many beats each rest receives in 4/4 time.

Time Signatures

A time signature tells you how many beats are in each measure and which note value receives one beat. On the staff below, write each of the following time signatures and label what each one means. Example: 4/4 = Four beats per measure; the quarter note gets one beat.

After writing each time signature, create one measure that correctly fits that rhythm. Use any combination of notes and rests as long as the total value matches the number of beats in the time signature.

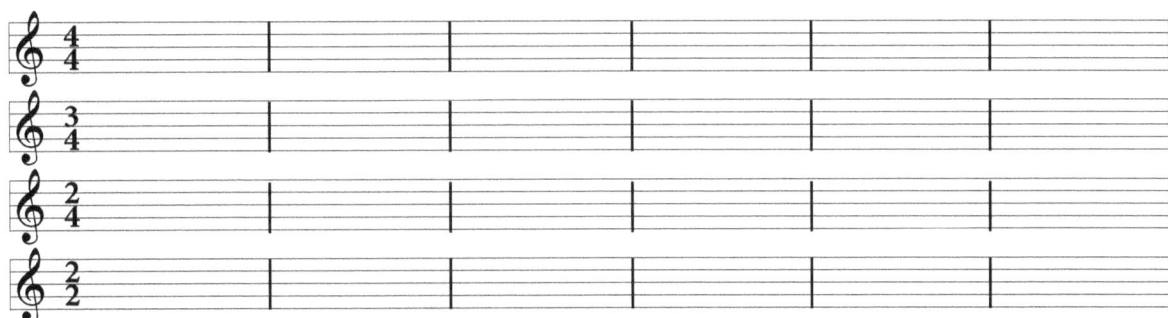

Notating Note Values

On the staff below, draw and label each of the following note types, then write how many beats each note receives in 4/4 time.

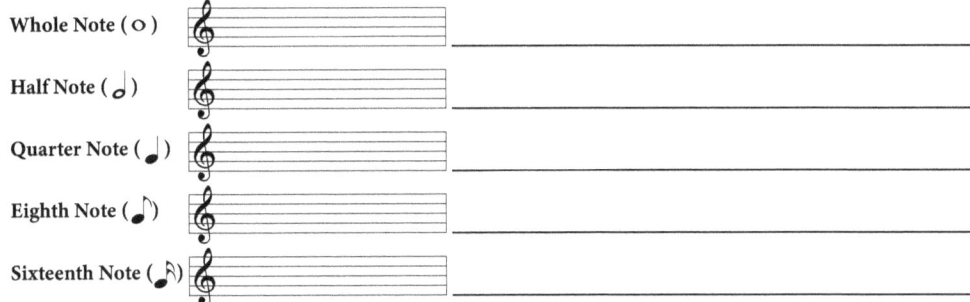

Notating Rest Values

Rests represent silence in music, just as important as the notes themselves. On the blank staff below, draw each of the following rest symbols, then write how many beats each rest receives in 4/4 time.

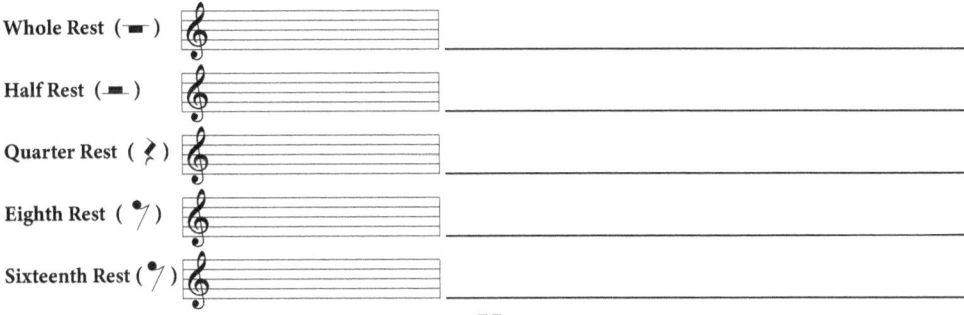

Time Signatures

A time signature tells you how many beats are in each measure and which note value receives one beat. On the staff below, write each of the following time signatures and label what each one means. Example: 4/4 = Four beats per measure; the quarter note gets one beat.

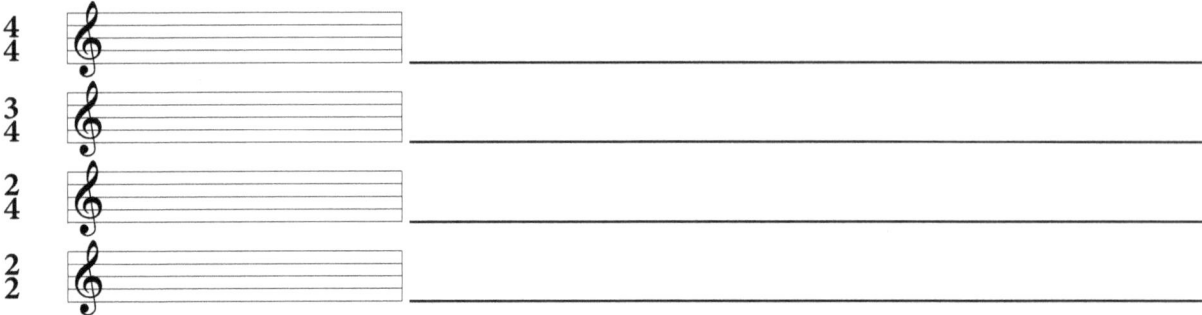

After writing each time signature, create one measure that correctly fits that rhythm. Use any combination of notes and rests as long as the total value matches the number of beats in the time signature.

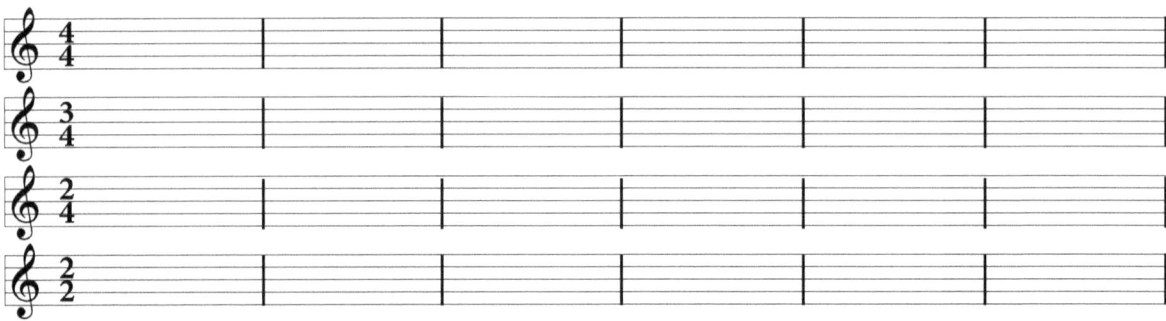

Notating Note Values

On the staff below, draw and label each of the following note types, then write how many beats each note receives in 4/4 time.

Notating Rest Values

Rests represent silence in music, just as important as the notes themselves. On the blank staff below, draw each of the following rest symbols, then write how many beats each rest receives in 4/4 time.

Time Signatures

A time signature tells you how many beats are in each measure and which note value receives one beat. On the staff below, write each of the following time signatures and label what each one means. Example: 4/4 = Four beats per measure; the quarter note gets one beat.

After writing each time signature, create one measure that correctly fits that rhythm. Use any combination of notes and rests as long as the total value matches the number of beats in the time signature.

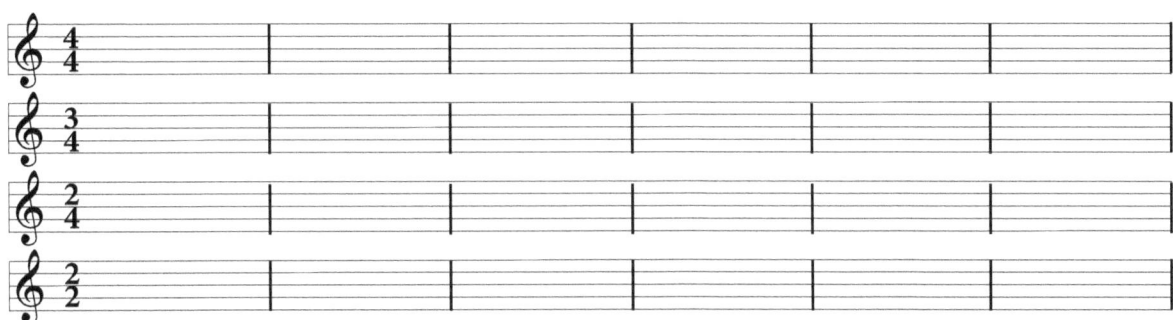

Notating Note Values

On the staff below, draw and label each of the following note types, then write how many beats each note receives in 4/4 time.

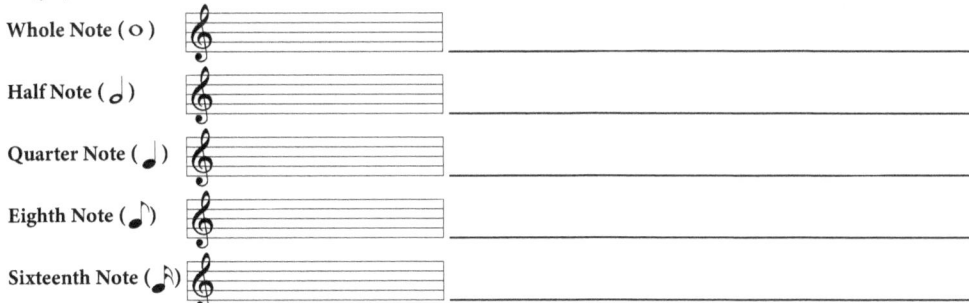

Notating Rest Values

Rests represent silence in music, just as important as the notes themselves. On the blank staff below, draw each of the following rest symbols, then write how many beats each rest receives in 4/4 time.

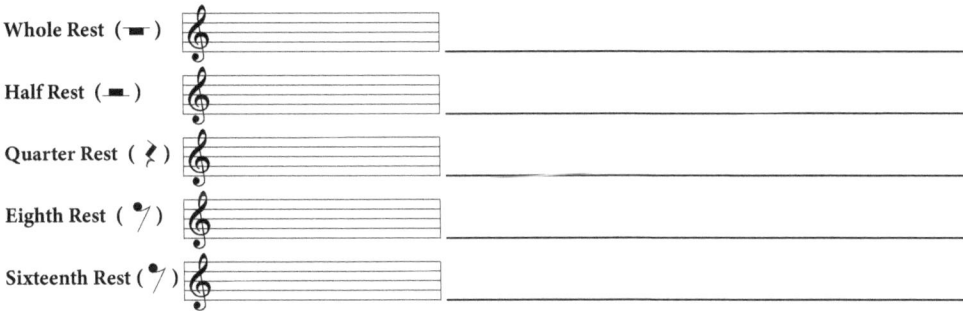

Time Signatures

A time signature tells you how many beats are in each measure and which note value receives one beat. On the staff below, write each of the following time signatures and label what each one means. Example: 4/4 = Four beats per measure; the quarter note gets one beat.

After writing each time signature, create one measure that correctly fits that rhythm. Use any combination of notes and rests as long as the total value matches the number of beats in the time signature.

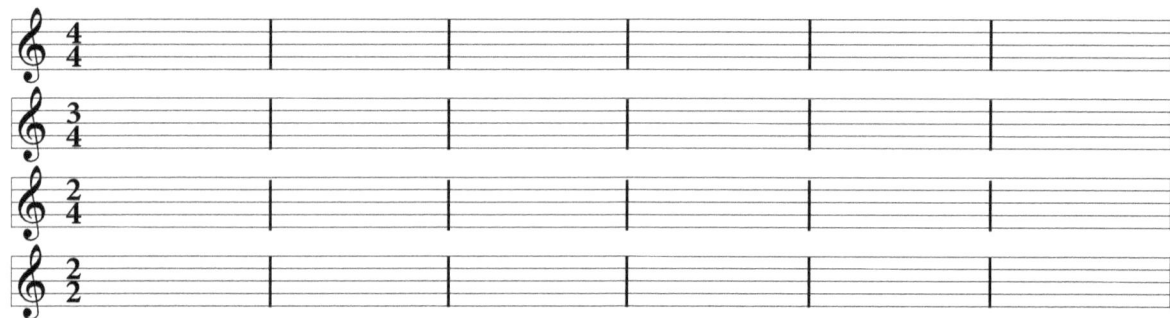

Notating Note Values

On the staff below, draw and label each of the following note types, then write how many beats each note receives in 4/4 time.

Notating Rest Values

Rests represent silence in music, just as important as the notes themselves. On the blank staff below, draw each of the following rest symbols, then write how many beats each rest receives in 4/4 time.

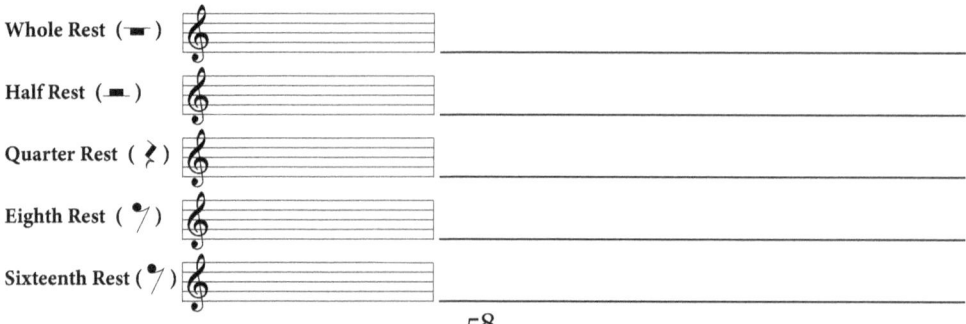

Time Signatures

A time signature tells you how many beats are in each measure and which note value receives one beat. On the staff below, write each of the following time signatures and label what each one means. Example: 4/4 = Four beats per measure; the quarter note gets one beat.

After writing each time signature, create one measure that correctly fits that rhythm. Use any combination of notes and rests as long as the total value matches the number of beats in the time signature.

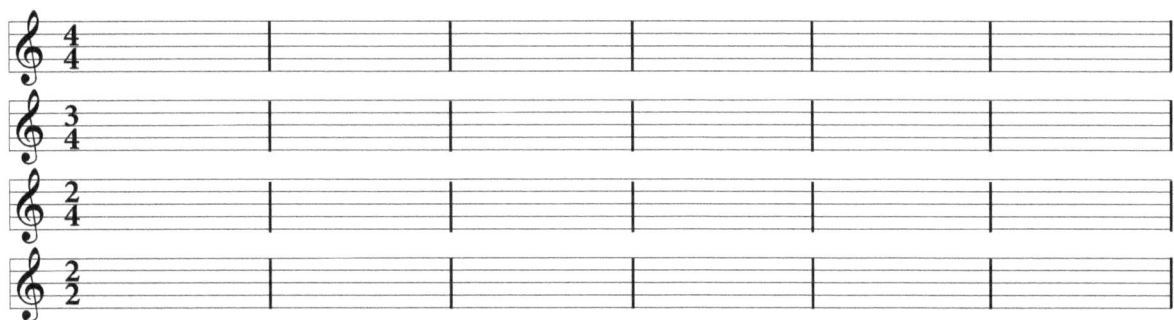

Notating Note Values

On the staff below, draw and label each of the following note types, then write how many beats each note receives in 4/4 time.

Notating Rest Values

Rests represent silence in music, just as important as the notes themselves. On the blank staff below, draw each of the following rest symbols, then write how many beats each rest receives in 4/4 time.

Time Signatures

A time signature tells you how many beats are in each measure and which note value receives one beat. On the staff below, write each of the following time signatures and label what each one means. Example: 4/4 = Four beats per measure; the quarter note gets one beat.

After writing each time signature, create one measure that correctly fits that rhythm. Use any combination of notes and rests as long as the total value matches the number of beats in the time signature.

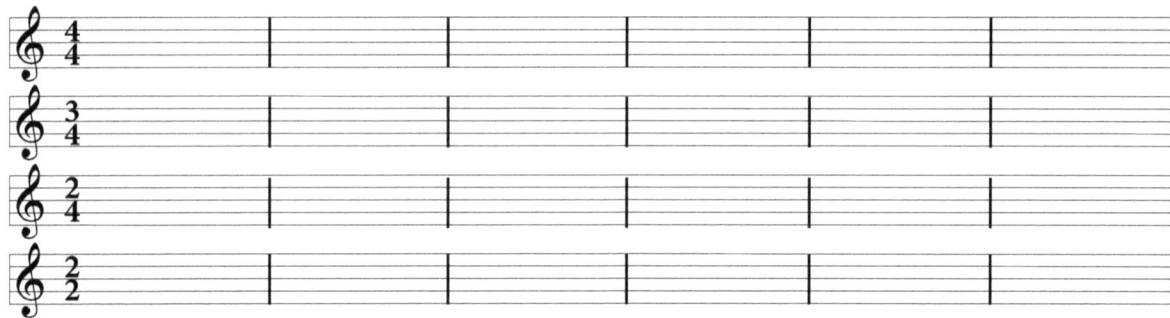

Notating Note Values

On the staff below, draw and label each of the following note types, then write how many beats each note receives in 4/4 time.

Notating Rest Values

Rests represent silence in music, just as important as the notes themselves. On the blank staff below, draw each of the following rest symbols, then write how many beats each rest receives in 4/4 time.

Section 2: Key Signature Memorization

SECTION 2: Key Signature Practice

Here you'll reinforce your ability to recognize, recall, and apply key signatures. Work through identification exercises, then move into writing the corresponding notes and diatonic chords. Each key signature worksheet includes ten identical practice sets, progressing from visual recognition to functional understanding.

Goal: To achieve instant recall of key signatures, associated scales, and related chords.

How to Use This Worksheet
This worksheet is designed to help you memorize key signatures, one of the most essential foundations in music theory. Understanding key signatures allows you to instantly identify which notes are sharp or flat in any key, making reading music, writing scales, and building chords easier and more intuitive.

Step 1: Identify Key Names: Major and Minor Keys
In the first set of exercises, key signatures are already written on the staff. Your task is to write the name of the key (C, G, D, etc.) in the blank provided. As you work:

Say the key name aloud.
Double-check the sharps or flats for each key signature.
Repeat until recalling the key becomes automatic.

Step 2: Circle of Fifths: Counting Sharps and Flats
The Circle of Fifths is already provided with key signatures. Your task is to write the number of sharps or flats for each key in the blanks. This exercise reinforces both visual memory and conceptual understanding of key signature patterns.

Step 3: Key Notes Identification
For this section, the key signature is already written. Your task is to:

Identify the key.
Write the notes of the key in proper scale order (I, ii, iii, etc.) in the blanks provided.
This exercise reinforces your ability to connect a key signature to its corresponding notes and internalize scale structure.

Step 4: Key Chords Identification
Again, the key signature is already provided. Your task is to:
Identify the key.
Write the chords that belong to that key in the blanks provided.

This final step ties together key signature recognition, note memorization, and chord construction, giving you a complete understanding of how each key functions musically.

Why This Matters
By completing these exercises consistently, key signatures will become second nature. You'll strengthen both your declarative memory (knowing what's correct) and procedural memory (applying it automatically), allowing you to read, analyze, and write music confidently without hesitation.

Key Signature Memorization Worksheet

Major Key Signatures

SHARPS

FLATS

Relative Minor Key Signatures

SHARPS

FLATS

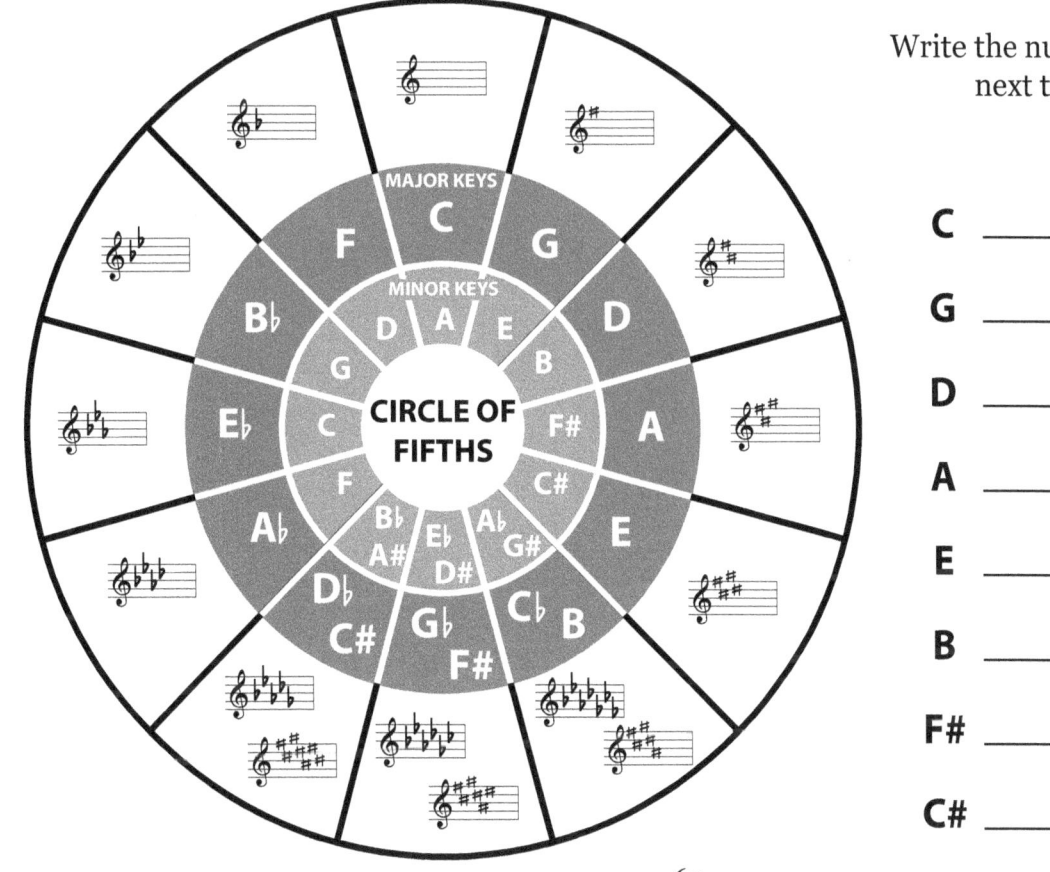

Write the number of sharps or flats
next to each Scale/Key

C _____   F _____

G _____   Bb _____

D _____   Eb _____

A _____   Ab _____

E _____   Db _____

B _____   Gb _____

F# _____   Cb _____

C# _____

Key Signature Memorization Worksheet

Major Key Signatures

SHARPS

_____ _____ _____ _____ _____ _____ _____ _____

FLATS

_____ _____ _____ _____ _____ _____ _____ _____

Relative Minor Key Signatures

SHARPS

_____ _____ _____ _____ _____ _____ _____ _____

FLATS

_____ _____ _____ _____ _____ _____ _____ _____

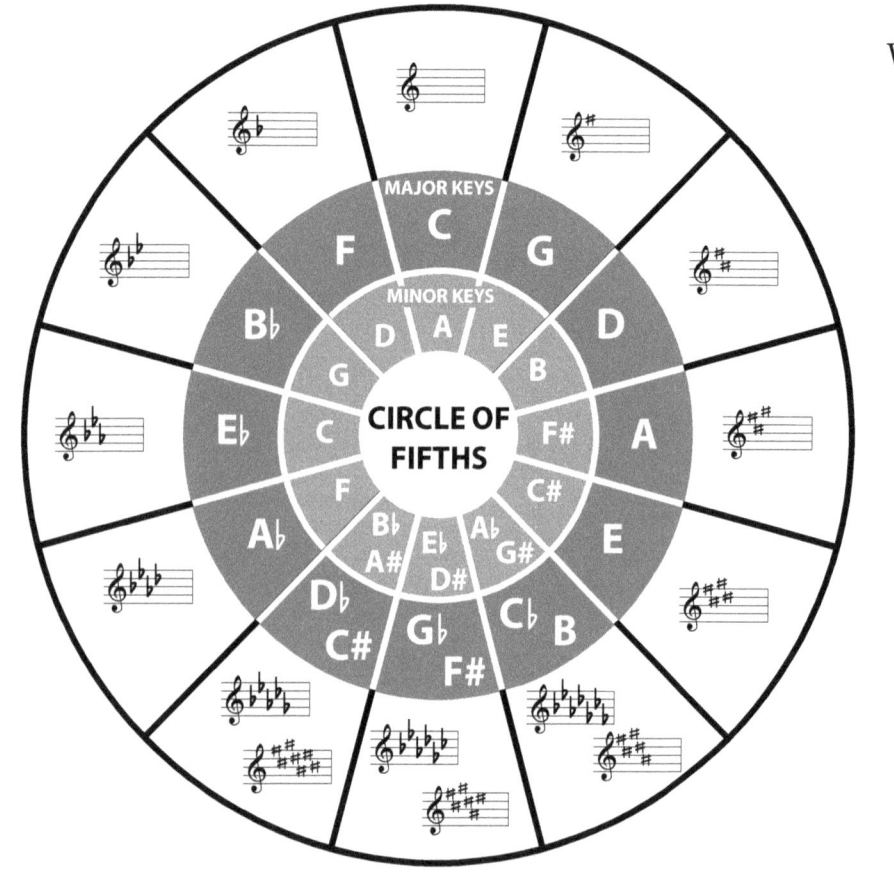

Write the number of sharps or flats
next to each Scale/Key

C _____   F _____

G _____   Bb _____

D _____   Eb _____

A _____   Ab _____

E _____   Db _____

B _____   Gb _____

F# _____   Cb _____

C# _____

Key Signature Memorization Worksheet

Major Key Signatures

SHARPS

_____ _____ _____ _____ _____ _____ _____ _____

FLATS

_____ _____ _____ _____ _____ _____ _____ _____

Relative Minor Key Signatures

SHARPS

_____ _____ _____ _____ _____ _____ _____ _____

FLATS

_____ _____ _____ _____ _____ _____ _____ _____

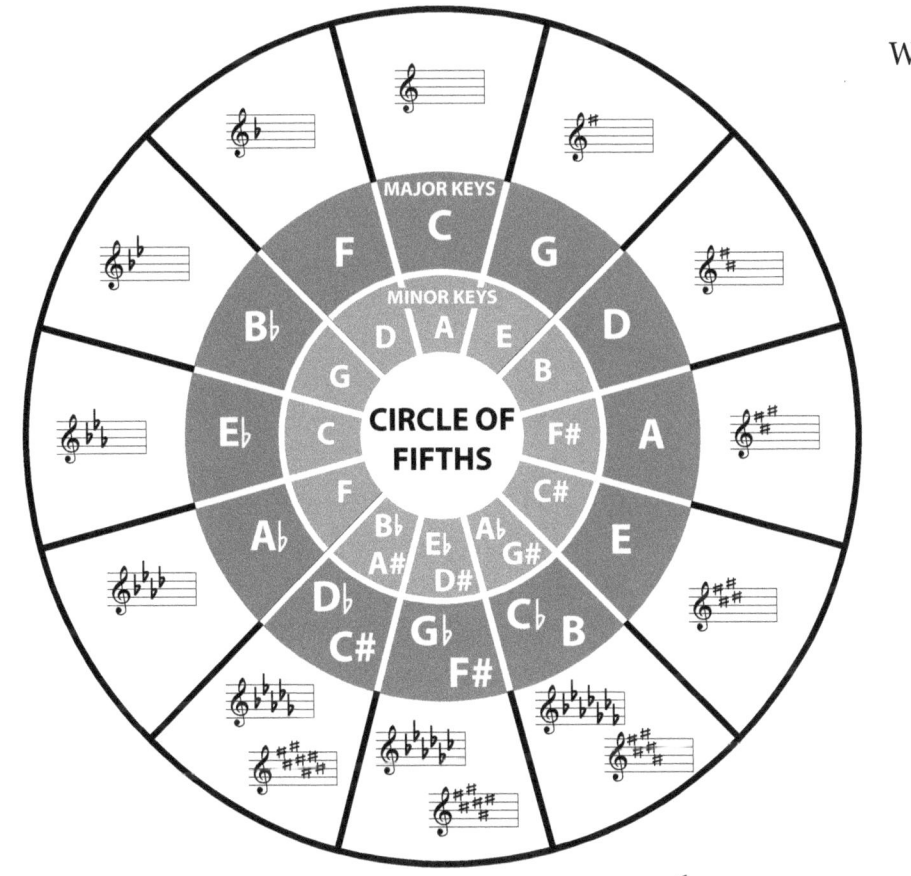

Write the number of sharps or flats
next to each Scale/Key

C _____   F _____

G _____   Bb _____

D _____   Eb _____

A _____   Ab _____

E _____   Db _____

B _____   Gb _____

F# _____   Cb _____

C# _____

Key Signature Memorization Worksheet

Major Key Signatures

SHARPS

FLATS

Relative Minor Key Signatures

SHARPS

FLATS

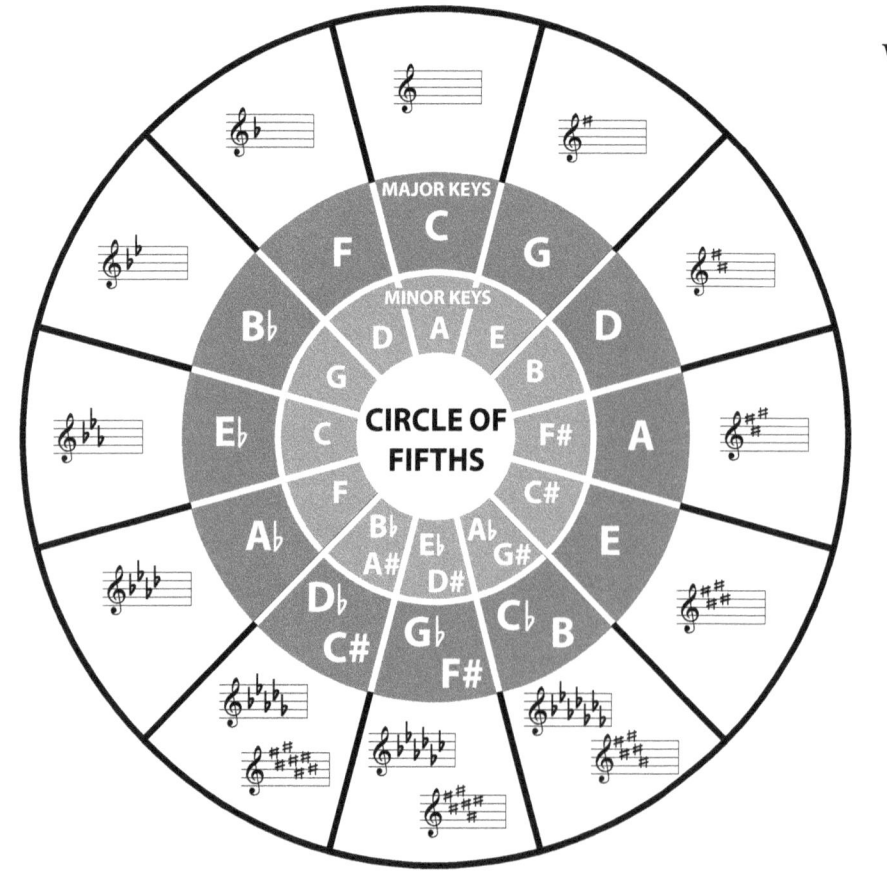

Write the number of sharps or flats
next to each Scale/Key

C _____	F _____
G _____	Bb _____
D _____	Eb _____
A _____	Ab _____
E _____	Db _____
B _____	Gb _____
F# _____	Cb _____
C# _____	

Key Signature Memorization Worksheet

Major Key Signatures

SHARPS
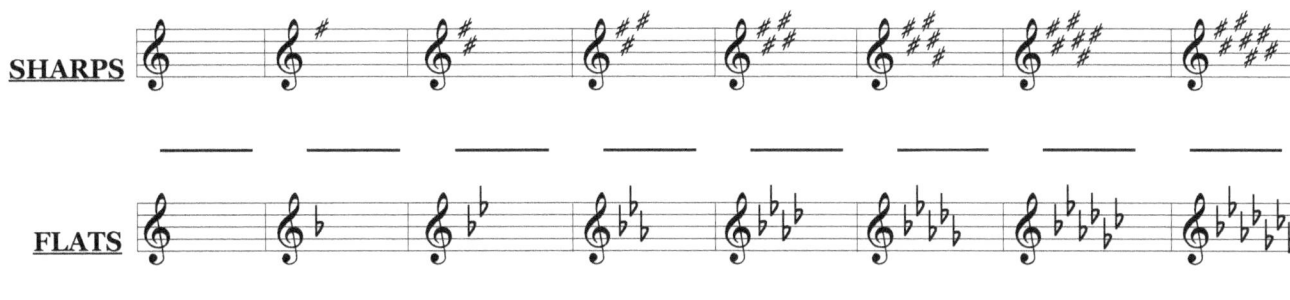

_____ _____ _____ _____ _____ _____ _____ _____

FLATS

_____ _____ _____ _____ _____ _____ _____ _____

Relative Minor Key Signatures

SHARPS

_____ _____ _____ _____ _____ _____ _____ _____

FLATS

_____ _____ _____ _____ _____ _____ _____ _____

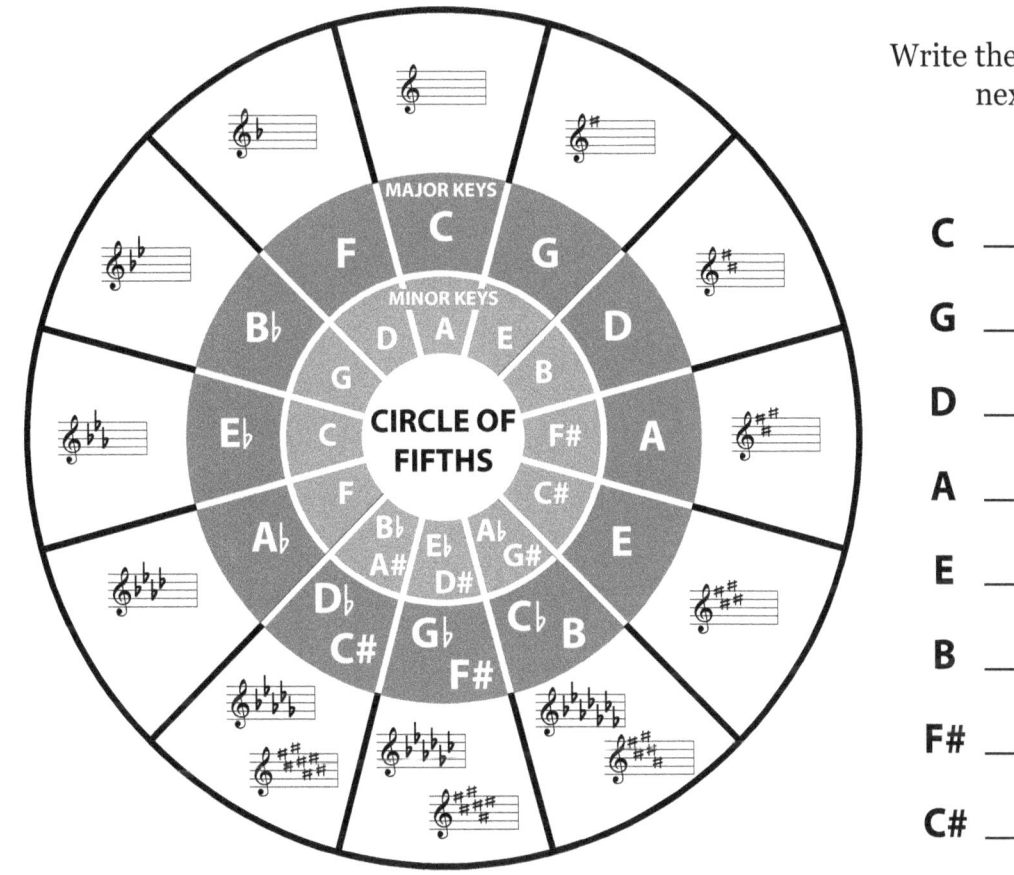

Write the number of sharps or flats
next to each Scale/Key

C _____   F _____

G _____   Bb _____

D _____   Eb _____

A _____   Ab _____

E _____   Db _____

B _____   Gb _____

F# _____   Cb _____

C# _____

Key Signature Memorization Worksheet

Major Key Signatures

SHARPS

_____ _____ _____ _____ _____ _____ _____ _____

FLATS

_____ _____ _____ _____ _____ _____ _____ _____

Relative Minor Key Signatures

SHARPS

_____ _____ _____ _____ _____ _____ _____ _____

FLATS

_____ _____ _____ _____ _____ _____ _____ _____

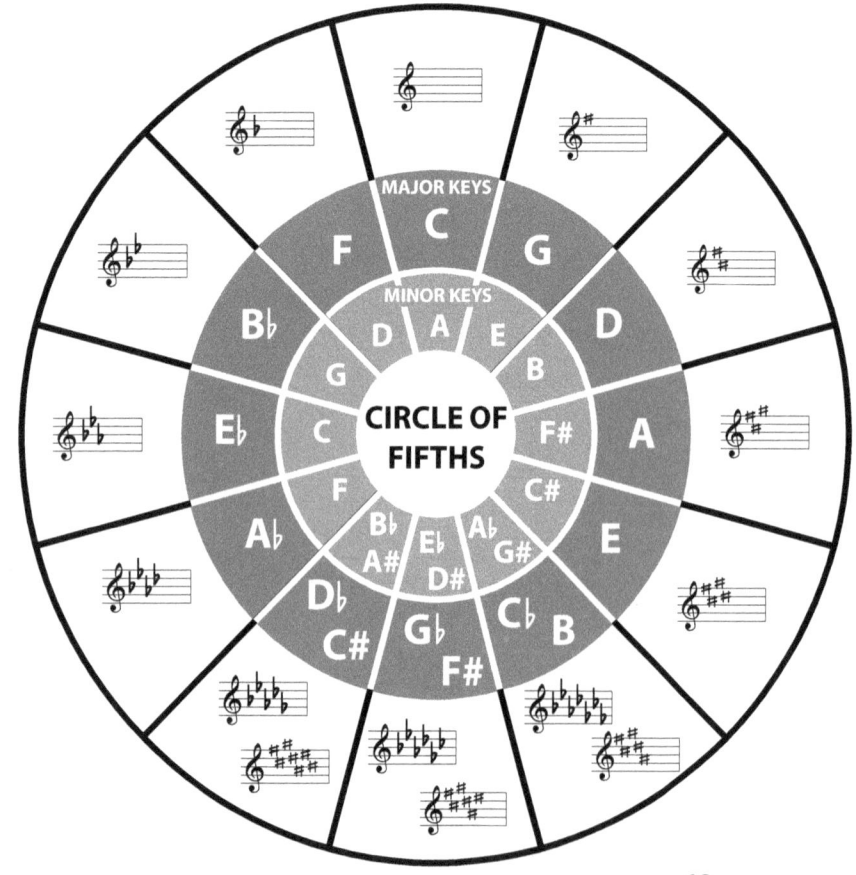

Write the number of sharps or flats
next to each Scale/Key

C _____   F _____

G _____   Bb _____

D _____   Eb _____

A _____   Ab _____

E _____   Db _____

B _____   Gb _____

F# _____   Cb _____

C# _____

68

Key Signature Memorization Worksheet

Major Key Signatures

SHARPS

_____ _____ _____ _____ _____ _____ _____ _____

FLATS

_____ _____ _____ _____ _____ _____ _____ _____

Relative Minor Key Signatures

SHARPS

_____ _____ _____ _____ _____ _____ _____ _____

FLATS

_____ _____ _____ _____ _____ _____ _____ _____

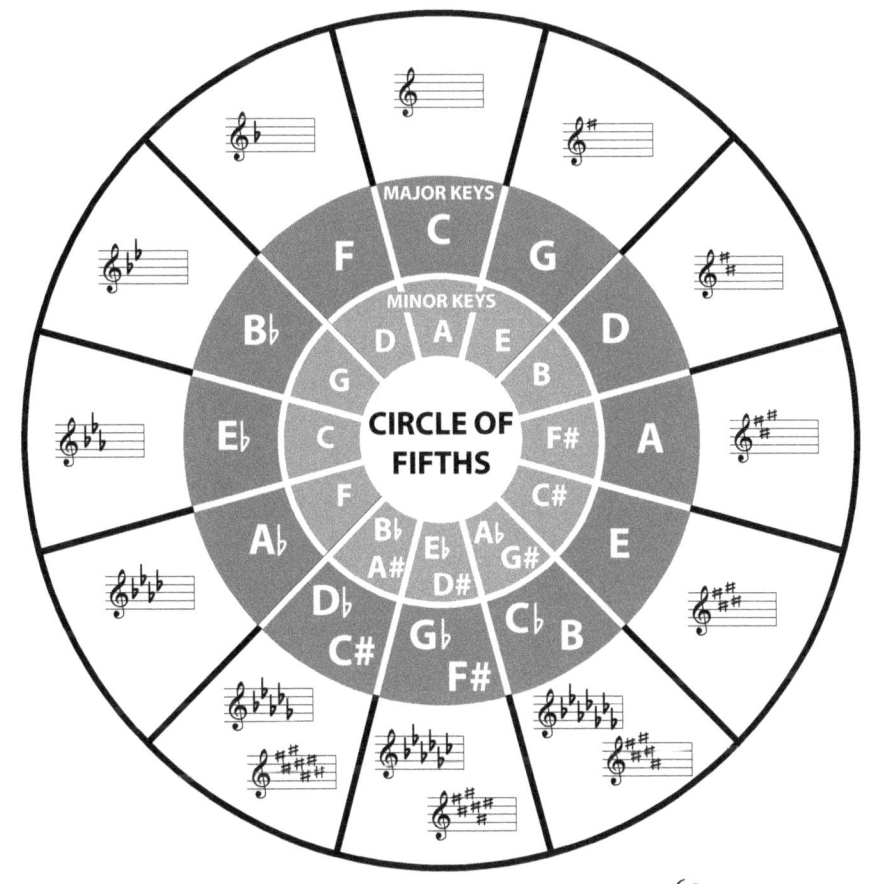

Write the number of sharps or flats
next to each Scale/Key

C _____   F _____

G _____   Bb _____

D _____   Eb _____

A _____   Ab _____

E _____   Db _____

B _____   Gb _____

F# _____   Cb _____

C# _____

Key Signature Memorization Worksheet

Major Key Signatures

SHARPS

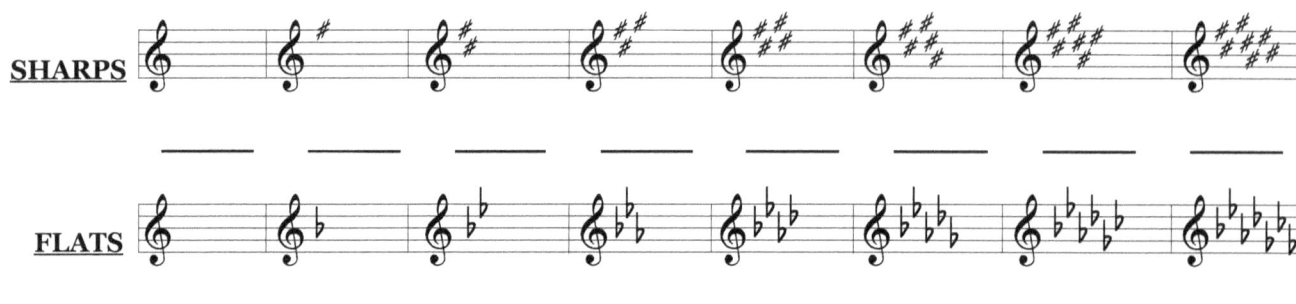

FLATS

Relative Minor Key Signatures

SHARPS

FLATS

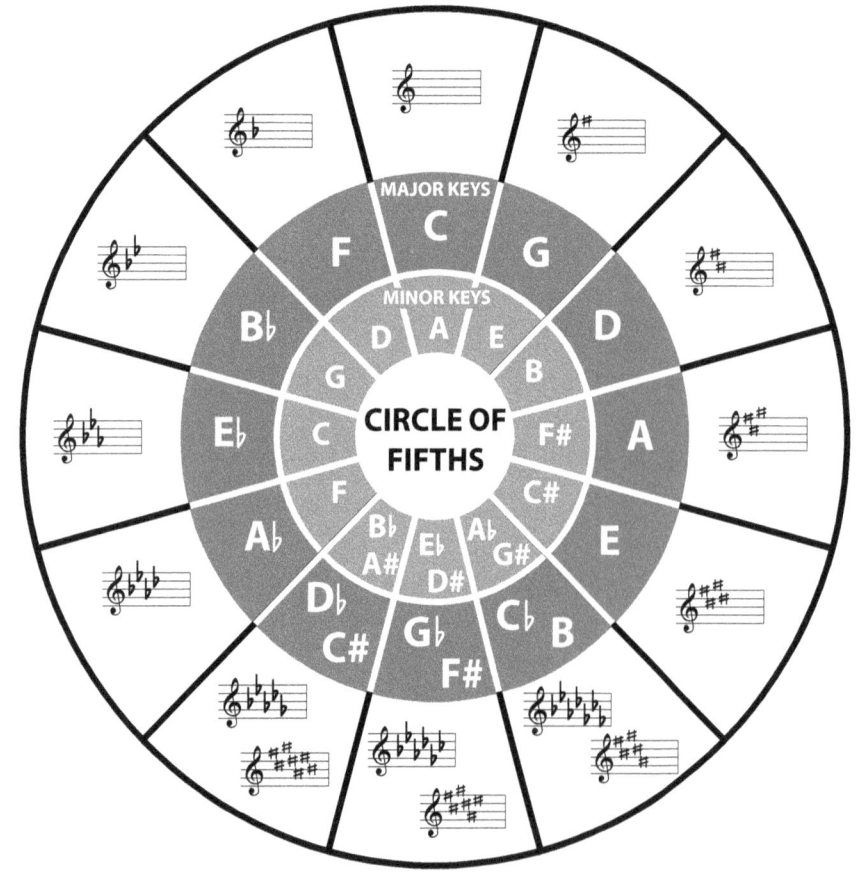

Write the number of sharps or flats
next to each Scale/Key

C _____   F _____

G _____   Bb _____

D _____   Eb _____

A _____   Ab _____

E _____   Db _____

B _____   Gb _____

F# _____   Cb _____

C# _____

Key Signature Memorization Worksheet

Major Key Signatures

SHARPS

_____ _____ _____ _____ _____ _____ _____ _____

FLATS

_____ _____ _____ _____ _____ _____ _____ _____

Relative Minor Key Signatures

SHARPS

_____ _____ _____ _____ _____ _____ _____ _____

FLATS

_____ _____ _____ _____ _____ _____ _____ _____

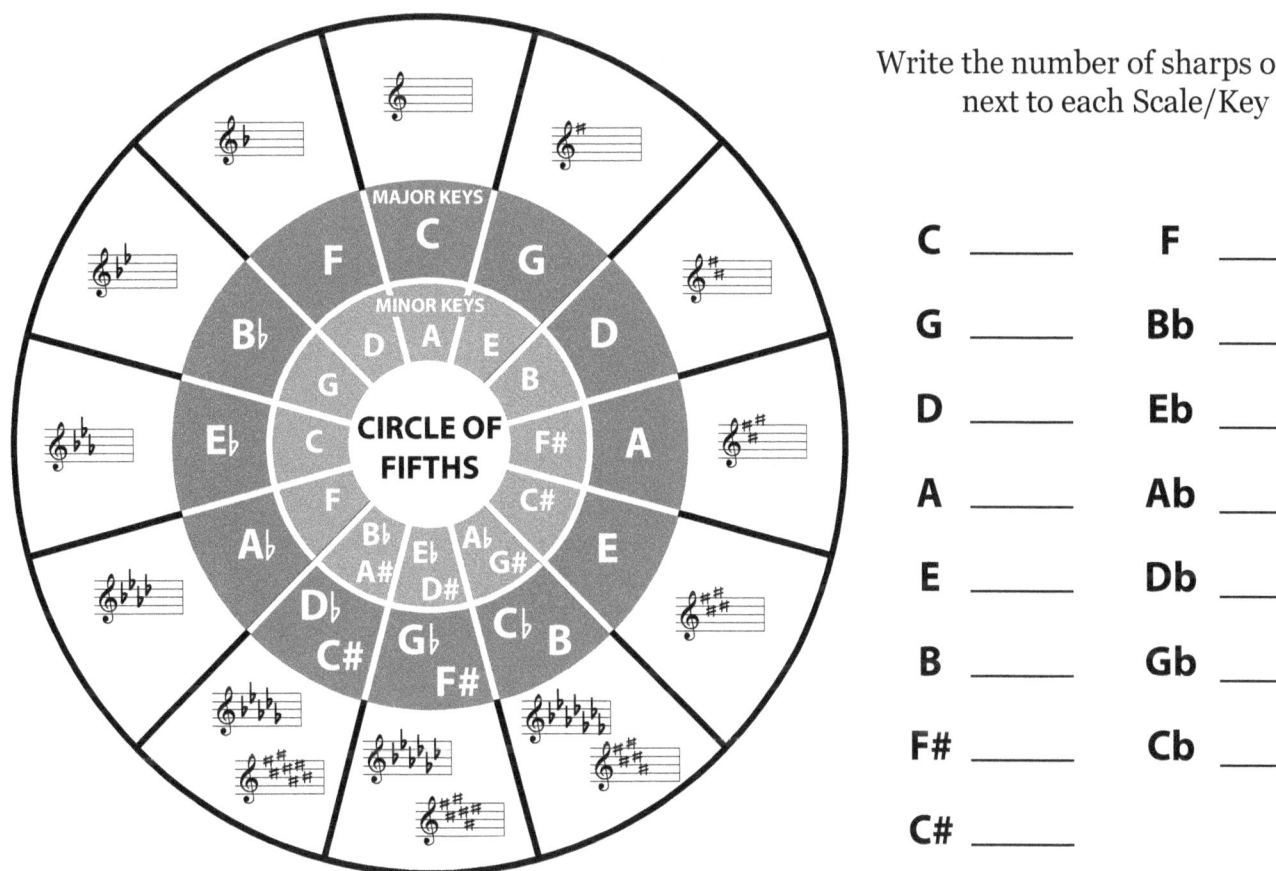

Write the number of sharps or flats
next to each Scale/Key

C _____   F _____

G _____   Bb _____

D _____   Eb _____

A _____   Ab _____

E _____   Db _____

B _____   Gb _____

F# _____   Cb _____

C# _____

71

Key Signature Memorization Worksheet

Major Key Signatures

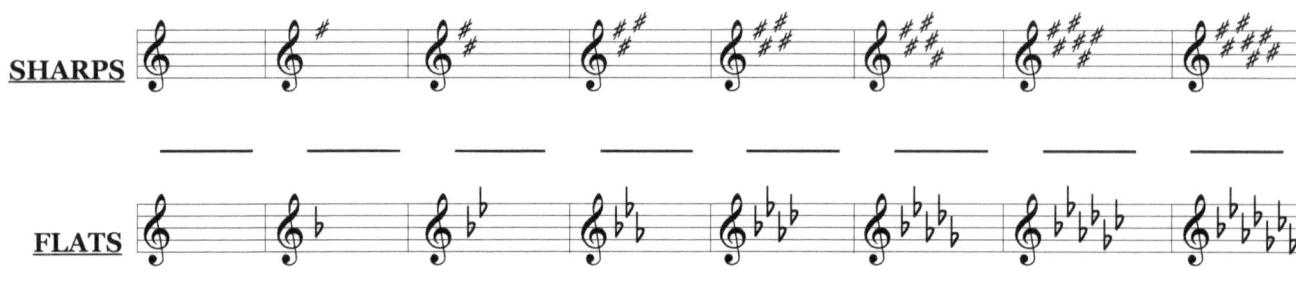

SHARPS

_____ _____ _____ _____ _____ _____ _____ _____

FLATS

_____ _____ _____ _____ _____ _____ _____ _____

Relative Minor Key Signatures

SHARPS

_____ _____ _____ _____ _____ _____ _____ _____

FLATS

_____ _____ _____ _____ _____ _____ _____ _____

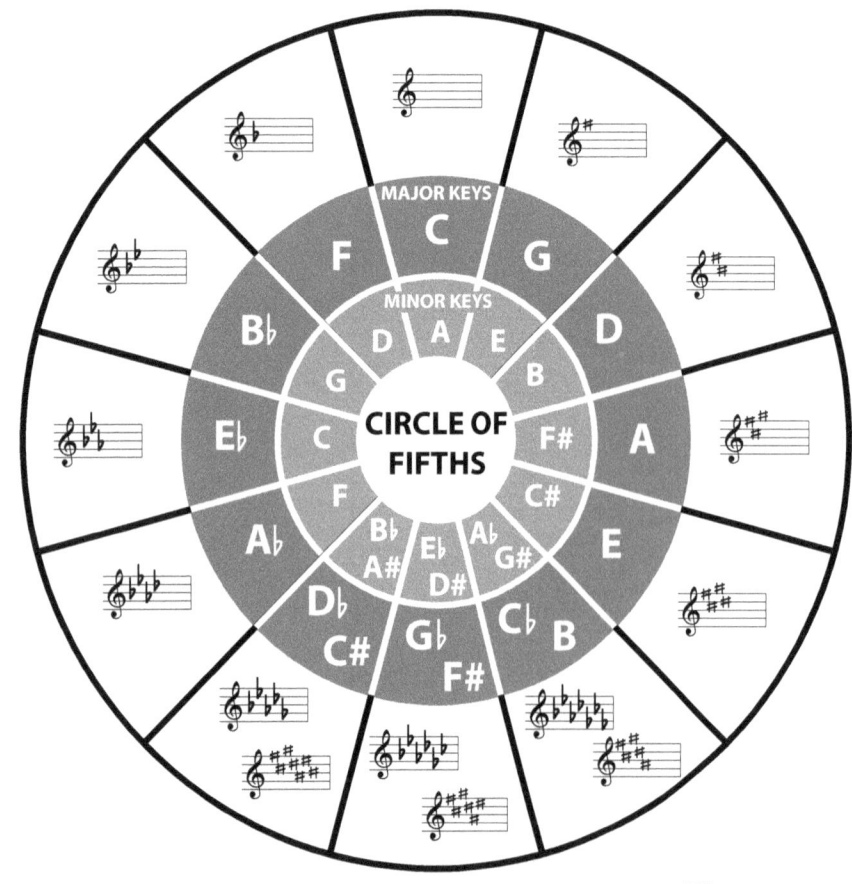

Write the number of sharps or flats next to each Scale/Key

C _____   F _____

G _____   Bb _____

D _____   Eb _____

A _____   Ab _____

E _____   Db _____

B _____   Gb _____

F# _____   Cb _____

C# _____

Key Signature Identification & Scale Practice

Use this worksheet to practice identifying key signatures and writing out the notes that belong to each key. For each illustration, first look at the key signature and write the correct key name on the blank line labeled "Key Signature." Then, using the degree numbers provided below, fill in the corresponding notes of the scale that belong to that key, starting with the tonic (1st degree) and continuing through the 7th degree. Be sure to include any sharps or flats shown in the key signature.

Key Signature _____

_____   _____   _____   _____   _____   _____   _____
I   ii   iii   IV   V   vi   vii°

Key Signature _____

_____   _____   _____   _____   _____   _____   _____
I   ii   iii   IV   V   vi   vii°

Key Signature _____

_____   _____   _____   _____   _____   _____   _____
I   ii   iii   IV   V   vi   vii°

Key Signature _____

_____   _____   _____   _____   _____   _____   _____
I   ii   iii   IV   V   vi   vii°

Key Signature _____

_____   _____   _____   _____   _____   _____   _____
I   ii   iii   IV   V   vi   vii°

Key Signature _____

_____   _____   _____   _____   _____   _____   _____
I   ii   iii   IV   V   vi   vii°

Key Signature _____

_____   _____   _____   _____   _____   _____   _____
I   ii   iii   IV   V   vi   vii°

Key Signature _____

_____   _____   _____   _____   _____   _____   _____
I   ii   iii   IV   V   vi   vii°

Use this worksheet to practice identifying and writing scales for key signatures that contain flats. For each example, begin by examining the key signature and writing the correct key name on the line labeled "Key Signature." Then, using the degree numbers shown below, fill in the notes of the scale that correspond to that key, starting on the tonic (1st degree) and continuing through the 7th degree. Remember to include all the flats indicated in the key signature as you write each note of the scale.

Key Signature _____

I	ii	iii	IV	V	vi	vii°

Key Signature _____

I	ii	iii	IV	V	vi	vii°

Key Signature _____

I	ii	iii	IV	V	vi	vii°

Key Signature _____

I	ii	iii	IV	V	vi	vii°

Key Signature _____

I	ii	iii	IV	V	vi	vii°

Key Signature _____

I	ii	iii	IV	V	vi	vii°

Key Signature _____

I	ii	iii	IV	V	vi	vii°

Key Signature _____

I	ii	iii	IV	V	vi	vii°

Key Signature Identification & Scale Practice

Use this worksheet to practice identifying key signatures and writing out the notes that belong to each key. For each illustration, first look at the key signature and write the correct key name on the blank line labeled "Key Signature." Then, using the degree numbers provided below, fill in the corresponding notes of the scale that belong to that key, starting with the tonic (1st degree) and continuing through the 7th degree. Be sure to include any sharps or flats shown in the key signature.

Key Signature _____

_____   _____   _____   _____   _____   _____   _____
I   ii   iii   IV   V   vi   vii°

Key Signature _____

_____   _____   _____   _____   _____   _____   _____
I   ii   iii   IV   V   vi   vii°

Key Signature _____

_____   _____   _____   _____   _____   _____   _____
I   ii   iii   IV   V   vi   vii°

Key Signature _____

_____   _____   _____   _____   _____   _____   _____
I   ii   iii   IV   V   vi   vii°

Key Signature _____

_____   _____   _____   _____   _____   _____   _____
I   ii   iii   IV   V   vi   vii°

Key Signature _____

_____   _____   _____   _____   _____   _____   _____
I   ii   iii   IV   V   vi   vii°

Key Signature _____

_____   _____   _____   _____   _____   _____   _____
I   ii   iii   IV   V   vi   vii°

Key Signature _____

_____   _____   _____   _____   _____   _____   _____
I   ii   iii   IV   V   vi   vii°

Use this worksheet to practice identifying and writing scales for key signatures that contain flats. For each example, begin by examining the key signature and writing the correct key name on the line labeled "Key Signature." Then, using the degree numbers shown below, fill in the notes of the scale that correspond to that key, starting on the tonic (1st degree) and continuing through the 7th degree. Remember to include all the flats indicated in the key signature as you write each note of the scale.

Key Signature _____

_____ _____ _____ _____ _____ _____ _____
I   ii   iii   IV   V   vi   vii°

Key Signature _____

_____ _____ _____ _____ _____ _____ _____
I   ii   iii   IV   V   vi   vii°

Key Signature _____

_____ _____ _____ _____ _____ _____ _____
I   ii   iii   IV   V   vi   vii°

Key Signature _____

_____ _____ _____ _____ _____ _____ _____
I   ii   iii   IV   V   vi   vii°

Key Signature _____

_____ _____ _____ _____ _____ _____ _____
I   ii   iii   IV   V   vi   vii°

Key Signature _____

_____ _____ _____ _____ _____ _____ _____
I   ii   iii   IV   V   vi   vii°

Key Signature _____

_____ _____ _____ _____ _____ _____ _____
I   ii   iii   IV   V   vi   vii°

Key Signature _____

_____ _____ _____ _____ _____ _____ _____
I   ii   iii   IV   V   vi   vii°

Key Signature Identification & Scale Practice

Use this worksheet to practice identifying key signatures and writing out the notes that belong to each key. For each illustration, first look at the key signature and write the correct key name on the blank line labeled "Key Signature." Then, using the degree numbers provided below, fill in the corresponding notes of the scale that belong to that key, starting with the tonic (1st degree) and continuing through the 7th degree. Be sure to include any sharps or flats shown in the key signature.

Key Signature _____

  I   ii   iii   IV   V   vi   vii°

Key Signature _____

  I   ii   iii   IV   V   vi   vii°

Key Signature _____

  I   ii   iii   IV   V   vi   vii°

Key Signature _____

  I   ii   iii   IV   V   vi   vii°

Key Signature _____

  I   ii   iii   IV   V   vi   vii°

Key Signature _____

  I   ii   iii   IV   V   vi   vii°

Key Signature _____

  I   ii   iii   IV   V   vi   vii°

Key Signature _____

  I   ii   iii   IV   V   vi   vii°

Use this worksheet to practice identifying and writing scales for key signatures that contain flats. For each example, begin by examining the key signature and writing the correct key name on the line labeled "Key Signature." Then, using the degree numbers shown below, fill in the notes of the scale that correspond to that key, starting on the tonic (1st degree) and continuing through the 7th degree. Remember to include all the flats indicated in the key signature as you write each note of the scale.

Key Signature _____

    I   ii   iii   IV   V   vi   vii°

Key Signature _____

    I   ii   iii   IV   V   vi   vii°

Key Signature _____

    I   ii   iii   IV   V   vi   vii°

Key Signature _____

    I   ii   iii   IV   V   vi   vii°

Key Signature _____

    I   ii   iii   IV   V   vi   vii°

Key Signature _____

    I   ii   iii   IV   V   vi   vii°

Key Signature _____

    I   ii   iii   IV   V   vi   vii°

Key Signature _____

    I   ii   iii   IV   V   vi   vii°

Key Signature Identification & Scale Practice

Use this worksheet to practice identifying key signatures and writing out the notes that belong to each key. For each illustration, first look at the key signature and write the correct key name on the blank line labeled "Key Signature." Then, using the degree numbers provided below, fill in the corresponding notes of the scale that belong to that key, starting with the tonic (1st degree) and continuing through the 7th degree. Be sure to include any sharps or flats shown in the key signature.

Key Signature _____

__ I ___ ii ___ iii ___ IV ___ V ___ vi ___ vii°

Key Signature _____

__ I ___ ii ___ iii ___ IV ___ V ___ vi ___ vii°

Key Signature _____

__ I ___ ii ___ iii ___ IV ___ V ___ vi ___ vii°

Key Signature _____

__ I ___ ii ___ iii ___ IV ___ V ___ vi ___ vii°

Key Signature _____

__ I ___ ii ___ iii ___ IV ___ V ___ vi ___ vii°

Key Signature _____

__ I ___ ii ___ iii ___ IV ___ V ___ vi ___ vii°

Key Signature _____

__ I ___ ii ___ iii ___ IV ___ V ___ vi ___ vii°

Key Signature _____

__ I ___ ii ___ iii ___ IV ___ V ___ vi ___ vii°

Use this worksheet to practice identifying and writing scales for key signatures that contain flats. For each example, begin by examining the key signature and writing the correct key name on the line labeled "Key Signature." Then, using the degree numbers shown below, fill in the notes of the scale that correspond to that key, starting on the tonic (1st degree) and continuing through the 7th degree. Remember to include all the flats indicated in the key signature as you write each note of the scale.

Key Signature _____

I	ii	iii	IV	V	vi	vii°

Key Signature _____

I	ii	iii	IV	V	vi	vii°

Key Signature _____

I	ii	iii	IV	V	vi	vii°

Key Signature _____

I	ii	iii	IV	V	vi	vii°

Key Signature _____

I	ii	iii	IV	V	vi	vii°

Key Signature _____

I	ii	iii	IV	V	vi	vii°

Key Signature _____

I	ii	iii	IV	V	vi	vii°

Key Signature _____

I	ii	iii	IV	V	vi	vii°

Key Signature Identification & Scale Practice

Use this worksheet to practice identifying key signatures and writing out the notes that belong to each key. For each illustration, first look at the key signature and write the correct key name on the blank line labeled "Key Signature." Then, using the degree numbers provided below, fill in the corresponding notes of the scale that belong to that key, starting with the tonic (1st degree) and continuing through the 7th degree. Be sure to include any sharps or flats shown in the key signature.

Key Signature _____

_____ _____ _____ _____ _____ _____ _____
I   ii   iii   IV   V   vi   vii°

Key Signature _____

_____ _____ _____ _____ _____ _____ _____
I   ii   iii   IV   V   vi   vii°

Key Signature _____

_____ _____ _____ _____ _____ _____ _____
I   ii   iii   IV   V   vi   vii°

Key Signature _____

_____ _____ _____ _____ _____ _____ _____
I   ii   iii   IV   V   vi   vii°

Key Signature _____

_____ _____ _____ _____ _____ _____ _____
I   ii   iii   IV   V   vi   vii°

Key Signature _____

_____ _____ _____ _____ _____ _____ _____
I   ii   iii   IV   V   vi   vii°

Key Signature _____

_____ _____ _____ _____ _____ _____ _____
I   ii   iii   IV   V   vi   vii°

Key Signature _____

_____ _____ _____ _____ _____ _____ _____
I   ii   iii   IV   V   vi   vii°

Use this worksheet to practice identifying and writing scales for key signatures that contain flats. For each example, begin by examining the key signature and writing the correct key name on the line labeled "Key Signature." Then, using the degree numbers shown below, fill in the notes of the scale that correspond to that key, starting on the tonic (1st degree) and continuing through the 7th degree. Remember to include all the flats indicated in the key signature as you write each note of the scale.

Key Signature _____

I   ii   iii   IV   V   vi   vii°

Key Signature _____

I   ii   iii   IV   V   vi   vii°

Key Signature _____

I   ii   iii   IV   V   vi   vii°

Key Signature _____

I   ii   iii   IV   V   vi   vii°

Key Signature _____

I   ii   iii   IV   V   vi   vii°

Key Signature _____

I   ii   iii   IV   V   vi   vii°

Key Signature _____

I   ii   iii   IV   V   vi   vii°

Key Signature _____

I   ii   iii   IV   V   vi   vii°

Key Signature Identification & Diatonic Chord Practice

Use this worksheet to practice identifying and writing the diatonic chords within each key that contains sharps. Begin by looking at the key signature and writing the key name on the line labeled "Key Signature." Then, using the degree numbers provided, write the chord built on each scale degree, starting with the tonic (I) and continuing through the seventh degree (vii°). Be sure to include the correct accidentals as indicated by the key signature and use the proper chord qualities (major, minor, or diminished) for each degree.

Key Signature _____

_____ _____ _____ _____ _____ _____ _____
I   ii   iii   IV   V   vi   vii°

Key Signature _____

_____ _____ _____ _____ _____ _____ _____
I   ii   iii   IV   V   vi   vii°

Key Signature _____

_____ _____ _____ _____ _____ _____ _____
I   ii   iii   IV   V   vi   vii°

Key Signature _____

_____ _____ _____ _____ _____ _____ _____
I   ii   iii   IV   V   vi   vii°

Key Signature _____

_____ _____ _____ _____ _____ _____ _____
I   ii   iii   IV   V   vi   vii°

Key Signature _____

_____ _____ _____ _____ _____ _____ _____
I   ii   iii   IV   V   vi   vii°

Key Signature _____

_____ _____ _____ _____ _____ _____ _____
I   ii   iii   IV   V   vi   vii°

Key Signature _____

_____ _____ _____ _____ _____ _____ _____
I   ii   iii   IV   V   vi   vii°

Use this worksheet to practice identifying and writing the diatonic chords within each key that contains flats. First, examine the key signature and write the correct key name on the line labeled "Key Signature." Then, using the degree numbers shown, fill in the chords that belong to that key, starting with the tonic (I) and continuing through the seventh degree (vii°). Make sure to include all flats indicated in the key signature and label each chord with its correct quality (major, minor, or diminished).

Key Signature _____

| I | ii | iii | IV | V | vi | vii° |

Key Signature _____

| I | ii | iii | IV | V | vi | vii° |

Key Signature _____

| I | ii | iii | IV | V | vi | vii° |

Key Signature _____

| I | ii | iii | IV | V | vi | vii° |

Key Signature _____

| I | ii | iii | IV | V | vi | vii° |

Key Signature _____

| I | ii | iii | IV | V | vi | vii° |

Key Signature _____

| I | ii | iii | IV | V | vi | vii° |

Key Signature _____

| I | ii | iii | IV | V | vi | vii° |

Key Signature Identification & Diatonic Chord Practice

Use this worksheet to practice identifying and writing the diatonic chords within each key that contains sharps. Begin by looking at the key signature and writing the key name on the line labeled "Key Signature." Then, using the degree numbers provided, write the chord built on each scale degree, starting with the tonic (I) and continuing through the seventh degree (vii°). Be sure to include the correct accidentals as indicated by the key signature and use the proper chord qualities (major, minor, or diminished) for each degree.

Key Signature _____

| I | ii | iii | IV | V | vi | vii° |

Key Signature _____

| I | ii | iii | IV | V | vi | vii° |

Key Signature _____

| I | ii | iii | IV | V | vi | vii° |

Key Signature _____

| I | ii | iii | IV | V | vi | vii° |

Key Signature _____

| I | ii | iii | IV | V | vi | vii° |

Key Signature _____

| I | ii | iii | IV | V | vi | vii° |

Key Signature _____

| I | ii | iii | IV | V | vi | vii° |

Key Signature _____

| I | ii | iii | IV | V | vi | vii° |

Use this worksheet to practice identifying and writing the diatonic chords within each key that contains flats. First, examine the key signature and write the correct key name on the line labeled "Key Signature." Then, using the degree numbers shown, fill in the chords that belong to that key, starting with the tonic (I) and continuing through the seventh degree (vii°). Make sure to include all flats indicated in the key signature and label each chord with its correct quality (major, minor, or diminished).

Key Signature _____

____ ____ ____ ____ ____ ____ ____
  I   ii   iii   IV   V   vi   vii°

Key Signature _____

____ ____ ____ ____ ____ ____ ____
  I   ii   iii   IV   V   vi   vii°

Key Signature _____

____ ____ ____ ____ ____ ____ ____
  I   ii   iii   IV   V   vi   vii°

Key Signature _____

____ ____ ____ ____ ____ ____ ____
  I   ii   iii   IV   V   vi   vii°

Key Signature _____

____ ____ ____ ____ ____ ____ ____
  I   ii   iii   IV   V   vi   vii°

Key Signature _____

____ ____ ____ ____ ____ ____ ____
  I   ii   iii   IV   V   vi   vii°

Key Signature _____

____ ____ ____ ____ ____ ____ ____
  I   ii   iii   IV   V   vi   vii°

Key Signature _____

____ ____ ____ ____ ____ ____ ____
  I   ii   iii   IV   V   vi   vii°

Key Signature Identification & Diatonic Chord Practice

Use this worksheet to practice identifying and writing the diatonic chords within each key that contains sharps. Begin by looking at the key signature and writing the key name on the line labeled "Key Signature." Then, using the degree numbers provided, write the chord built on each scale degree, starting with the tonic (I) and continuing through the seventh degree (vii°). Be sure to include the correct accidentals as indicated by the key signature and use the proper chord qualities (major, minor, or diminished) for each degree.

Key Signature _____

    I   ii   iii   IV   V   vi   vii°

Key Signature _____

    I   ii   iii   IV   V   vi   vii°

Key Signature _____

    I   ii   iii   IV   V   vi   vii°

Key Signature _____

    I   ii   iii   IV   V   vi   vii°

Key Signature _____

    I   ii   iii   IV   V   vi   vii°

Key Signature _____

    I   ii   iii   IV   V   vi   vii°

Key Signature _____

    I   ii   iii   IV   V   vi   vii°

Key Signature _____

    I   ii   iii   IV   V   vi   vii°

Use this worksheet to practice identifying and writing the diatonic chords within each key that contains flats. First, examine the key signature and write the correct key name on the line labeled "Key Signature." Then, using the degree numbers shown, fill in the chords that belong to that key, starting with the tonic (I) and continuing through the seventh degree (vii°). Make sure to include all flats indicated in the key signature and label each chord with its correct quality (major, minor, or diminished).

Key Signature _____

I ___ ii ___ iii ___ IV ___ V ___ vi ___ vii°

Key Signature _____

I ___ ii ___ iii ___ IV ___ V ___ vi ___ vii°

Key Signature _____

I ___ ii ___ iii ___ IV ___ V ___ vi ___ vii°

Key Signature _____

I ___ ii ___ iii ___ IV ___ V ___ vi ___ vii°

Key Signature _____

I ___ ii ___ iii ___ IV ___ V ___ vi ___ vii°

Key Signature _____

I ___ ii ___ iii ___ IV ___ V ___ vi ___ vii°

Key Signature _____

I ___ ii ___ iii ___ IV ___ V ___ vi ___ vii°

Key Signature _____

I ___ ii ___ iii ___ IV ___ V ___ vi ___ vii°

Key Signature Identification & Diatonic Chord Practice

Use this worksheet to practice identifying and writing the diatonic chords within each key that contains sharps. Begin by looking at the key signature and writing the key name on the line labeled "Key Signature." Then, using the degree numbers provided, write the chord built on each scale degree, starting with the tonic (I) and continuing through the seventh degree (vii°). Be sure to include the correct accidentals as indicated by the key signature and use the proper chord qualities (major, minor, or diminished) for each degree.

Key Signature _____

I	ii	iii	IV	V	vi	vii°

Key Signature _____

I	ii	iii	IV	V	vi	vii°

Key Signature _____

I	ii	iii	IV	V	vi	vii°

Key Signature _____

I	ii	iii	IV	V	vi	vii°

Key Signature _____

I	ii	iii	IV	V	vi	vii°

Key Signature _____

I	ii	iii	IV	V	vi	vii°

Key Signature _____

I	ii	iii	IV	V	vi	vii°

Key Signature _____

I	ii	iii	IV	V	vi	vii°

Use this worksheet to practice identifying and writing the diatonic chords within each key that contains flats. First, examine the key signature and write the correct key name on the line labeled "Key Signature." Then, using the degree numbers shown, fill in the chords that belong to that key, starting with the tonic (I) and continuing through the seventh degree (vii°). Make sure to include all flats indicated in the key signature and label each chord with its correct quality (major, minor, or diminished).

Key Signature _____

_____ _____ _____ _____ _____ _____ _____
I   ii   iii   IV   V   vi   vii°

Key Signature _____

_____ _____ _____ _____ _____ _____ _____
I   ii   iii   IV   V   vi   vii°

Key Signature _____

_____ _____ _____ _____ _____ _____ _____
I   ii   iii   IV   V   vi   vii°

Key Signature _____

_____ _____ _____ _____ _____ _____ _____
I   ii   iii   IV   V   vi   vii°

Key Signature _____

_____ _____ _____ _____ _____ _____ _____
I   ii   iii   IV   V   vi   vii°

Key Signature _____

_____ _____ _____ _____ _____ _____ _____
I   ii   iii   IV   V   vi   vii°

Key Signature _____

_____ _____ _____ _____ _____ _____ _____
I   ii   iii   IV   V   vi   vii°

Key Signature _____

_____ _____ _____ _____ _____ _____ _____
I   ii   iii   IV   V   vi   vii°

Key Signature Identification & Diatonic Chord Practice

Use this worksheet to practice identifying and writing the diatonic chords within each key that contains sharps. Begin by looking at the key signature and writing the key name on the line labeled "Key Signature." Then, using the degree numbers provided, write the chord built on each scale degree, starting with the tonic (I) and continuing through the seventh degree (vii°). Be sure to include the correct accidentals as indicated by the key signature and use the proper chord qualities (major, minor, or diminished) for each degree.

Key Signature _____

I   ii   iii   IV   V   vi   vii°

Key Signature _____

I   ii   iii   IV   V   vi   vii°

Key Signature _____

I   ii   iii   IV   V   vi   vii°

Key Signature _____

I   ii   iii   IV   V   vi   vii°

Key Signature _____

I   ii   iii   IV   V   vi   vii°

Key Signature _____

I   ii   iii   IV   V   vi   vii°

Key Signature _____

I   ii   iii   IV   V   vi   vii°

Key Signature _____

I   ii   iii   IV   V   vi   vii°

Use this worksheet to practice identifying and writing the diatonic chords within each key that contains flats. First, examine the key signature and write the correct key name on the line labeled "Key Signature." Then, using the degree numbers shown, fill in the chords that belong to that key, starting with the tonic (I) and continuing through the seventh degree (vii°). Make sure to include all flats indicated in the key signature and label each chord with its correct quality (major, minor, or diminished).

Key Signature _____

_____ _____ _____ _____ _____ _____ _____
I   ii   iii   IV   V   vi   vii°

Key Signature _____

_____ _____ _____ _____ _____ _____ _____
I   ii   iii   IV   V   vi   vii°

Key Signature _____

_____ _____ _____ _____ _____ _____ _____
I   ii   iii   IV   V   vi   vii°

Key Signature _____

_____ _____ _____ _____ _____ _____ _____
I   ii   iii   IV   V   vi   vii°

Key Signature _____

_____ _____ _____ _____ _____ _____ _____
I   ii   iii   IV   V   vi   vii°

Key Signature _____

_____ _____ _____ _____ _____ _____ _____
I   ii   iii   IV   V   vi   vii°

Key Signature _____

_____ _____ _____ _____ _____ _____ _____
I   ii   iii   IV   V   vi   vii°

Key Signature _____

_____ _____ _____ _____ _____ _____ _____
I   ii   iii   IV   V   vi   vii°

Section 3: Interval Practice

SECTION 3: Interval Practice

This section connects sight, sound, and touch through interval recognition and mapping. Write intervals on the staff, find their positions on the guitar neck, and locate them on the piano keyboard. By visualizing and hearing intervals across different instruments, you'll develop both theoretical and practical fluency.

Goal: To accurately identify, hear, and perform intervals across instruments.

Use this page to reinforce your understanding of interval names, distances in half steps, and how they appear on your instrument. Practicing intervals helps improve your ear, your improvisation, and your understanding of scales and chords. Pair this with a metronome and your instrument for maximum effect.

Interval Reference Chart (Declarative Practice)

Interval Name	Semitones	Abbreviation	Example (C as root)
Unison	0	P1	C–C
Minor 2nd	1	m2	C–Db
Major 2nd	2	M2	C–D
Minor 3rd	3	m3	C–Eb
Major 3rd	4	M3	C–E
Perfect 4th	5	P4	C–F
Tritone	6	TT or A4/d5	C–F#/Gb
Perfect 5th	7	P5	C–G
Minor 6th	8	m6	C–Ab
Major 6th	9	M6	C–A
Minor 7th	10	m7	C–Bb
Major 7th	11	M7	C–B
Octave	12	P8	C–C (octave)

Using C for the root note, Here is an example of an exercise you can use to identify and memorize intervals. Simply, select a root note and write the intervals as demonstrated.

TIP: Intervals are counted from the tonic note (1st) to the target note (e.g., C to G = 5 = Perfect 5th).

Intervals on the Staff

Choose a root note and write a second note above it that corresponds an interval. Use whole notes and label the interval chosen (e.g., M3, P5, m6).

Example: Root note: C, Interval: Major 3rd, You write C and E

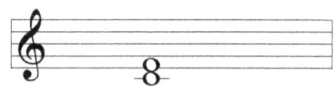

Root: C Interval: M3

Intervals on the Fretboard (Guitar-Focused)

Choose a root note and label it. Then write in the fret positions for different intervals (M3, P5, m7, etc.) from that root on the same string or across strings. This helps you visualize and memorize interval shapes.

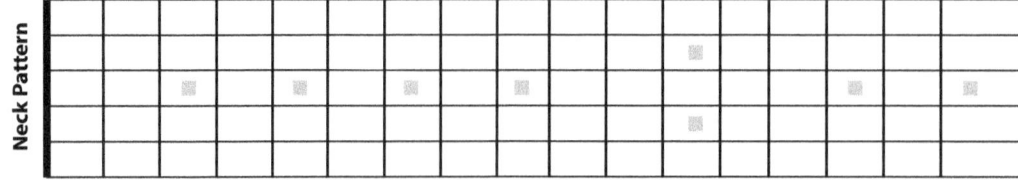

Tip: Use colored pencils to associate the intervals. Example: Root- Black, m3-Red, P5-Green.

Intervals on Piano Keys

Using the blank staff and keyboard diagram, select a root note and interval. Write the interval on the staff and mark the keyboard with the interval:

Root: ___ Interval: ___

Ear Training Ideas

Using your guitar or piano, play two notes back to back and name the interval. Start with a root note play the random second note and try and identify the interval. Once you believe you've identified the interval double check your answer by counting the semitones.

Another exercise is to sing the interval from a reference note. Don't worry how you sound. This is not a vocal exercise.

Interval Practice Blanks

Root: ___ Interval: ___   Root: ___ Interval: ___   Root: ___ Interval: ___

Root: ___ Interval: ___   Root: ___ Interval: ___   Root: ___ Interval: ___

Root: ___ Interval: ___   Root: ___ Interval: ___   Root: ___ Interval: ___

Root: ___ Interval: ___   Root: ___ Interval: ___   Root: ___ Interval: ___

Root: ___ Interval: ___   Root: ___ Interval: ___   Root: ___ Interval: ___

Intervals on Piano Keys

Using the blank staff and keyboard diagram, select a root note and interval. Write the interval on the staff and mark the keyboard with the interval:

Root: ___ Interval: ___

Ear Training Ideas

Using your guitar or piano, play two notes back to back and name the interval. Start with a root note play the random second note and try and identify the interval. Once you believe you've identified the interval double check your answer by counting the semitones.

Another exercise is to sing the interval from a reference note. Don't worry how you sound. This is not a vocal exercise.

Interval Practice Blanks

Root: ___ Interval: ___   Root: ___ Interval: ___   Root: ___ Interval: ___

Root: ___ Interval: ___   Root: ___ Interval: ___   Root: ___ Interval: ___

Root: ___ Interval: ___   Root: ___ Interval: ___   Root: ___ Interval: ___

Root: ___ Interval: ___   Root: ___ Interval: ___   Root: ___ Interval: ___

Root: ___ Interval: ___   Root: ___ Interval: ___   Root: ___ Interval: ___

Intervals on Piano Keys

Using the blank staff and keyboard diagram, select a root note and interval. Write the interval on the staff and mark the keyboard with the interval:

Root: ___ Interval: ___

Ear Training Ideas

Using your guitar or piano, play two notes back to back and name the interval. Start with a root note play the random second note and try and identify the interval. Once you believe you've identified the interval double check your answer by counting the semitones.

Another exercise is to sing the interval from a reference note. Don't worry how you sound. This is not a vocal exercise.

Interval Practice Blanks

Root: ___ Interval: ___   Root: ___ Interval: ___   Root: ___ Interval: ___

Root: ___ Interval: ___   Root: ___ Interval: ___   Root: ___ Interval: ___

Root: ___ Interval: ___   Root: ___ Interval: ___   Root: ___ Interval: ___

Root: ___ Interval: ___   Root: ___ Interval: ___   Root: ___ Interval: ___

Root: ___ Interval: ___   Root: ___ Interval: ___   Root: ___ Interval: ___

Intervals on Piano Keys

Using the blank staff and keyboard diagram, select a root note and interval. Write the interval on the staff and mark the keyboard with the interval:

Root: ___ Interval: ___

Ear Training Ideas

Using your guitar or piano, play two notes back to back and name the interval. Start with a root note play the random second note and try and identify the interval. Once you believe you've identified the interval double check your answer by counting the semitones.

Another exercise is to sing the interval from a reference note. Don't worry how you sound. This is not a vocal exercise.

Interval Practice Blanks

Root: ___ Interval: ___   Root: ___ Interval: ___   Root: ___ Interval: ___

Root: ___ Interval: ___   Root: ___ Interval: ___   Root: ___ Interval: ___

Root: ___ Interval: ___   Root: ___ Interval: ___   Root: ___ Interval: ___

Root: ___ Interval: ___   Root: ___ Interval: ___   Root: ___ Interval: ___

Root: ___ Interval: ___   Root: ___ Interval: ___   Root: ___ Interval: ___

Intervals on Piano Keys

Using the blank staff and keyboard diagram, select a root note and interval. Write the interval on the staff and mark the keyboard with the interval:

Root: ___ Interval: ___

Ear Training Ideas

Using your guitar or piano, play two notes back to back and name the interval. Start with a root note play the random second note and try and identify the interval. Once you believe you've identified the interval double check your answer by counting the semitones.

Another exercise is to sing the interval from a reference note. Don't worry how you sound. This is not a vocal exercise.

Interval Practice Blanks

Root: ___ Interval: ___   Root: ___ Interval: ___   Root: ___ Interval: ___

Root: ___ Interval: ___   Root: ___ Interval: ___   Root: ___ Interval: ___

Root: ___ Interval: ___   Root: ___ Interval: ___   Root: ___ Interval: ___

Root: ___ Interval: ___   Root: ___ Interval: ___   Root: ___ Interval: ___

Root: ___ Interval: ___   Root: ___ Interval: ___   Root: ___ Interval: ___

Intervals on Piano Keys

Using the blank staff and keyboard diagram, select a root note and interval. Write the interval on the staff and mark the keyboard with the interval:

Root: ___ Interval: ___

Ear Training Ideas

Using your guitar or piano, play two notes back to back and name the interval. Start with a root note play the random second note and try and identify the interval. Once you believe you've identified the interval double check your answer by counting the semitones.

Another exercise is to sing the interval from a reference note. Don't worry how you sound. This is not a vocal exercise.

Interval Practice Blanks

Root: ___ Interval: ___   Root: ___ Interval: ___   Root: ___ Interval: ___

Root: ___ Interval: ___   Root: ___ Interval: ___   Root: ___ Interval: ___

Root: ___ Interval: ___   Root: ___ Interval: ___   Root: ___ Interval: ___

Root: ___ Interval: ___   Root: ___ Interval: ___   Root: ___ Interval: ___

Root: ___ Interval: ___   Root: ___ Interval: ___   Root: ___ Interval: ___

Intervals on Piano Keys

Using the blank staff and keyboard diagram, select a root note and interval. Write the interval on the staff and mark the keyboard with the interval:

Root: ___ Interval: ___

Ear Training Ideas

Using your guitar or piano, play two notes back to back and name the interval. Start with a root note play the random second note and try and identify the interval. Once you believe you've identified the interval double check your answer by counting the semitones.

Another exercise is to sing the interval from a reference note. Don't worry how you sound. This is not a vocal exercise.

Interval Practice Blanks

Root: ___ Interval: ___   Root: ___ Interval: ___   Root: ___ Interval: ___

Root: ___ Interval: ___   Root: ___ Interval: ___   Root: ___ Interval: ___

Root: ___ Interval: ___   Root: ___ Interval: ___   Root: ___ Interval: ___

Root: ___ Interval: ___   Root: ___ Interval: ___   Root: ___ Interval: ___

Root: ___ Interval: ___   Root: ___ Interval: ___   Root: ___ Interval: ___

Intervals on Piano Keys

Using the blank staff and keyboard diagram, select a root note and interval. Write the interval on the staff and mark the keyboard with the interval:

Root: ___ Interval: ___

Ear Training Ideas

Using your guitar or piano, play two notes back to back and name the interval. Start with a root note play the random second note and try and identify the interval. Once you believe you've identified the interval double check your answer by counting the semitones.

Another exercise is to sing the interval from a reference note. Don't worry how you sound. This is not a vocal exercise.

Interval Practice Blanks

Root: ___ Interval: ___   Root: ___ Interval: ___   Root: ___ Interval: ___

Root: ___ Interval: ___   Root: ___ Interval: ___   Root: ___ Interval: ___

Root: ___ Interval: ___   Root: ___ Interval: ___   Root: ___ Interval: ___

Root: ___ Interval: ___   Root: ___ Interval: ___   Root: ___ Interval: ___

Root: ___ Interval: ___   Root: ___ Interval: ___   Root: ___ Interval: ___

Intervals on Piano Keys

Using the blank staff and keyboard diagram, select a root note and interval. Write the interval on the staff and mark the keyboard with the interval:

Root: ___ Interval: ___

Ear Training Ideas

Using your guitar or piano, play two notes back to back and name the interval. Start with a root note play the random second note and try and identify the interval. Once you believe you've identified the interval double check your answer by counting the semitones.

Another exercise is to sing the interval from a reference note. Don't worry how you sound. This is not a vocal exercise.

Interval Practice Blanks

Root: ___ Interval: ___   **Root: ___ Interval: ___**   **Root: ___ Interval: ___**

Root: ___ Interval: ___   **Root: ___ Interval: ___**   **Root: ___ Interval: ___**

Root: ___ Interval: ___   **Root: ___ Interval: ___**   **Root: ___ Interval: ___**

Root: ___ Interval: ___   **Root: ___ Interval: ___**   **Root: ___ Interval: ___**

Root: ___ Interval: ___   **Root: ___ Interval: ___**   **Root: ___ Interval: ___**

Intervals on Piano Keys

Using the blank staff and keyboard diagram, select a root note and interval. Write the interval on the staff and mark the keyboard with the interval:

Root: ___ Interval: ___

Ear Training Ideas

Using your guitar or piano, play two notes back to back and name the interval. Start with a root note play the random second note and try and identify the interval. Once you believe you've identified the interval double check your answer by counting the semitones.

Another exercise is to sing the interval from a reference note. Don't worry how you sound. This is not a vocal exercise.

Interval Practice Blanks

Root: ___ Interval: ___

Root: ___ Interval: ___

Root: ___ Interval: ___

Root: ___ Interval: ___

Root: ___ Interval: ___

Root: ___ Interval: ___

Root: ___ Interval: ___

Root: ___ Interval: ___

Root: ___ Interval: ___

Root: ___ Interval: ___

Root: ___ Interval: ___

Root: ___ Interval: ___

Root: ___ Interval: ___

Root: ___ Interval: ___

Root: ___ Interval: ___

Fretboard Blanks

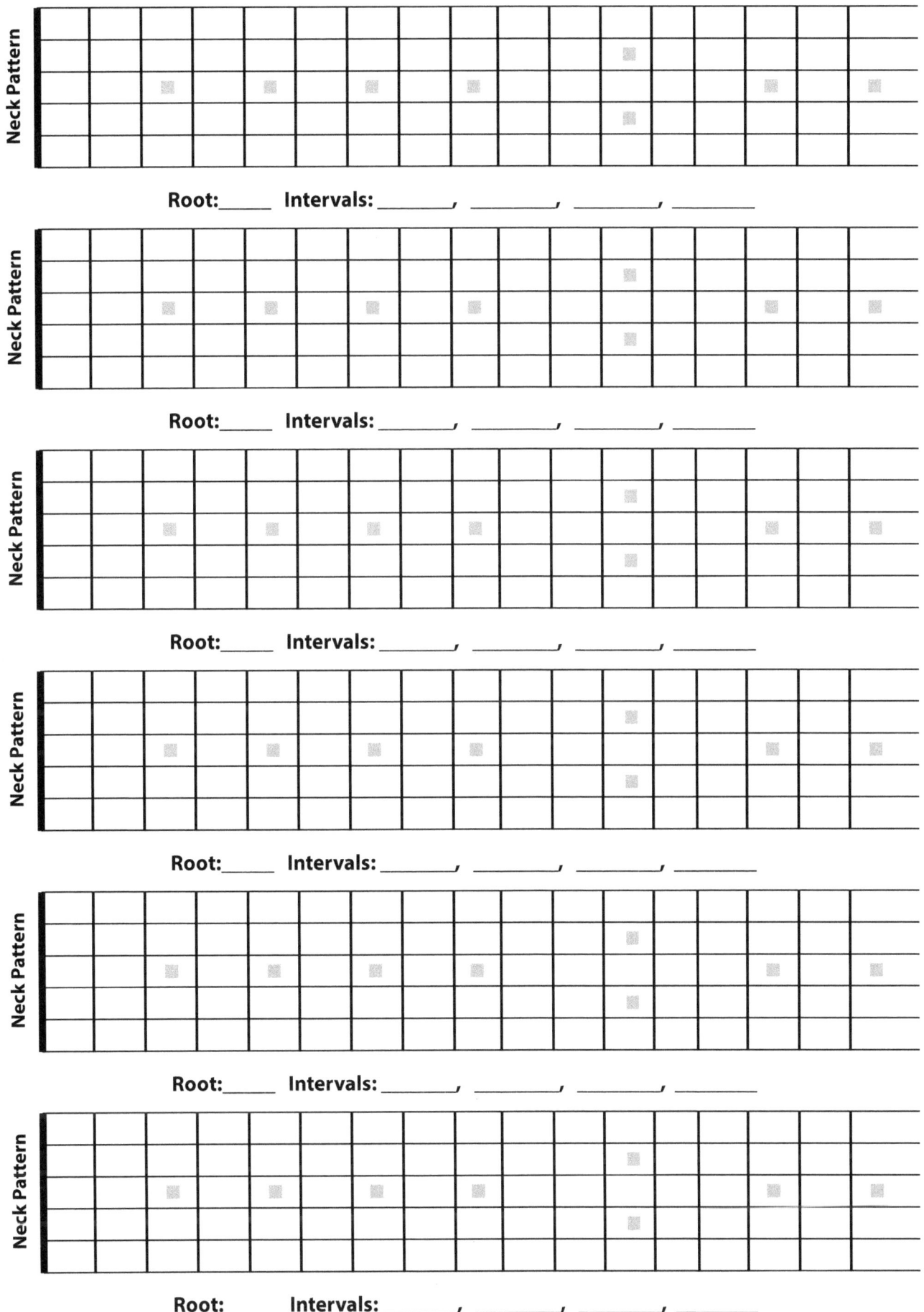

Neck Pattern

Root:_____ Intervals: _____, _____, _____, _____

Neck Pattern

Root:_____ Intervals: _____, _____, _____, _____

Neck Pattern

Root:_____ Intervals: _____, _____, _____, _____

Neck Pattern

Root:_____ Intervals: _____, _____, _____, _____

Neck Pattern

Root:_____ Intervals: _____, _____, _____, _____

Neck Pattern

Root:_____ Intervals: _____, _____, _____, _____

Fretboard Blanks

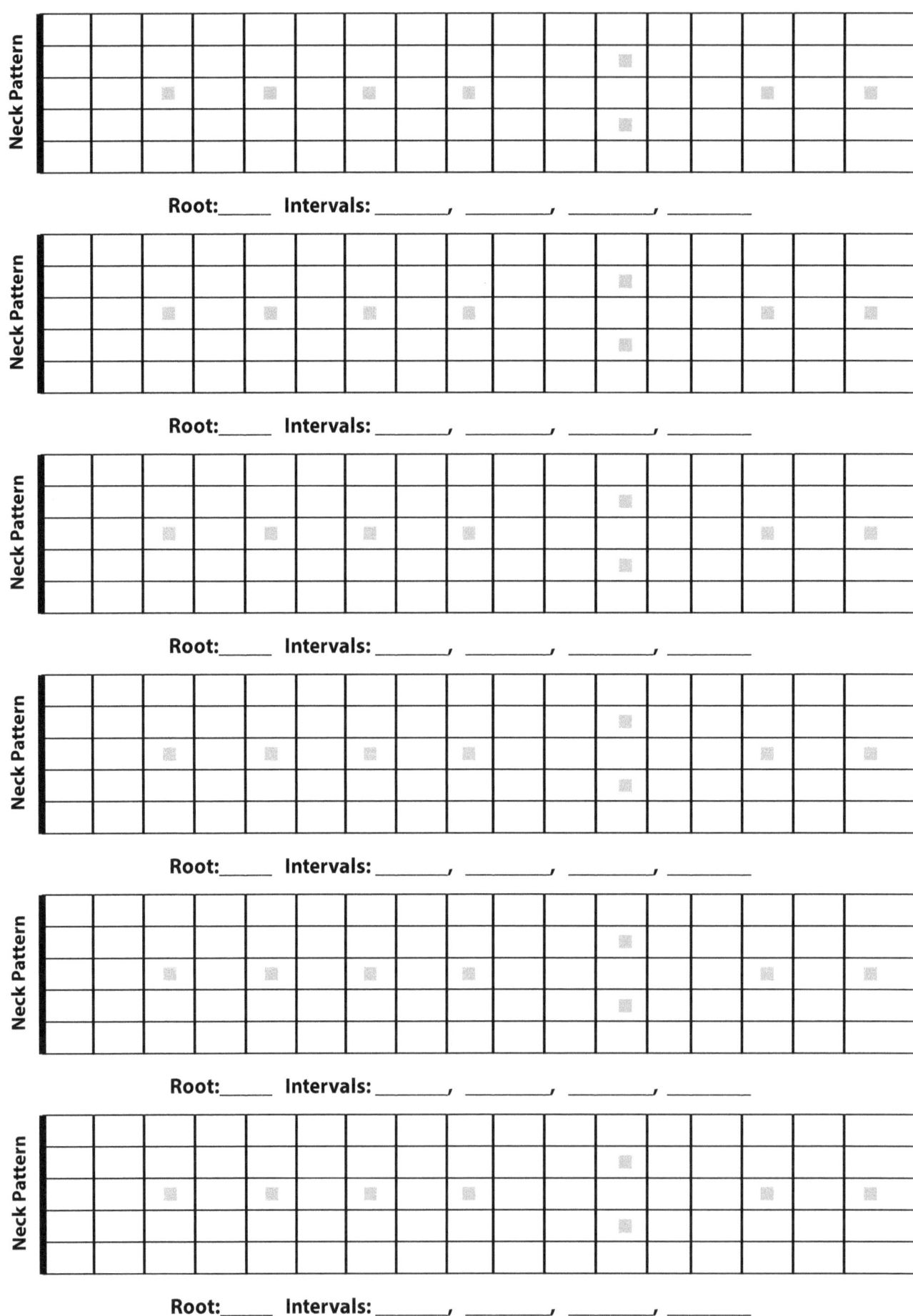

Root:_____ Intervals: _____ , _____ , _____ , _____

Root:_____ Intervals: _____ , _____ , _____ , _____

Root:_____ Intervals: _____ , _____ , _____ , _____

Root:_____ Intervals: _____ , _____ , _____ , _____

Root:_____ Intervals: _____ , _____ , _____ , _____

Root:_____ Intervals: _____ , _____ , _____ , _____

Fretboard Blanks

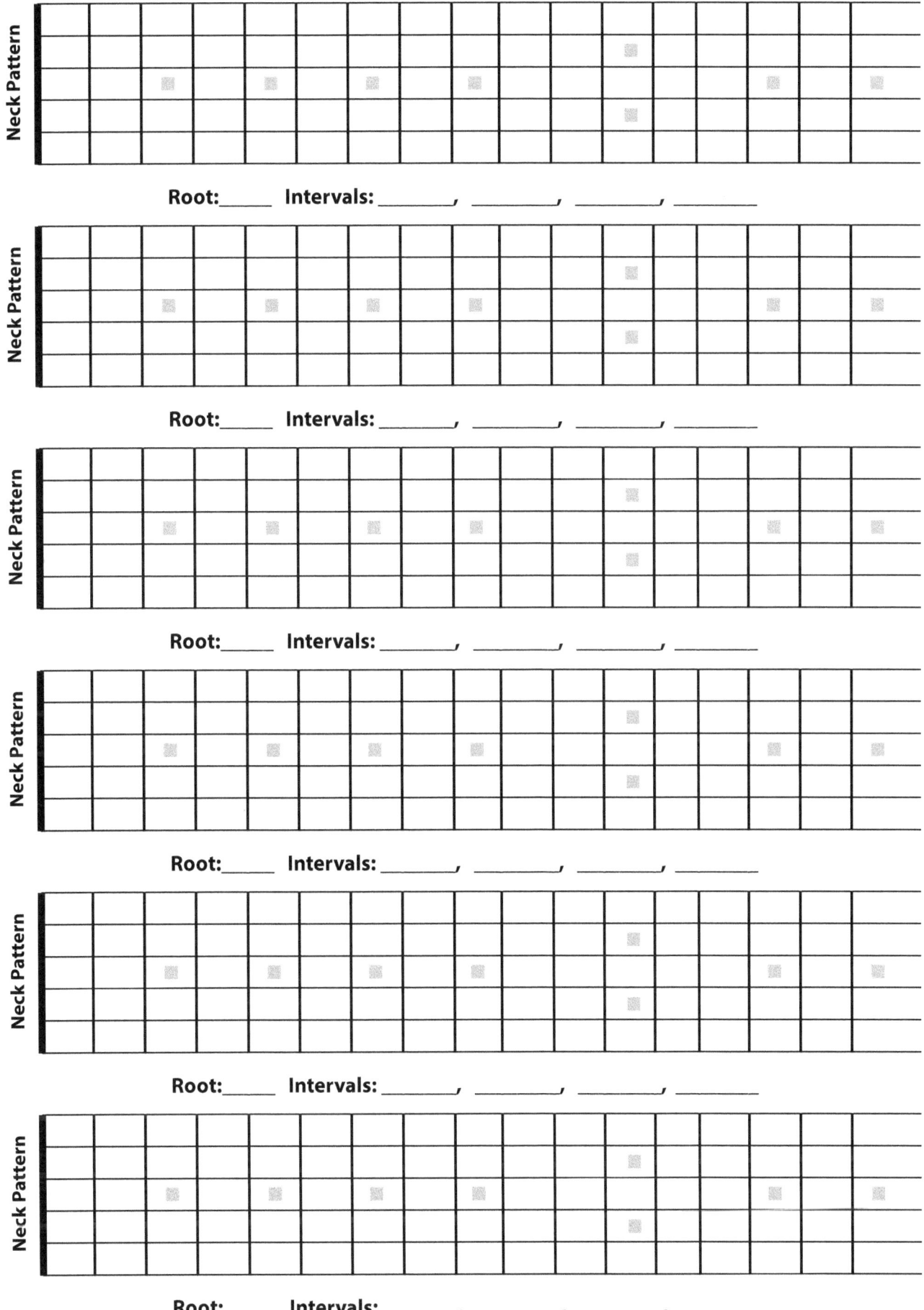

Neck Pattern

Root:_____   Intervals: _____, _____, _____, _____

Neck Pattern

Root:_____   Intervals: _____, _____, _____, _____

Neck Pattern

Root:_____   Intervals: _____, _____, _____, _____

Neck Pattern

Root:_____   Intervals: _____, _____, _____, _____

Neck Pattern

Root:_____   Intervals: _____, _____, _____, _____

Neck Pattern

Root:_____   Intervals: _____, _____, _____, _____

Fretboard Blanks

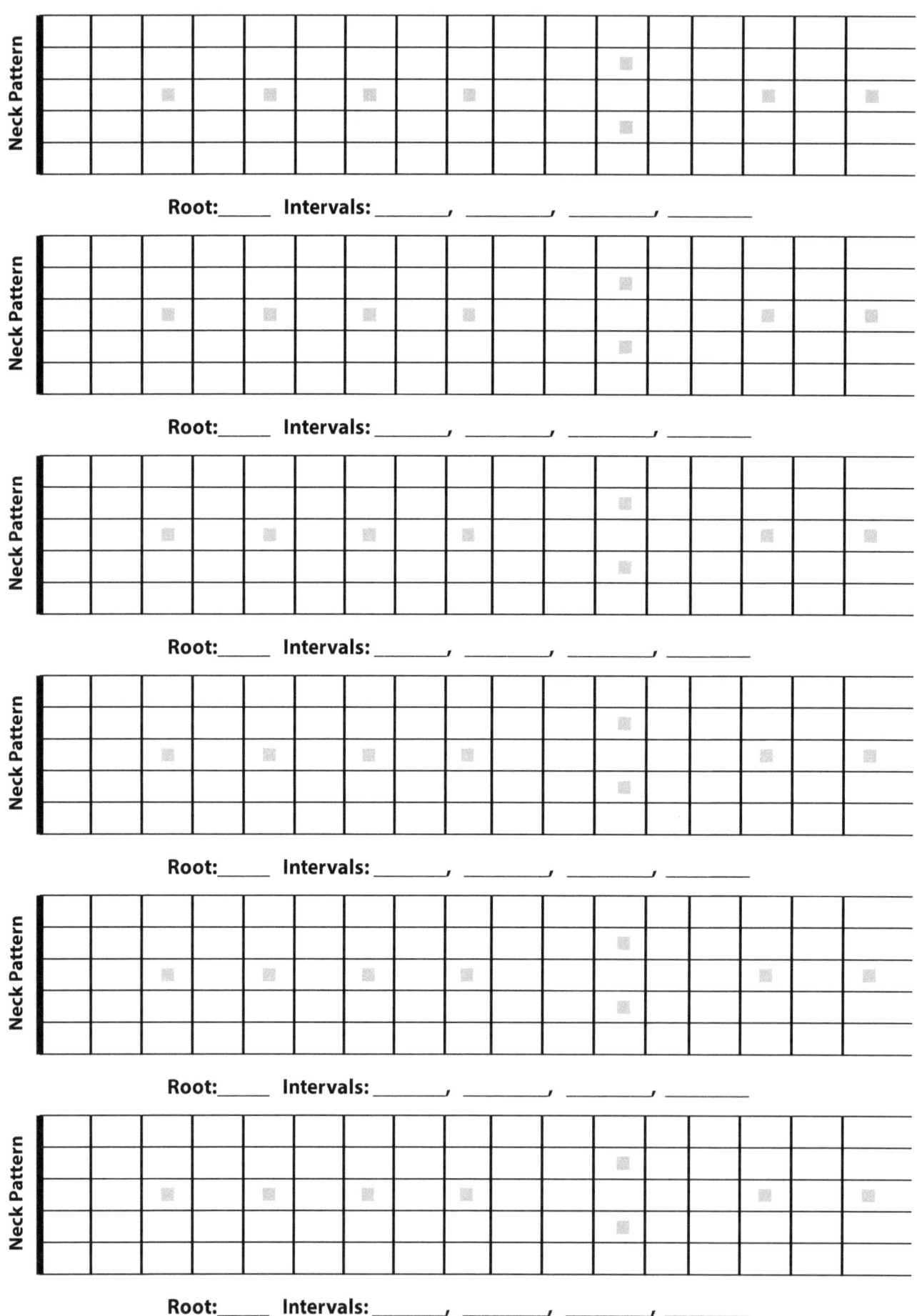

Root:_____ Intervals: _____, _____, _____, _____

Root:_____ Intervals: _____, _____, _____, _____

Root:_____ Intervals: _____, _____, _____, _____

Root:_____ Intervals: _____, _____, _____, _____

Root:_____ Intervals: _____, _____, _____, _____

Root:_____ Intervals: _____, _____, _____, _____

Fretboard Blanks

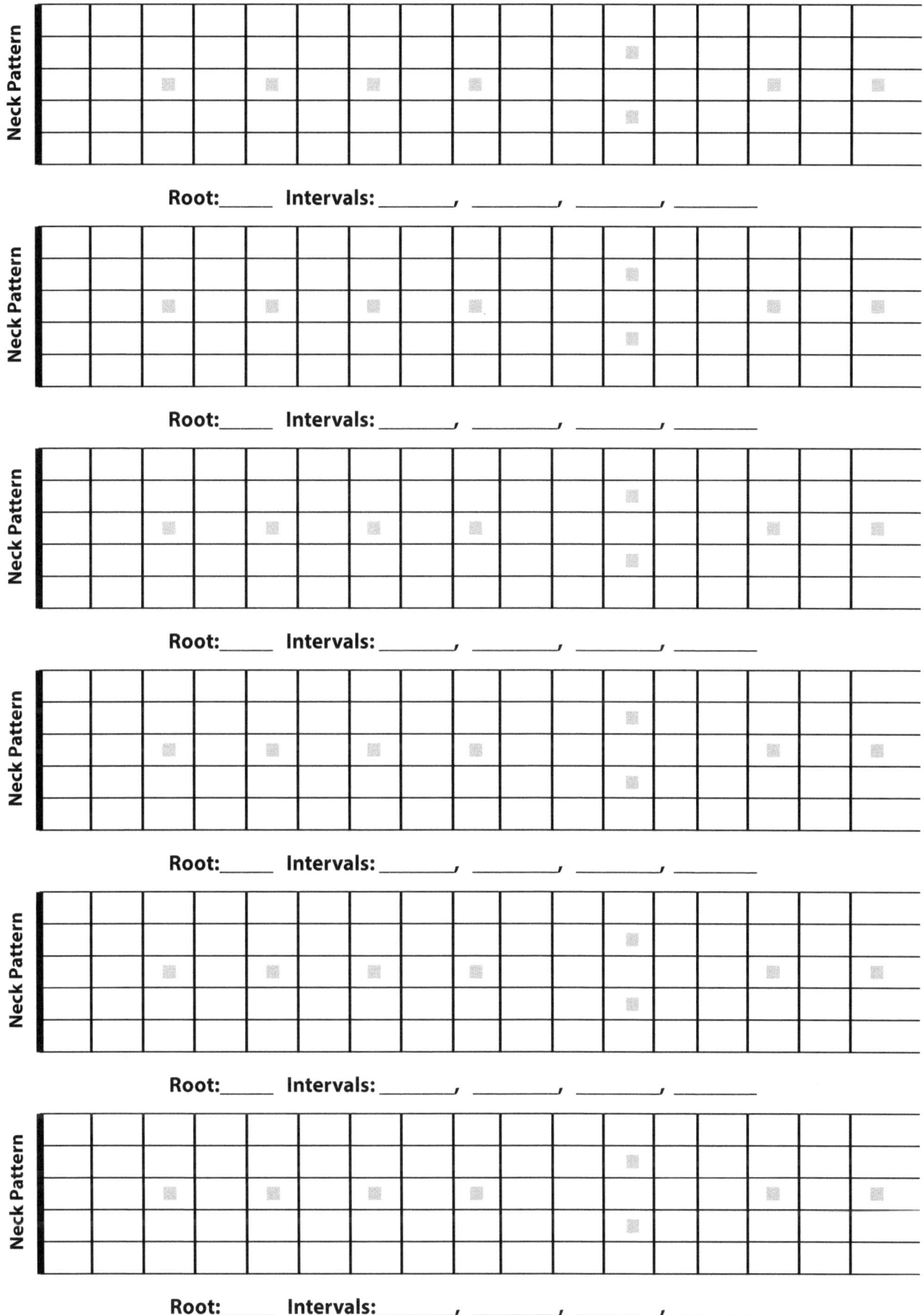

Root:_____ **Intervals:** _____, _____, _____, _____

Root:_____ **Intervals:** _____, _____, _____, _____

Root:_____ **Intervals:** _____, _____, _____, _____

Root:_____ **Intervals:** _____, _____, _____, _____

Root:_____ **Intervals:** _____, _____, _____, _____

Root:_____ **Intervals:** _____, _____, _____, _____

Fretboard Blanks

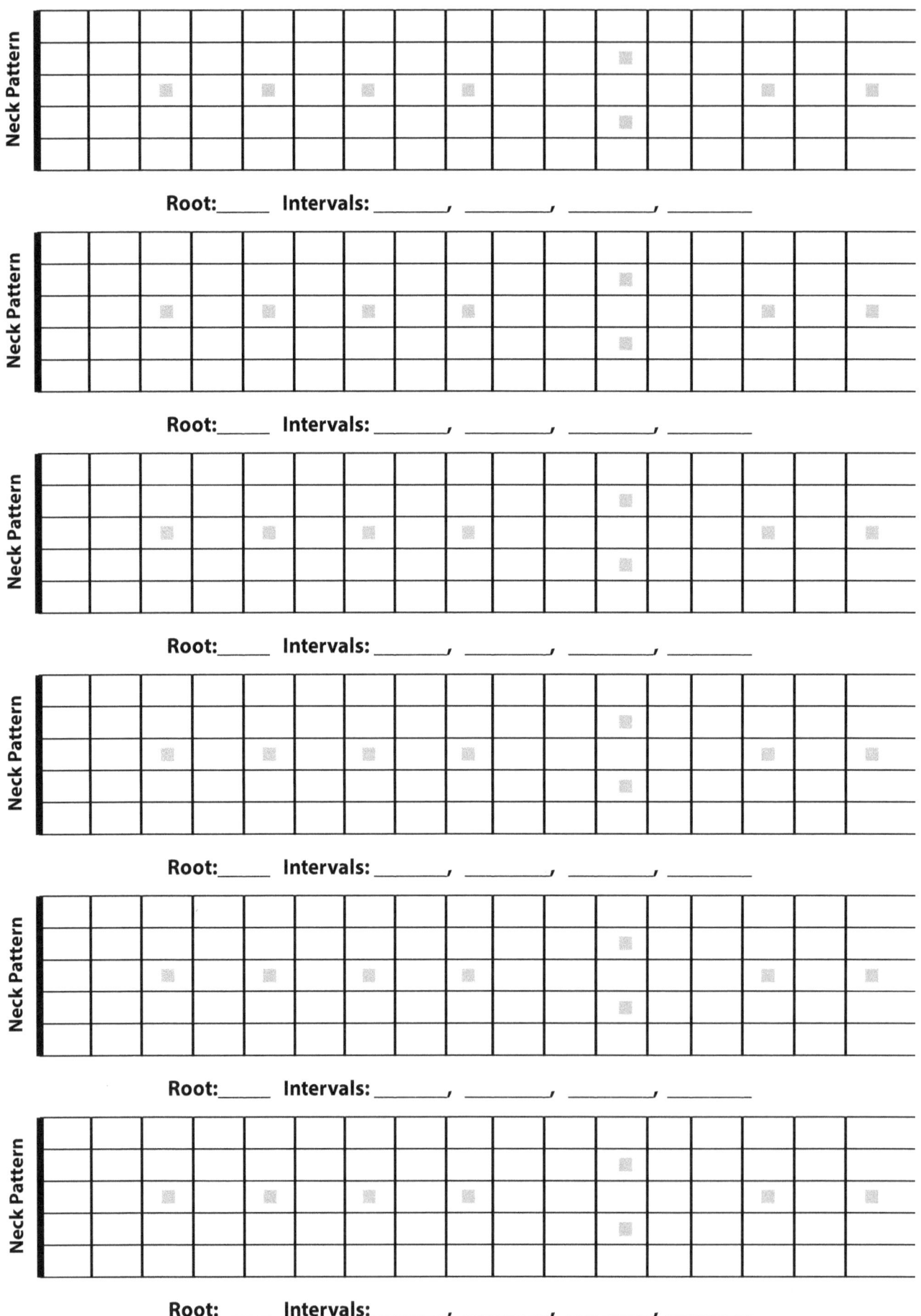

Root:_____ Intervals: _____, _____, _____, _____

Root:_____ Intervals: _____, _____, _____, _____

Root:_____ Intervals: _____, _____, _____, _____

Root:_____ Intervals: _____, _____, _____, _____

Root:_____ Intervals: _____, _____, _____, _____

Root:_____ Intervals: _____, _____, _____, _____

Fretboard Blanks

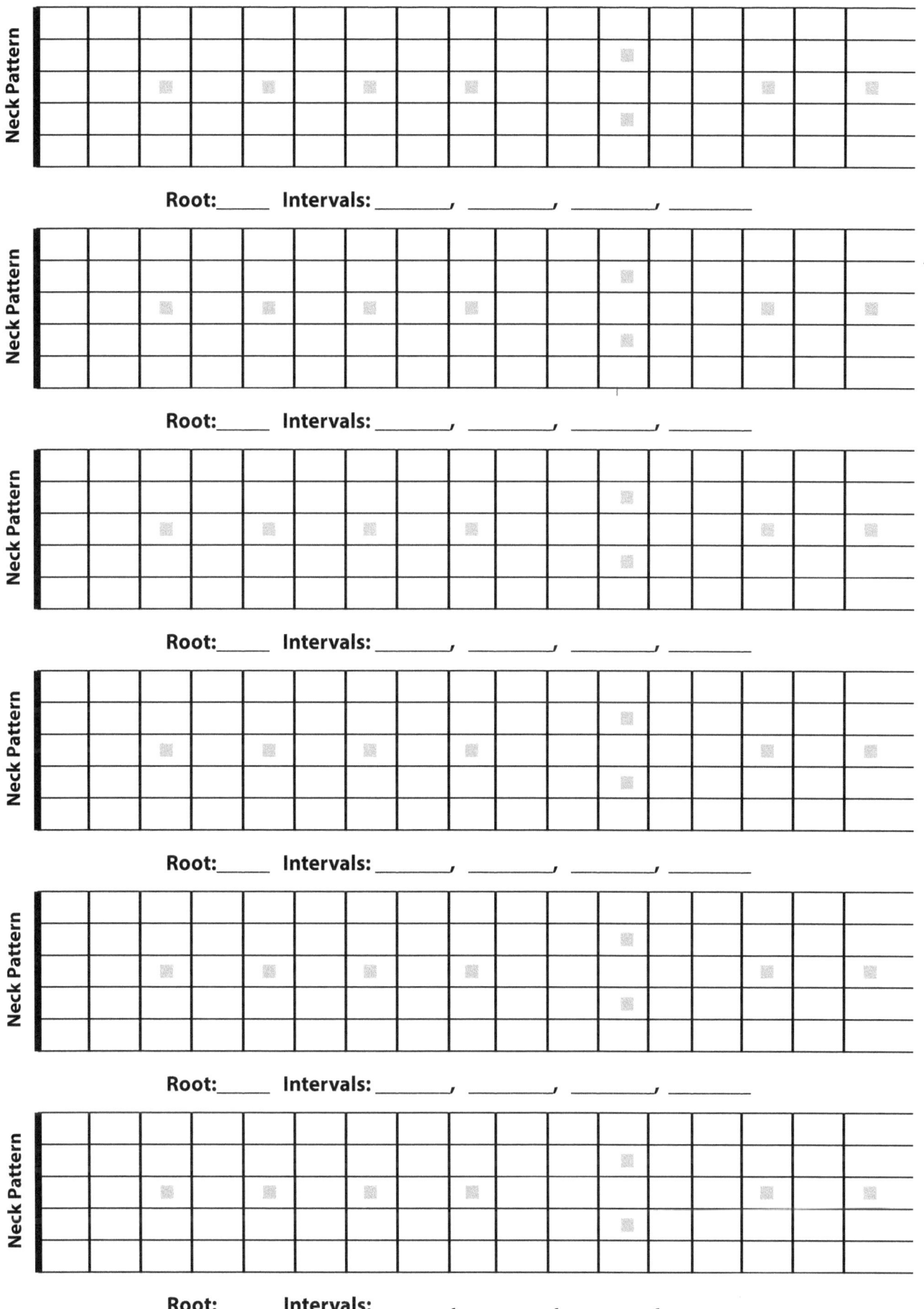

Root:_____ Intervals: _____, _____, _____, _____

Root:_____ Intervals: _____, _____, _____, _____

Root:_____ Intervals: _____, _____, _____, _____

Root:_____ Intervals: _____, _____, _____, _____

Root:_____ Intervals: _____, _____, _____, _____

Fretboard Blanks

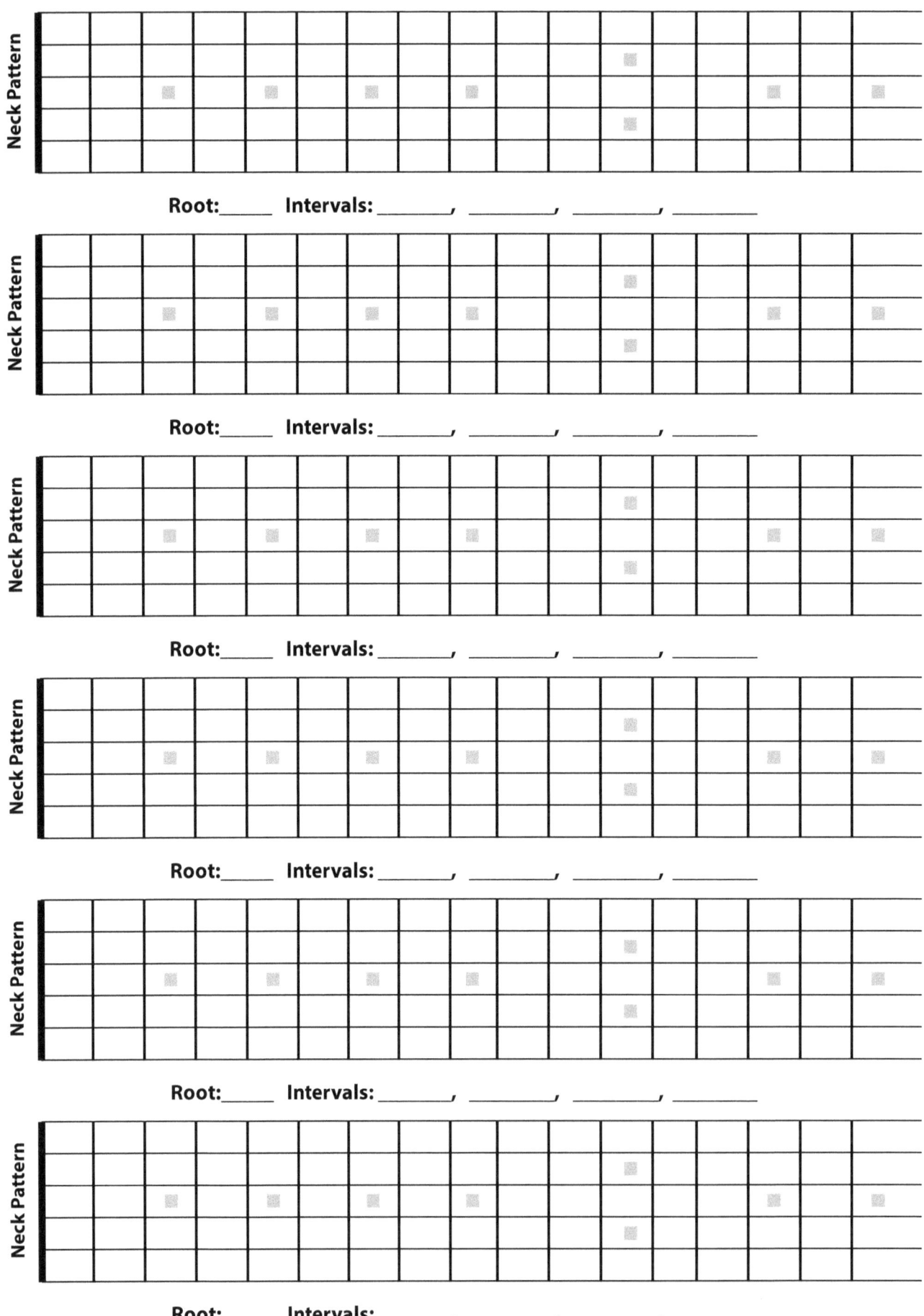

Neck Pattern

Root:_____ **Intervals:** _____, _____, _____, _____

Neck Pattern

Root:_____ **Intervals:** _____, _____, _____, _____

Neck Pattern

Root:_____ **Intervals:** _____, _____, _____, _____

Neck Pattern

Root:_____ **Intervals:** _____, _____, _____, _____

Neck Pattern

Root:_____ **Intervals:** _____, _____, _____, _____

Neck Pattern

Root:_____ **Intervals:** _____, _____, _____, _____

Fretboard Blanks

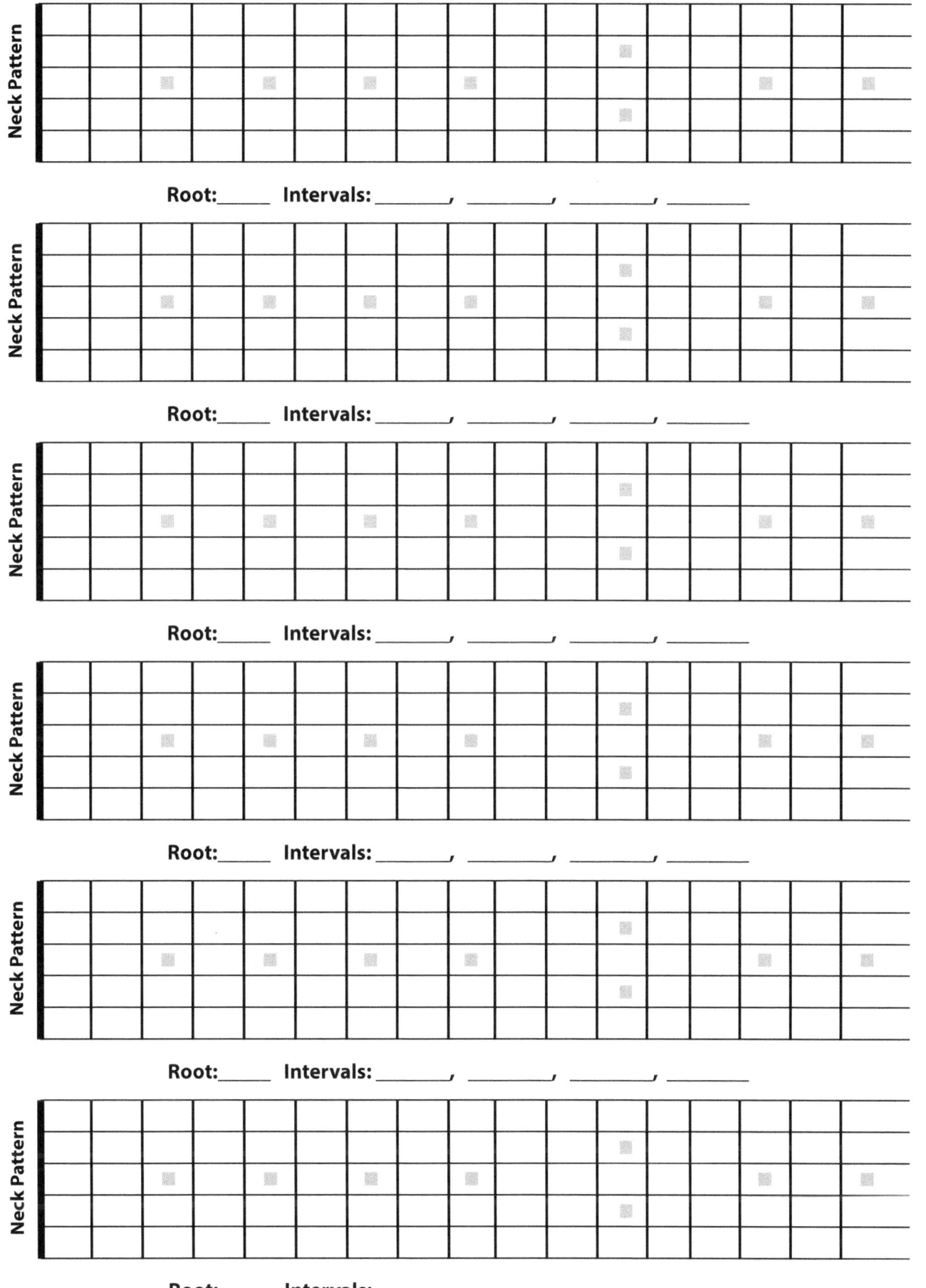

Root:_____   Intervals: _____, _____, _____, _____

Root:_____   Intervals: _____, _____, _____, _____

Root:_____   Intervals: _____, _____, _____, _____

Root:_____   Intervals: _____, _____, _____, _____

Root:_____   Intervals: _____, _____, _____, _____

Root:_____   Intervals: _____, _____, _____, _____

Fretboard Blanks

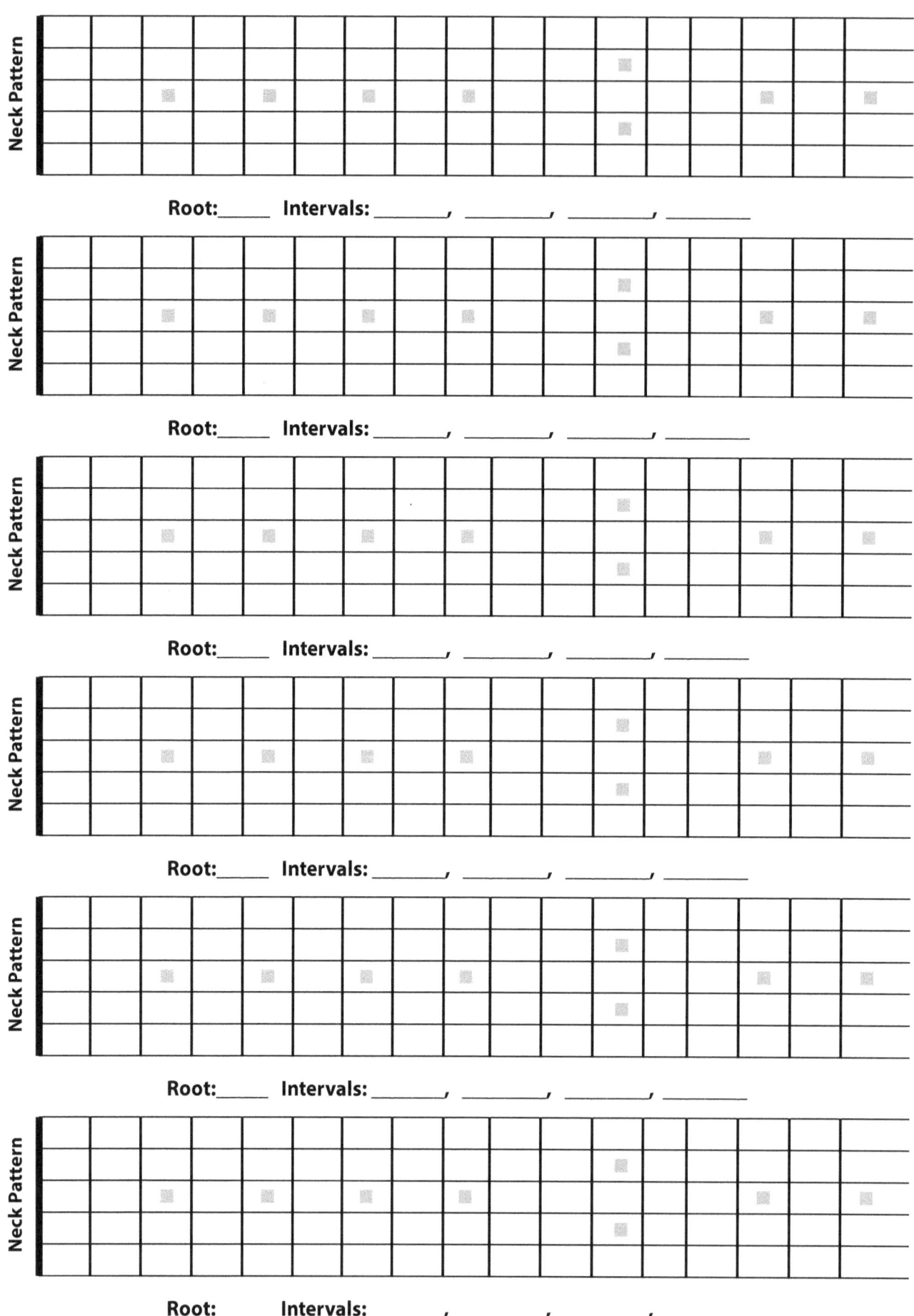

Root:_____ Intervals: _____, _____, _____, _____

Root:_____ Intervals: _____, _____, _____, _____

Root:_____ Intervals: _____, _____, _____, _____

Root:_____ Intervals: _____, _____, _____, _____

Root:_____ Intervals: _____, _____, _____, _____

Root:_____ Intervals: _____, _____, _____, _____

Piano Blanks

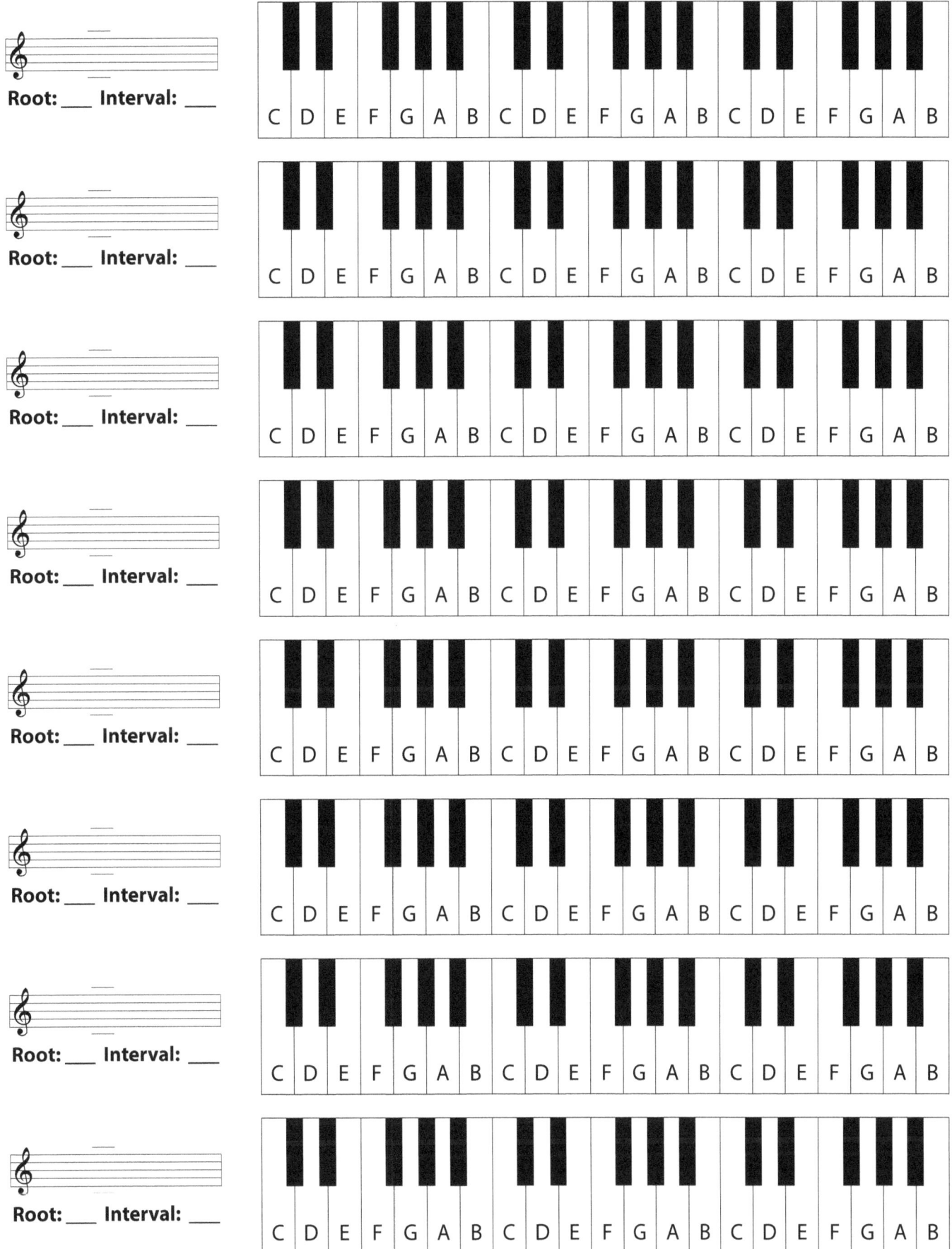

Root: ___ Interval: ___

Root: ___ Interval: ___

Root: ___ Interval: ___

Root: ___ Interval: ___

Root: ___ Interval: ___

Root: ___ Interval: ___

Root: ___ Interval: ___

Root: ___ Interval: ___

Piano Blanks

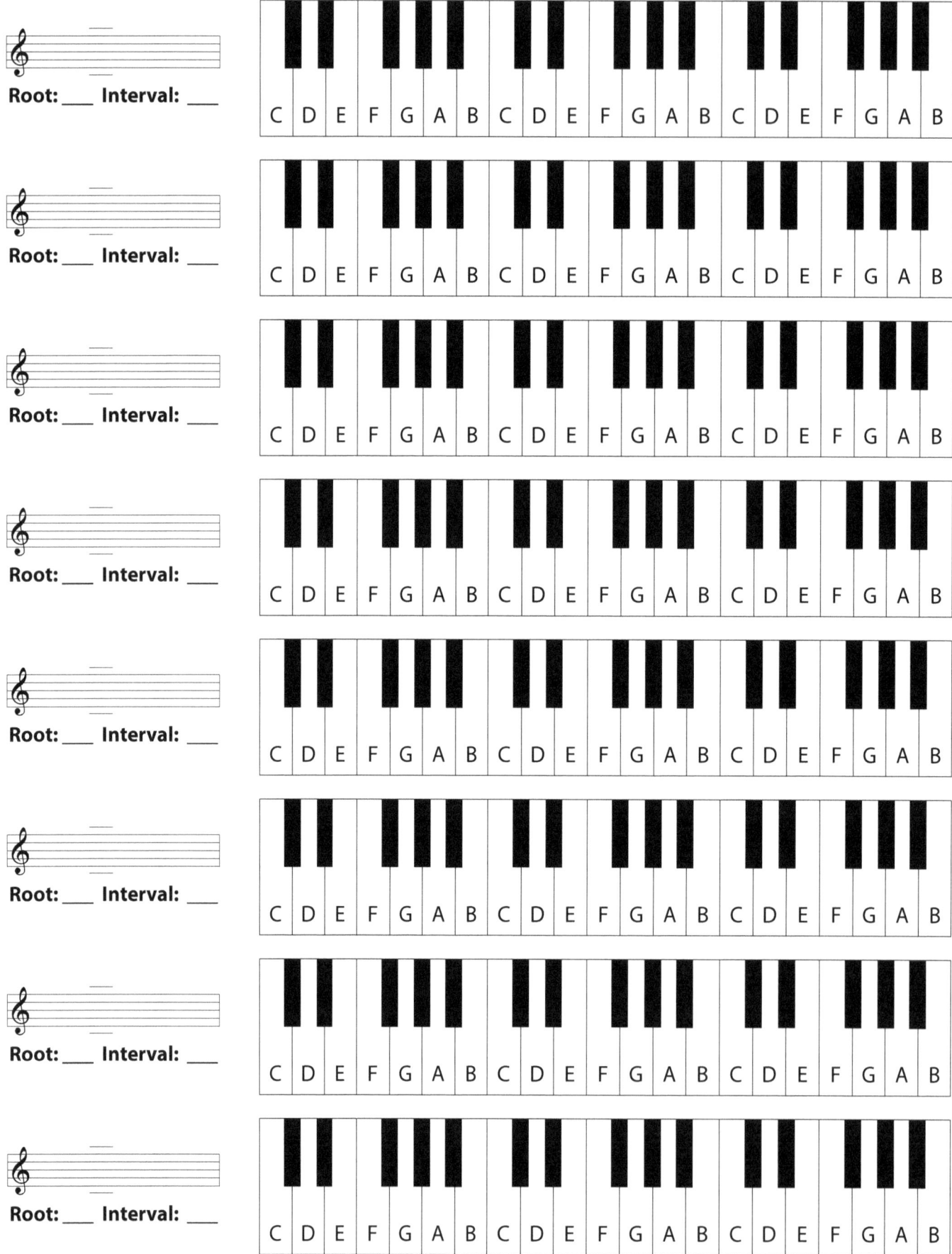

Root: ___ Interval: ___

Root: ___ Interval: ___

Root: ___ Interval: ___

Root: ___ Interval: ___

Root: ___ Interval: ___

Root: ___ Interval: ___

Root: ___ Interval: ___

Root: ___ Interval: ___

Piano Blanks

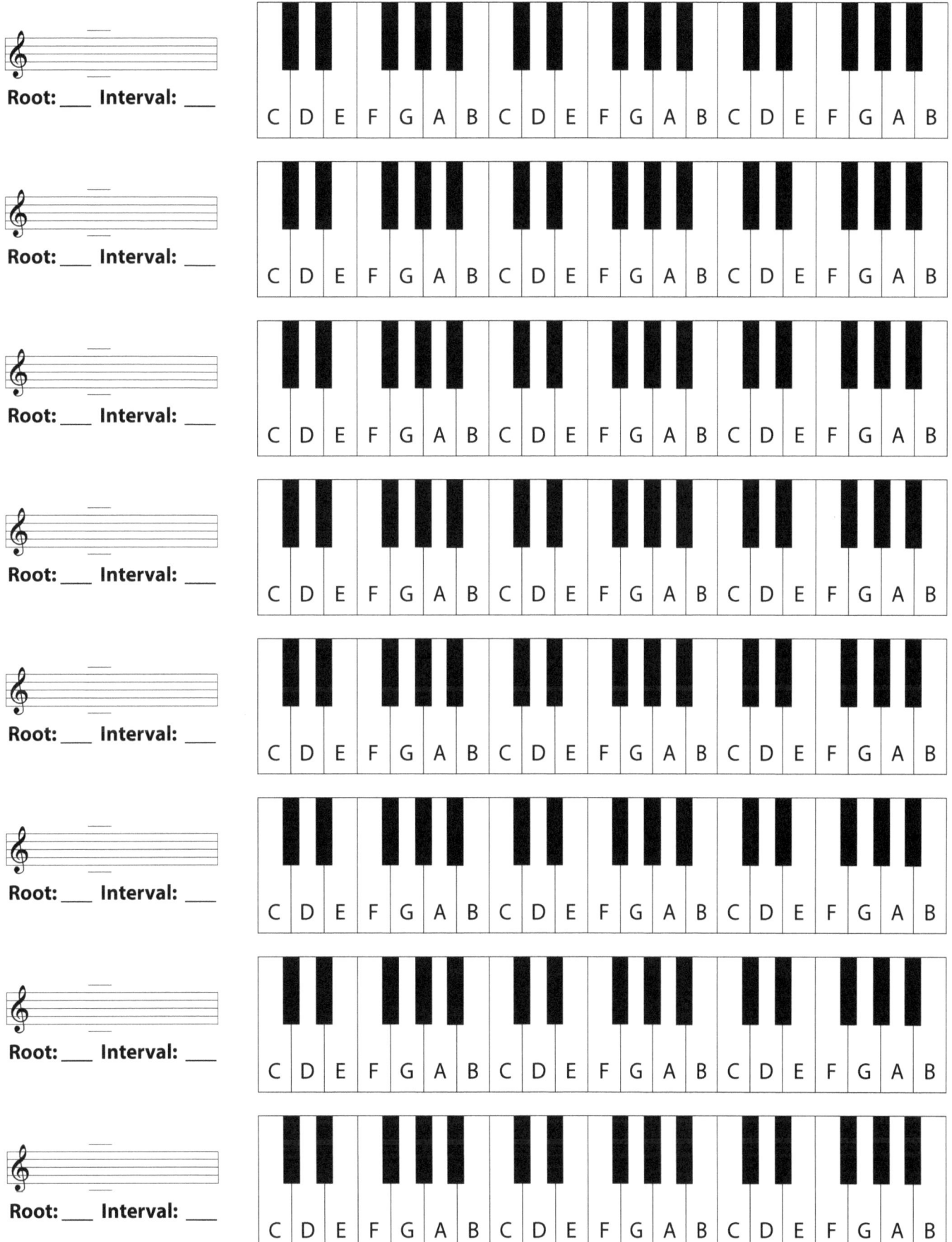

Root: ___ Interval: ___

Root: ___ Interval: ___

Root: ___ Interval: ___

Root: ___ Interval: ___

Root: ___ Interval: ___

Root: ___ Interval: ___

Root: ___ Interval: ___

Root: ___ Interval: ___

Piano Blanks

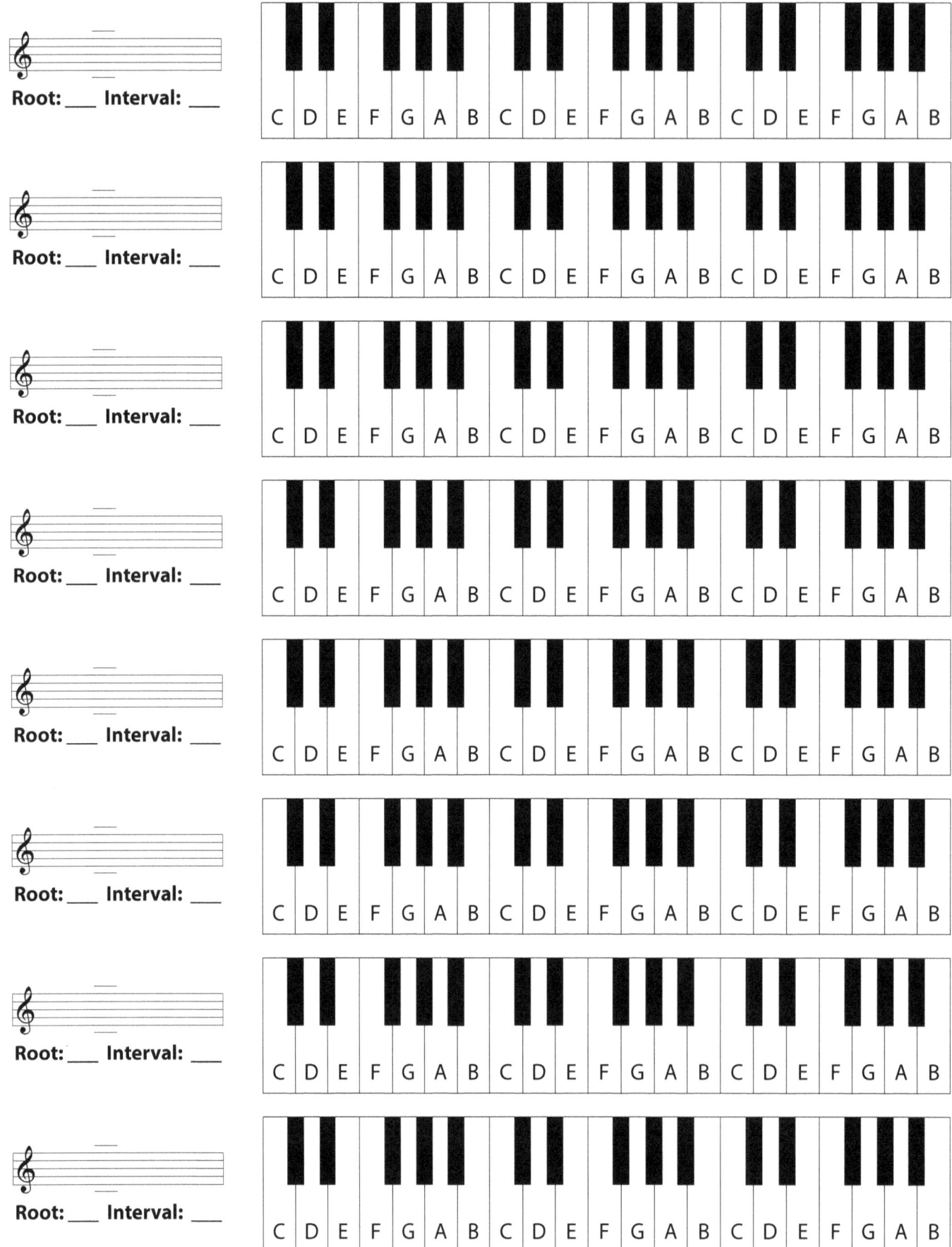

Piano Blanks

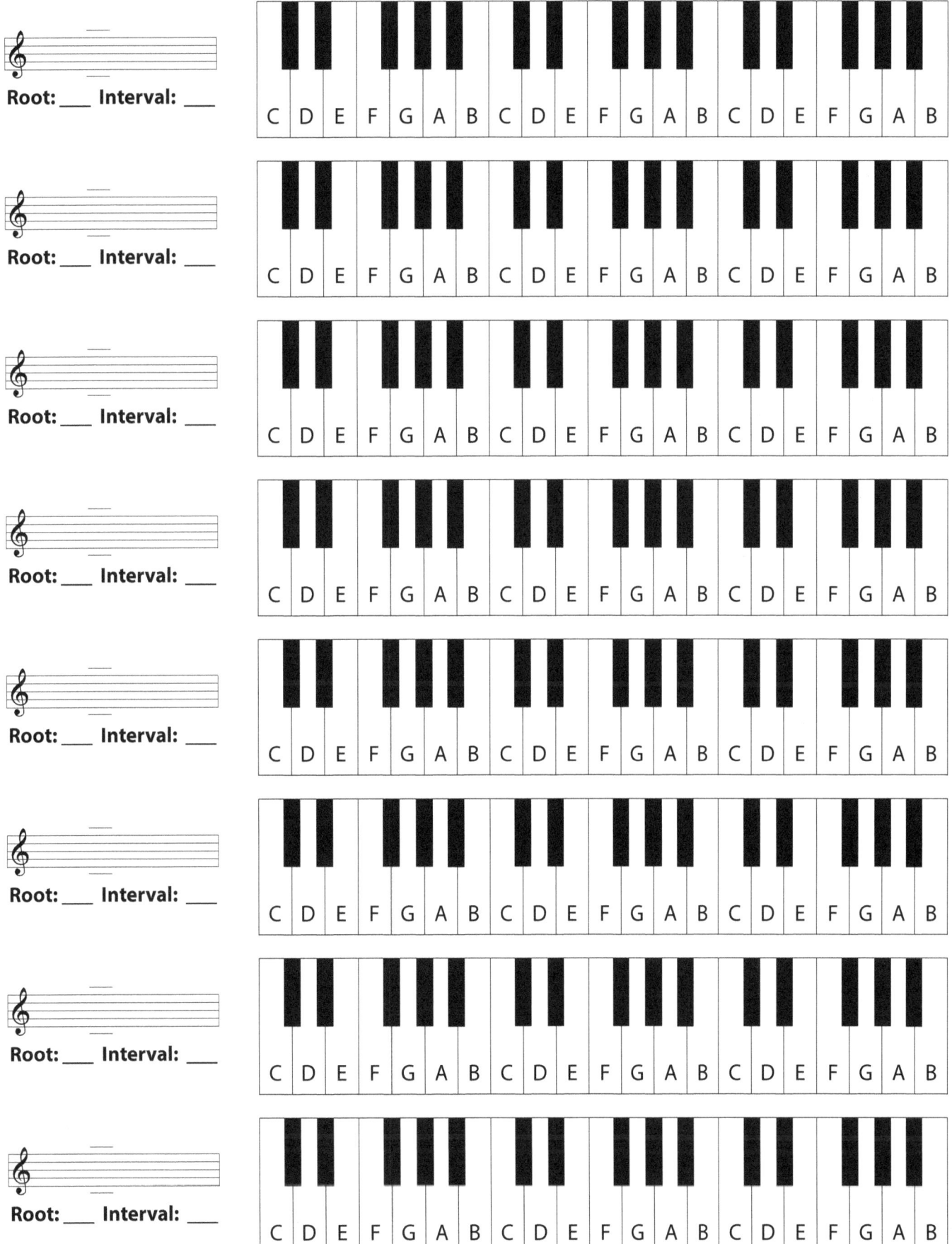

Root: ___ Interval: ___

Root: ___ Interval: ___

Root: ___ Interval: ___

Root: ___ Interval: ___

Root: ___ Interval: ___

Root: ___ Interval: ___

Root: ___ Interval: ___

Root: ___ Interval: ___

Piano Blanks

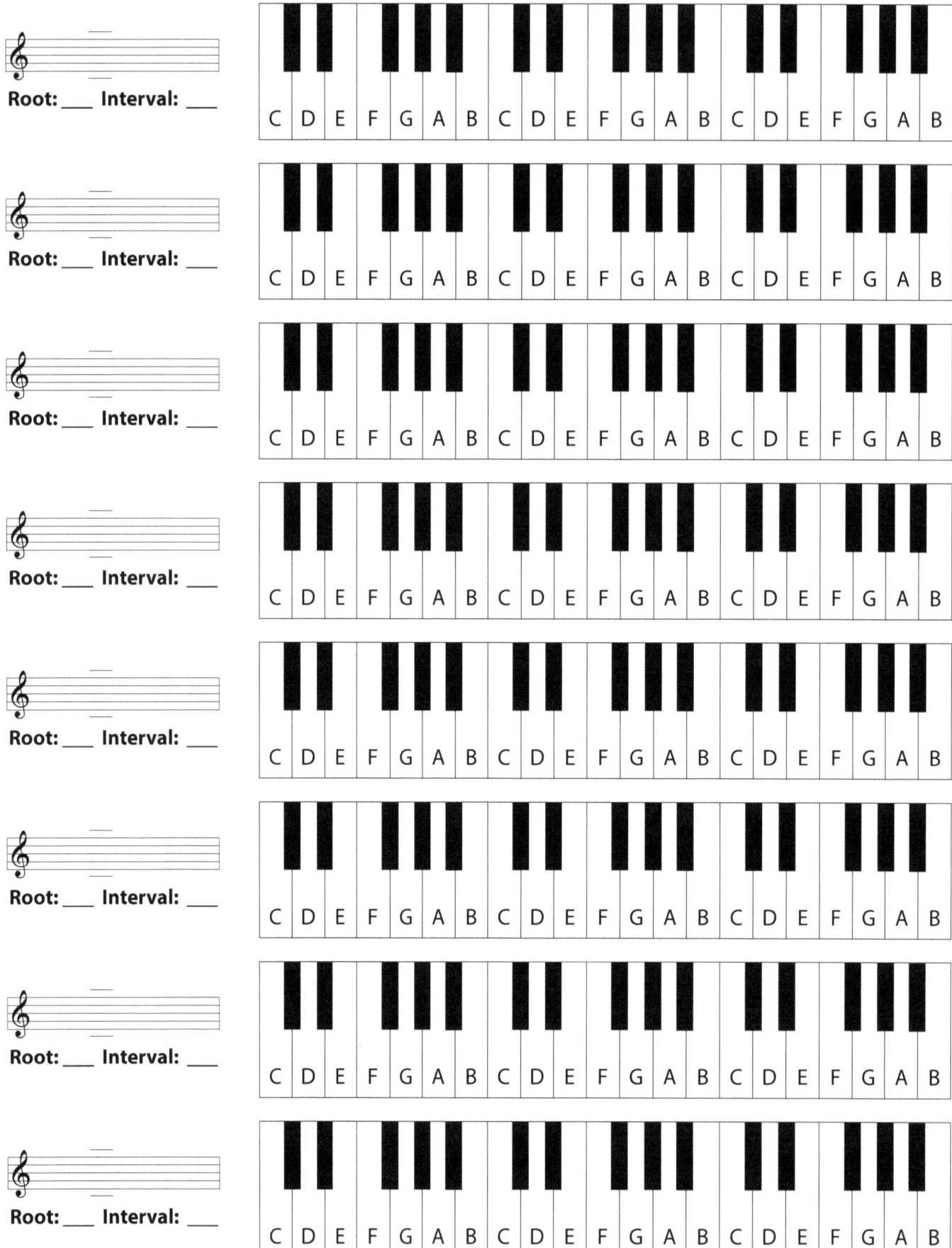

Root: ___ Interval: ___

Root: ___ Interval: ___

Root: ___ Interval: ___

Root: ___ Interval: ___

Root: ___ Interval: ___

Root: ___ Interval: ___

Root: ___ Interval: ___

Root: ___ Interval: ___

Piano Blanks

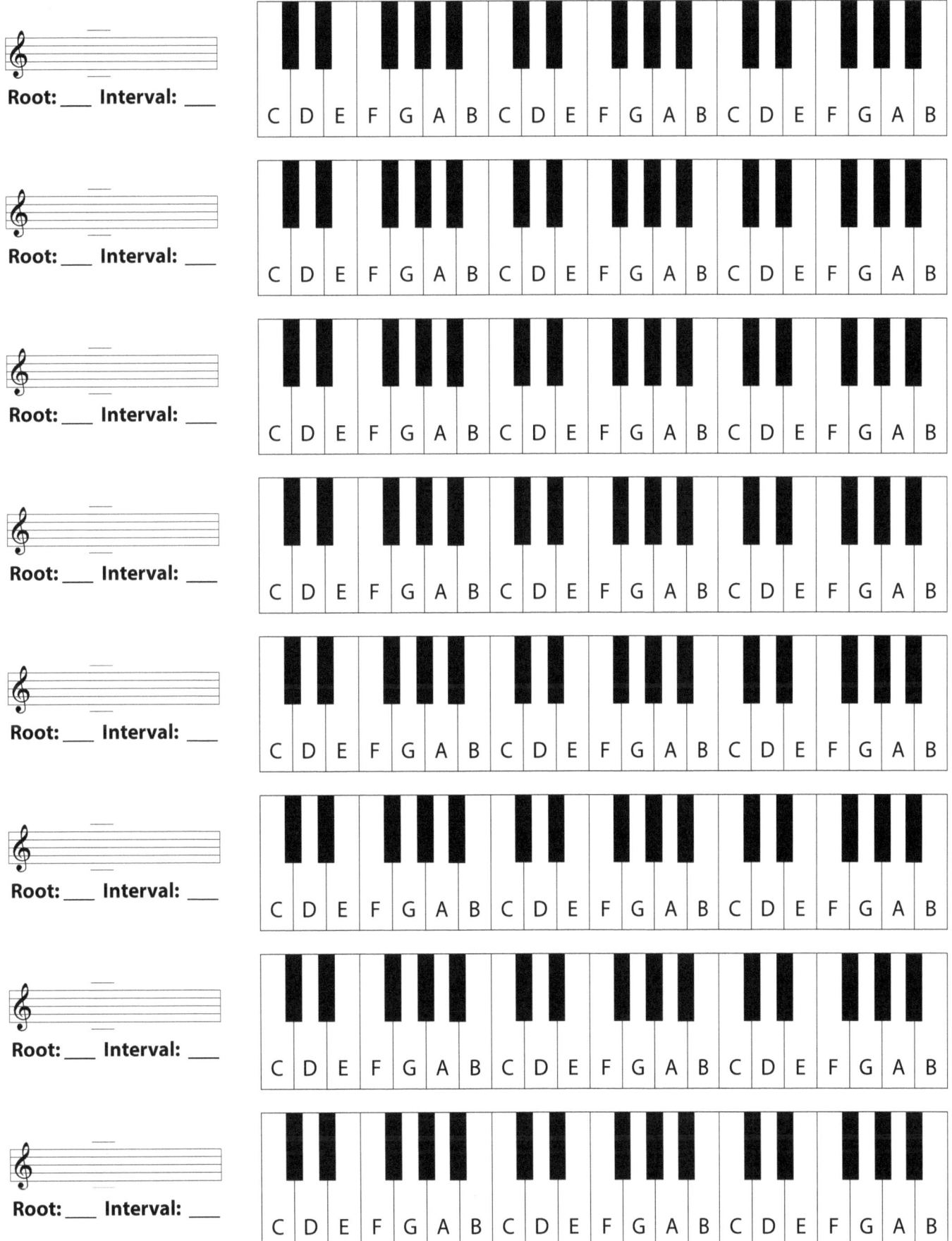

Piano Blanks

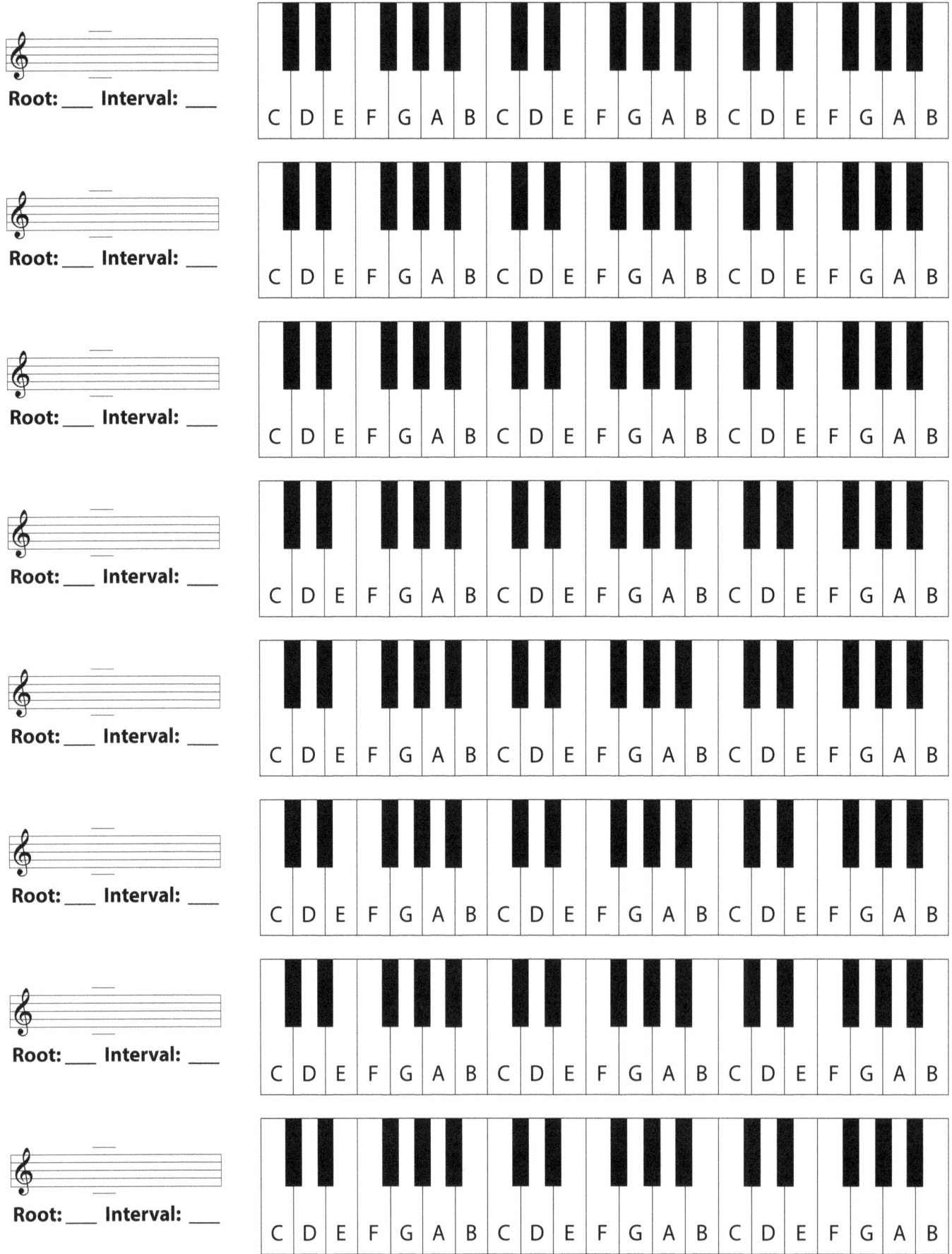

Piano Blanks

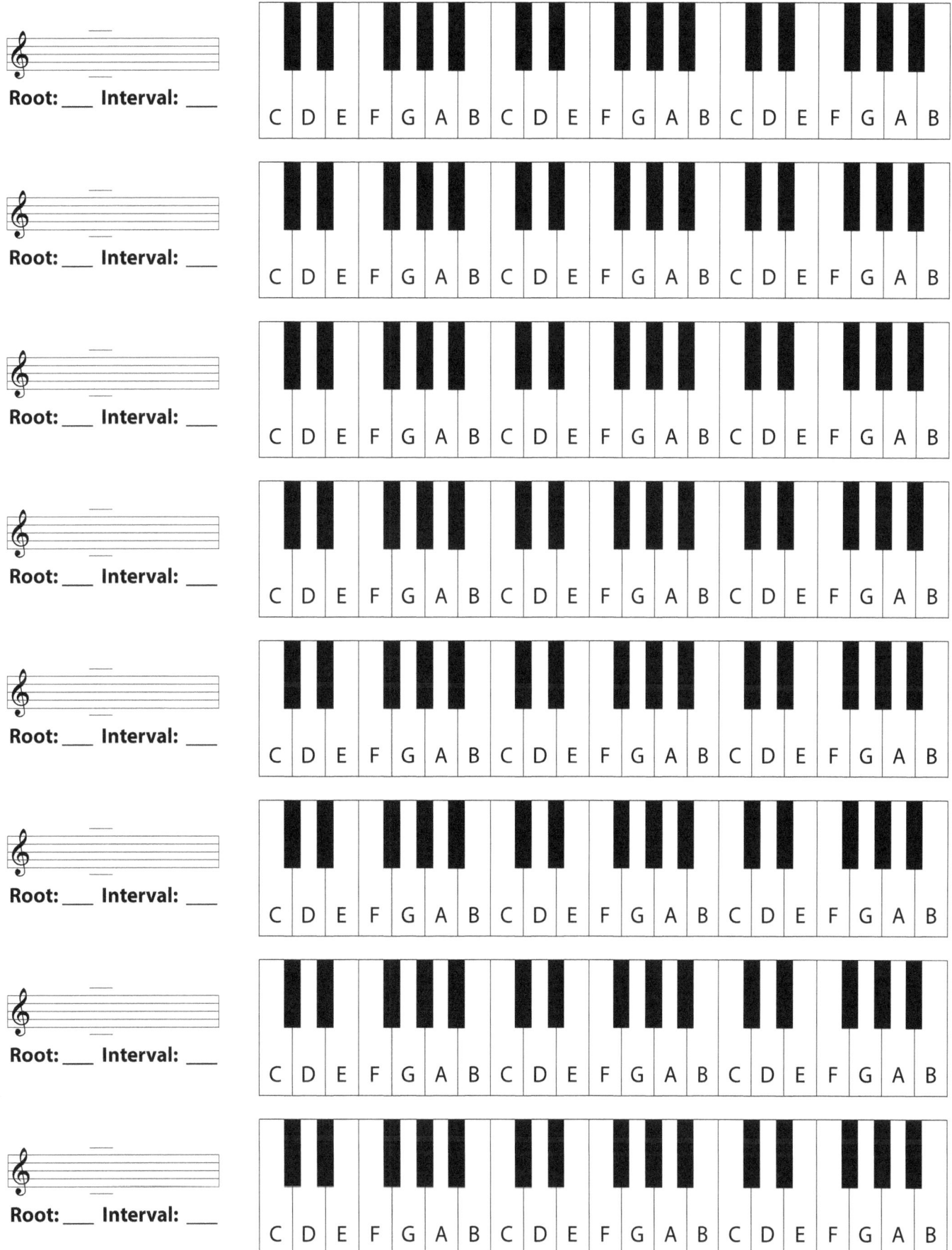

Root: ___ Interval: ___

Root: ___ Interval: ___

Root: ___ Interval: ___

Root: ___ Interval: ___

Root: ___ Interval: ___

Root: ___ Interval: ___

Root: ___ Interval: ___

Root: ___ Interval: ___

Piano Blanks

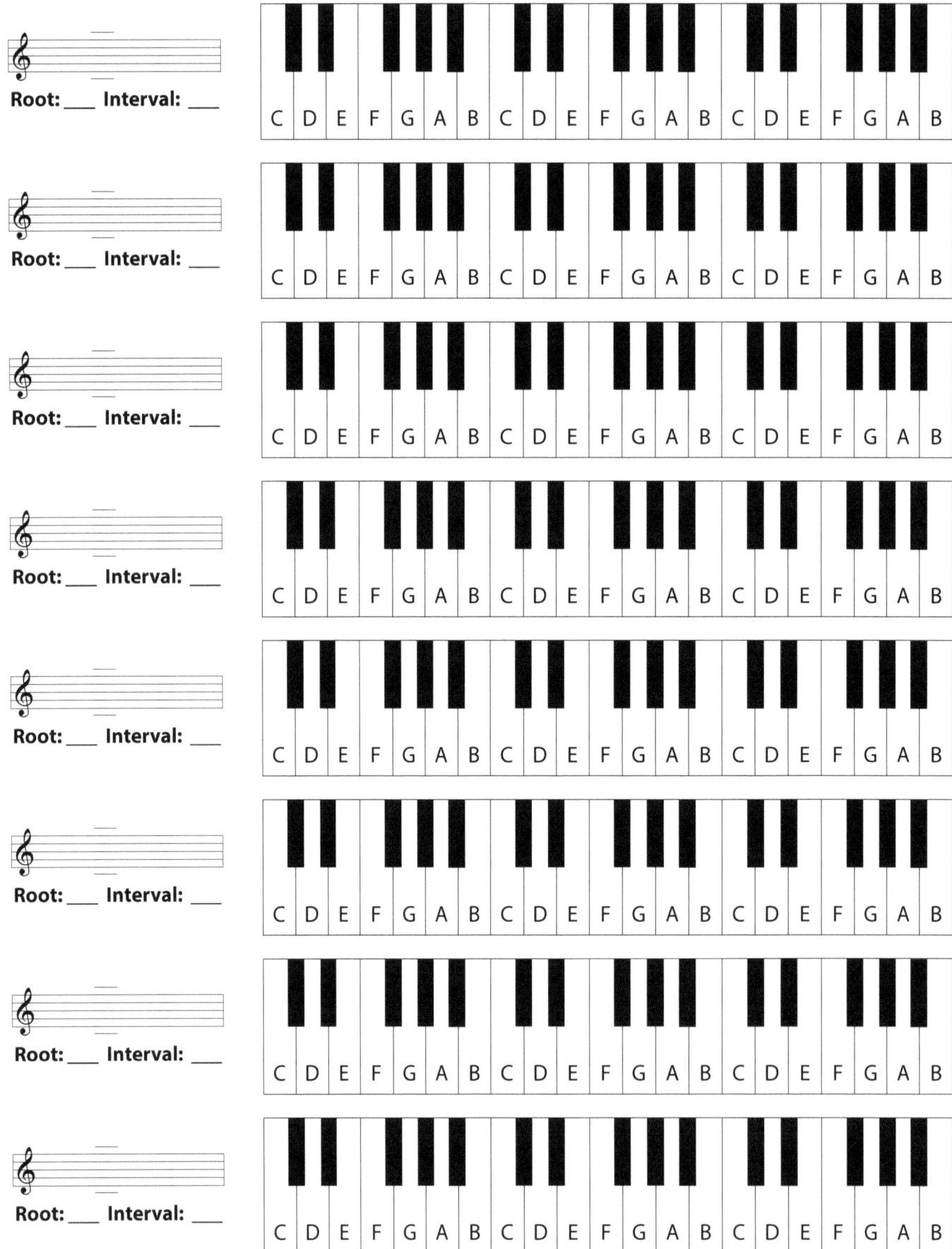

Section 4: Keys, Scales, & Chords

SECTION 4: Key, Scale & Chord Worksheets

Here, you'll apply all prior learning to real-world musical mapping. Each exercise begins with writing out the notes of a scale, followed by building its diatonic triads. Then, transfer that information to the provided piano and guitar diagrams. This section transforms theory into applied musicianship, connecting sound, sight, and physical movement.

Goal: To construct chords and scales in any key, understanding their structure both visually and physically.

Key Signature and Scale Notation
Start by selecting a scale (or tonic note). Write the corresponding key signature on the staff. This will help you quickly identify and recall key signatures.

Next, write out the notes of the scale on the staff. Say each note aloud as you write it. This helps reinforce your visual and auditory recognition.

Don't worry if you're unsure which note to use at first. This exercise is about improving your music reading fluency. With practice, you'll read music as naturally as you read a book.

Scale Structure & Chord Qualities
In this section, you'll write the interval pattern of the scale (e.g., W–W–H–W–W–W–H for major).

Then, write the notes of the scale, and memorize:
> The degree numbers (1st, 2nd, 3rd, etc.)
> The functional names (Tonic, Supertonic, Mediant, etc.)
> The modes associated with each scale degree (Ionian, Dorian, etc.)
> Lastly, identify the chord qualities for each degree (e.g., Major, Minor, Minor, Major, Major, Minor, Diminished). This is often referred to as the Chord Key.

Chord Names and Neck Visualization
Now identify the chord names built on each degree of the scale. Under each chord, you'll find a blank fretboard diagram.

Use these to identify and mark the notes that make up each chord. This helps you visualize how chords appear on the guitar neck, making it easier to apply them while playing.

Scale Mapping Across the Neck
This final section helps you memorize the notes across the guitar neck and understand how a scale moves across individual strings and the full fretboard.

Start with an open string (e.g., low E).
Identify its open note, then fill in the notes of the scale down the neck on that one string.
Repeat for each of the six strings.

As you work through all the strings, you'll begin to see patterns and visual shapes emerge that will help you navigate the fretboard with ease.

Scale/Chord Worksheet

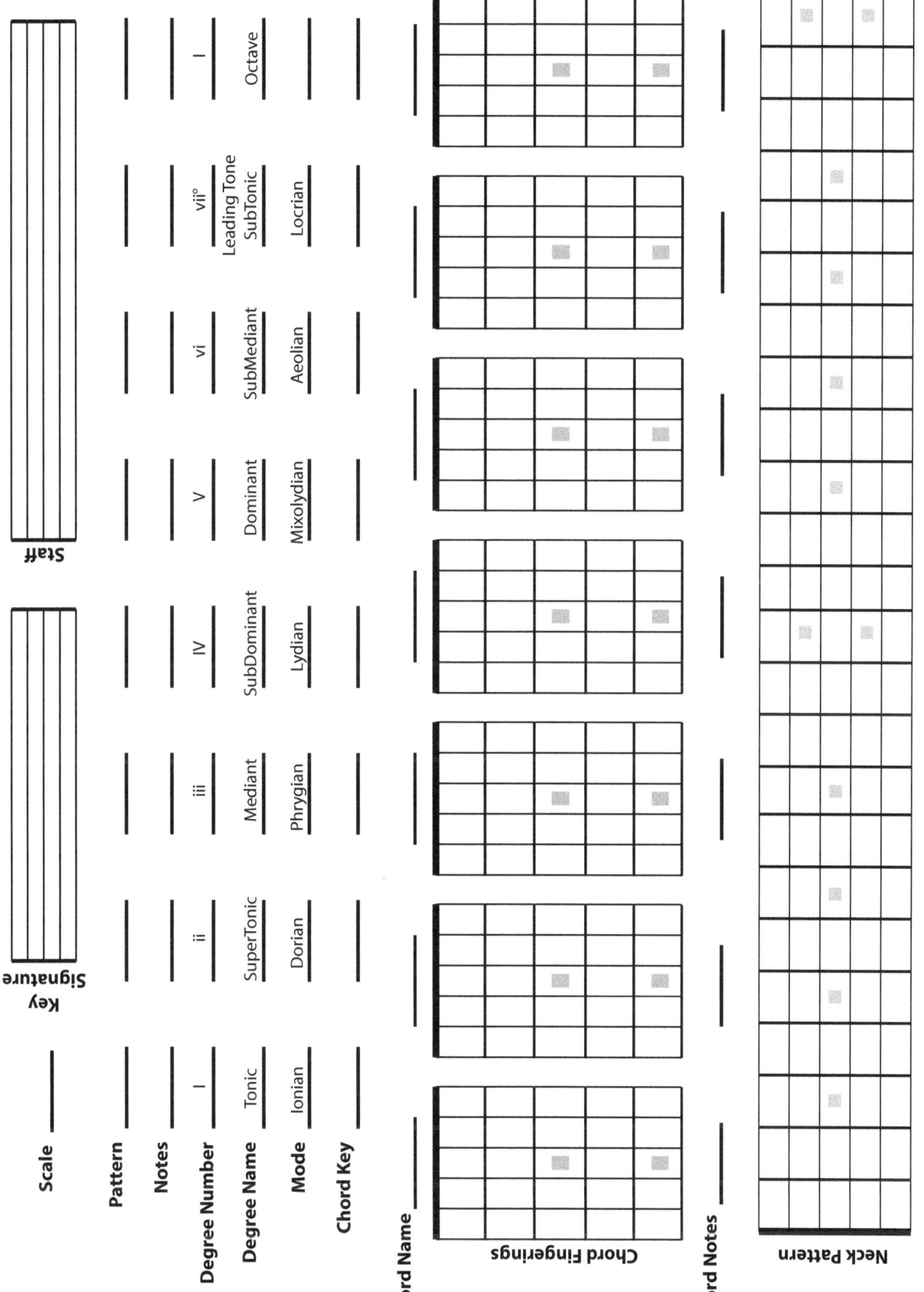

Staff

Key Signature

Scale ____

Pattern ____

Notes ____

Degree Number	I	ii	iii	IV	V	vi	vii°
Degree Name	Tonic	SuperTonic	Mediant	SubDominant	Dominant	SubMediant	Leading Tone / SubTonic
Mode	Ionian	Dorian	Phrygian	Lydian	Mixolydian	Aeolian	Locrian
								I / Octave

Chord Key ____

Chord Name ____

Chord Fingerings

Chord Notes ____

Neck Pattern

Scale/Chord Worksheet

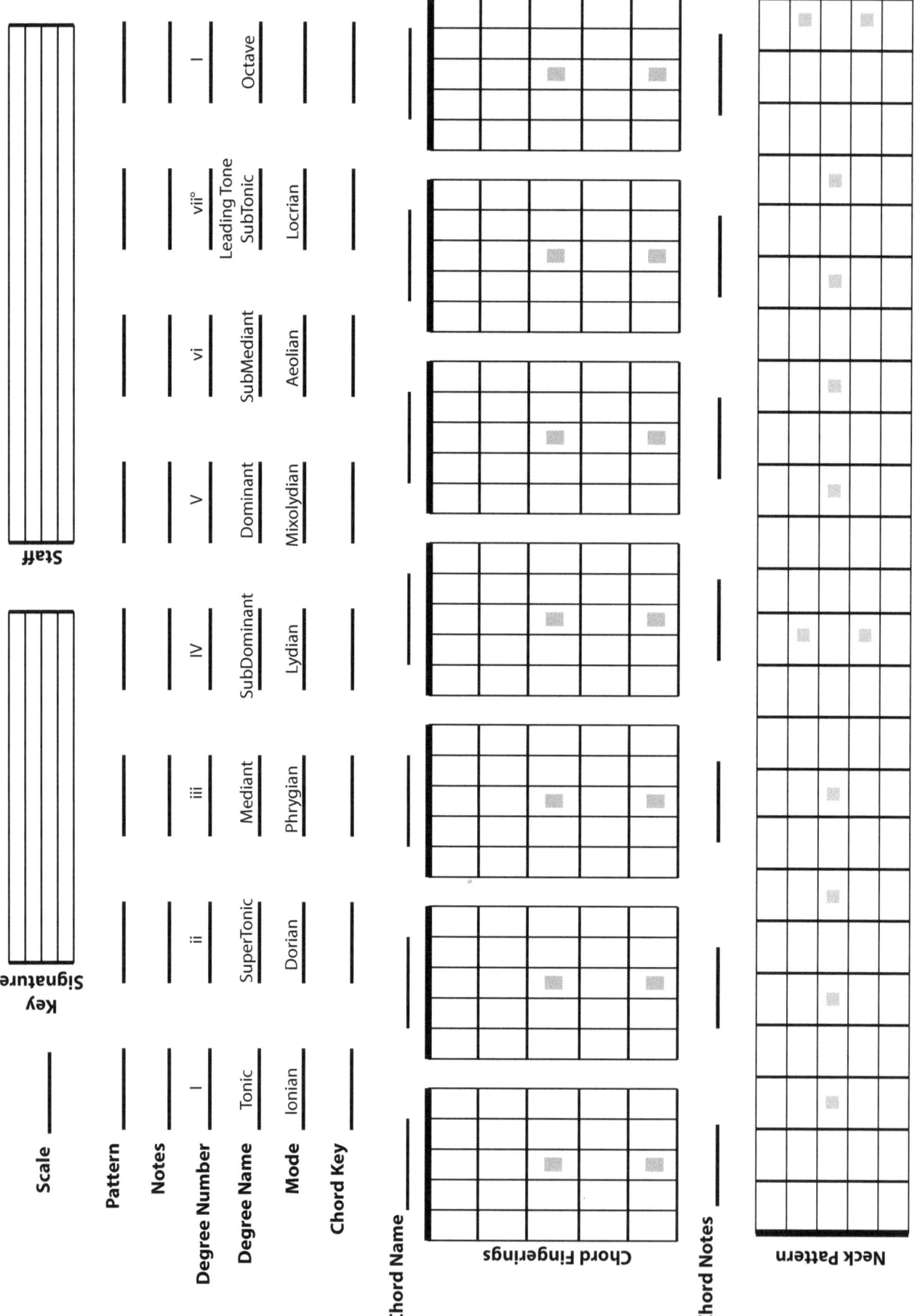

Staff

Key Signature

Scale _____

Pattern _____

Notes _____

Degree Number	I	ii	iii	IV	V	vi	vii°	
Degree Name	Tonic	SuperTonic	Mediant	SubDominant	Dominant	SubMediant	Leading Tone SubTonic	
Mode	Ionian	Dorian	Phrygian	Lydian	Mixolydian	Aeolian	Locrian	Octave

Chord Key _____

Chord Name _____

Chord Fingerings

Chord Notes _____

Neck Pattern

Scale/Chord Worksheet

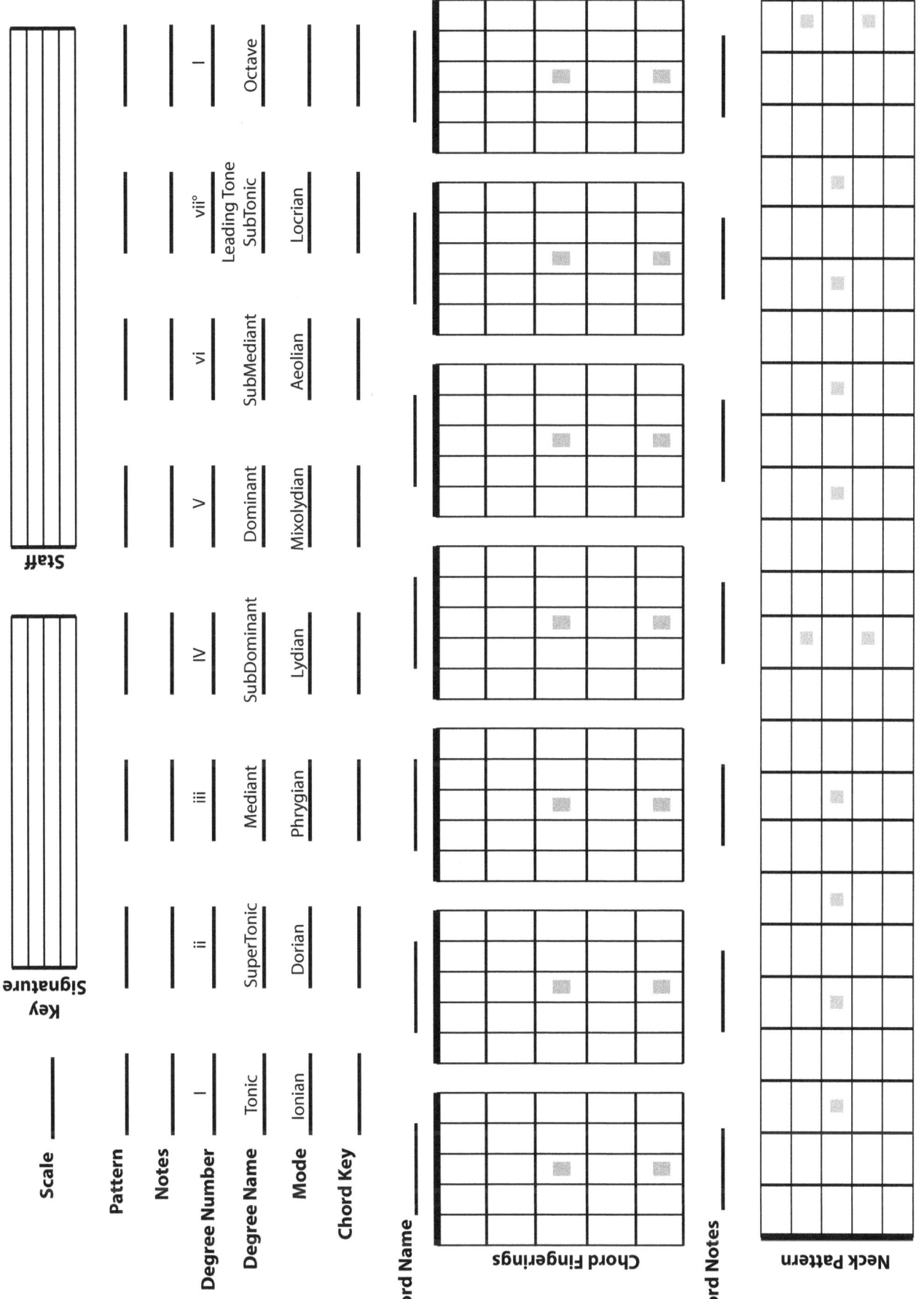

Scale ___

Staff

Key Signature

Pattern ___

Notes ___

Degree Number	I	ii	iii	IV	V	vi	vii°	I
Degree Name	Tonic	SuperTonic	Mediant	SubDominant	Dominant	SubMediant	Leading Tone / SubTonic	Octave
Mode	Ionian	Dorian	Phrygian	Lydian	Mixolydian	Aeolian	Locrian	

Chord Key ___

Chord Name ___

Chord Fingerings

Chord Notes ___

Neck Pattern

129

Scale/Chord Worksheet

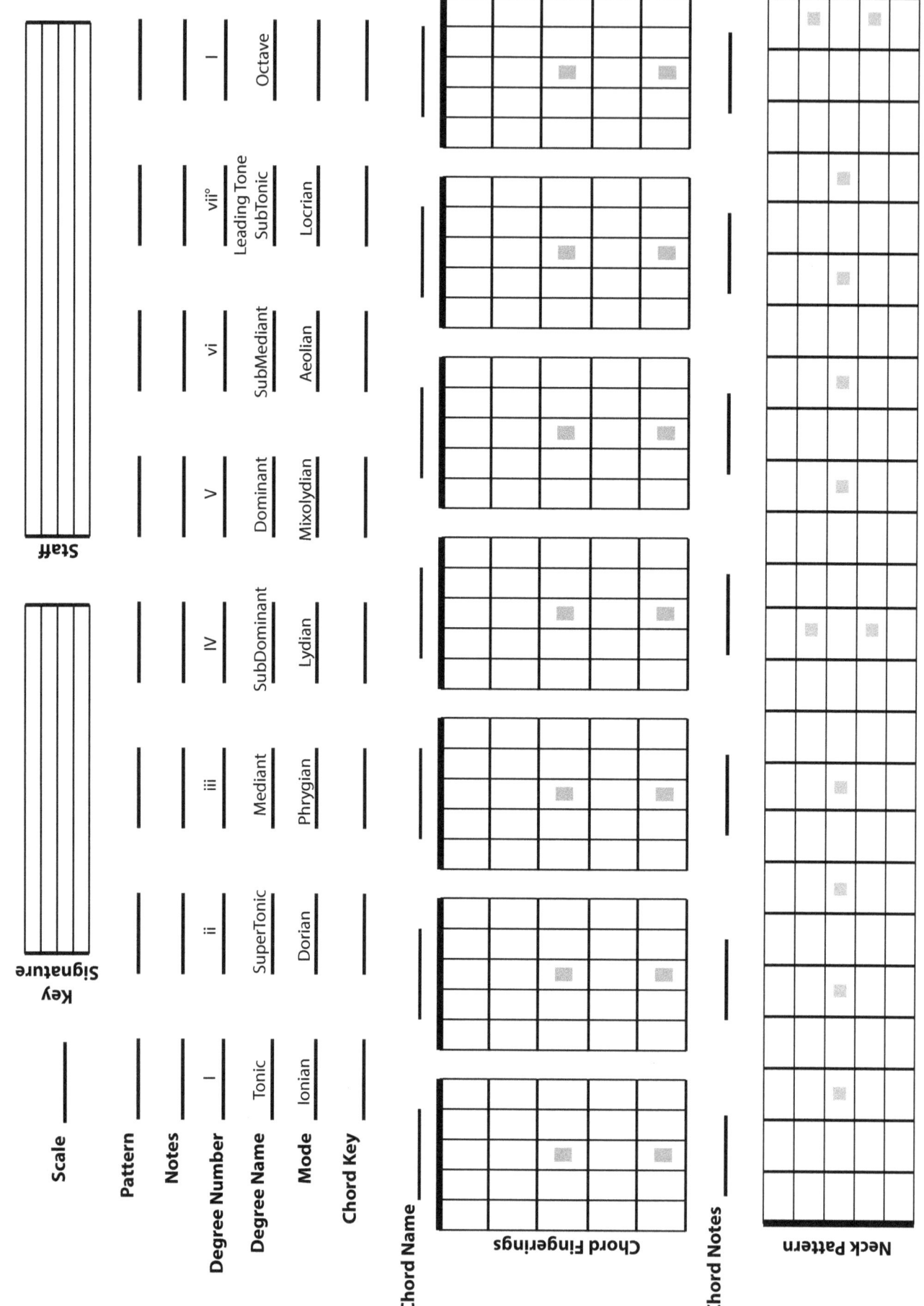

Staff

Key Signature

Scale ___

Pattern ___

Notes ___

Degree Number	I	ii	iii	IV	V	vi	vii°
Degree Name	Tonic	SuperTonic	Mediant	SubDominant	Dominant	SubMediant	Leading Tone / SubTonic
Mode	Ionian	Dorian	Phrygian	Lydian	Mixolydian	Aeolian	Locrian

| | | | | | | | Octave |

Chord Key ___

Chord Name ___

Chord Fingerings

Chord Notes ___

Neck Pattern

Scale/Chord Worksheet

Staff

Key Signature

Scale _____

Pattern _____

Notes _____

Degree Number	I	ii	iii	IV	V	vi	vii°	I
Degree Name	Tonic	SuperTonic	Mediant	SubDominant	Dominant	SubMediant	Leading Tone SubTonic	Octave
Mode	Ionian	Dorian	Phrygian	Lydian	Mixolydian	Aeolian	Locrian	

Chord Key _____

Chord Name _____

Chord Fingerings

Chord Notes _____

Neck Pattern

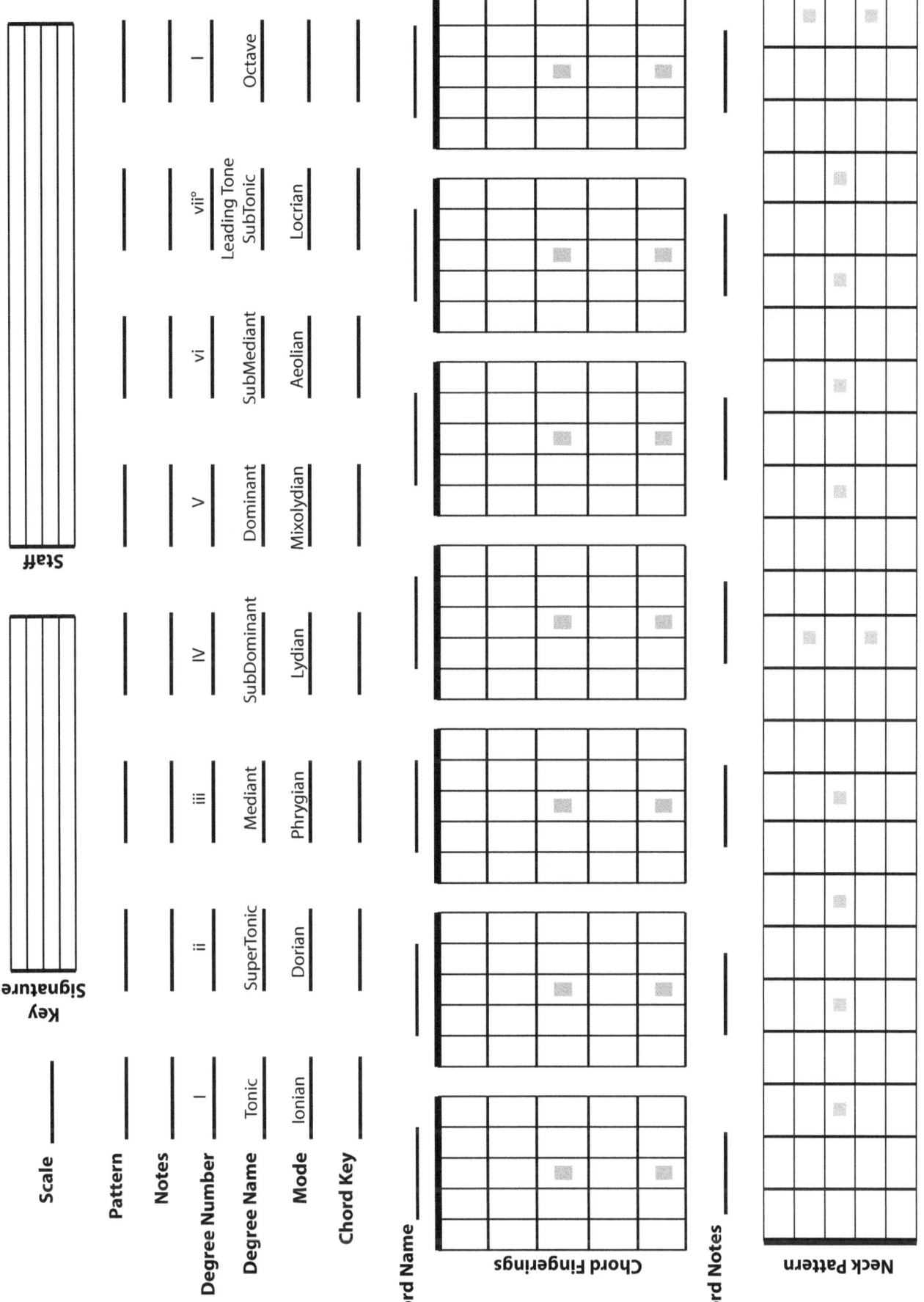

Scale/Chord Worksheet

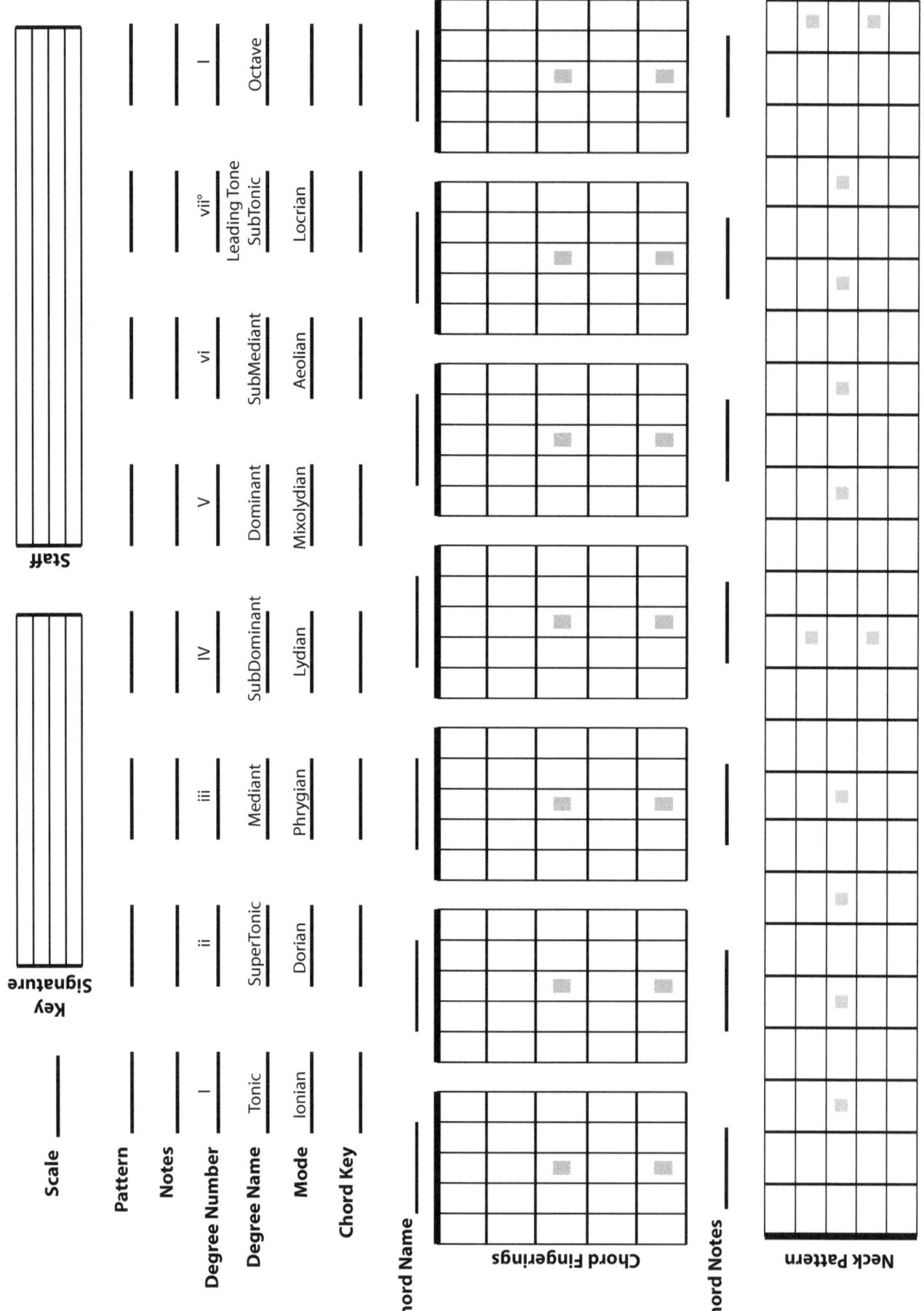

Staff

Key Signature

Scale ____

Pattern ____

Notes ____

Degree Number	I	ii	iii	IV	V	vi	vii°
Degree Name	Tonic	SuperTonic	Mediant	SubDominant	Dominant	SubMediant	Leading Tone / SubTonic
Mode	Ionian	Dorian	Phrygian	Lydian	Mixolydian	Aeolian	Locrian

I — Octave

Chord Key ____

Chord Name ____

Chord Fingerings

Chord Notes ____

Neck Pattern

Scale/Chord Worksheet

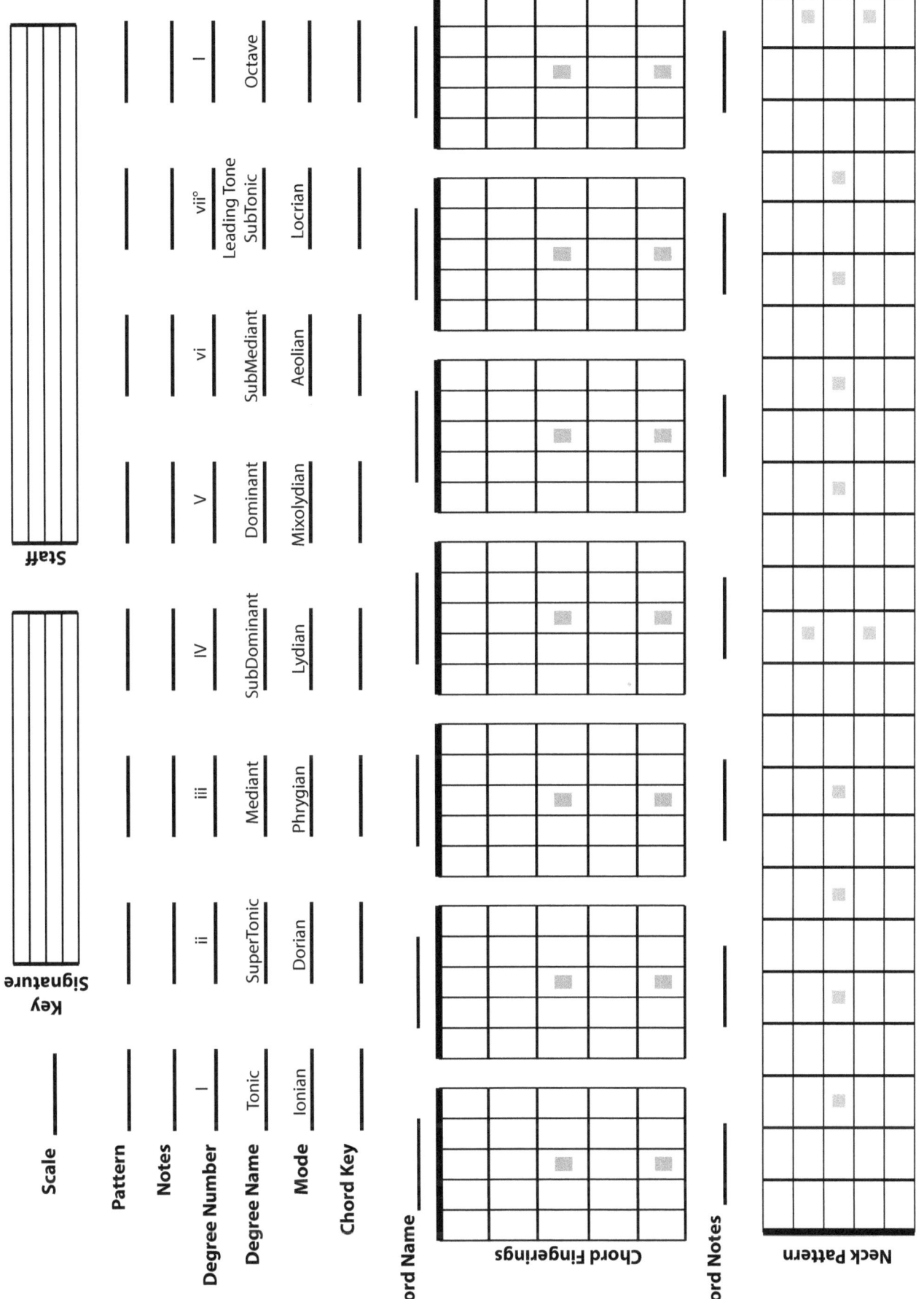

Staff

Key Signature

Scale ____

Pattern ____

Notes ____

Degree Number | I | ii | iii | IV | V | vi | vii° | I
Degree Name | Tonic | SuperTonic | Mediant | SubDominant | Dominant | SubMediant | Leading Tone / SubTonic | Octave
Mode | Ionian | Dorian | Phrygian | Lydian | Mixolydian | Aeolian | Locrian |

Chord Key ____

Chord Name ____

Chord Fingerings

Chord Notes ____

Neck Pattern

Scale/Chord Worksheet

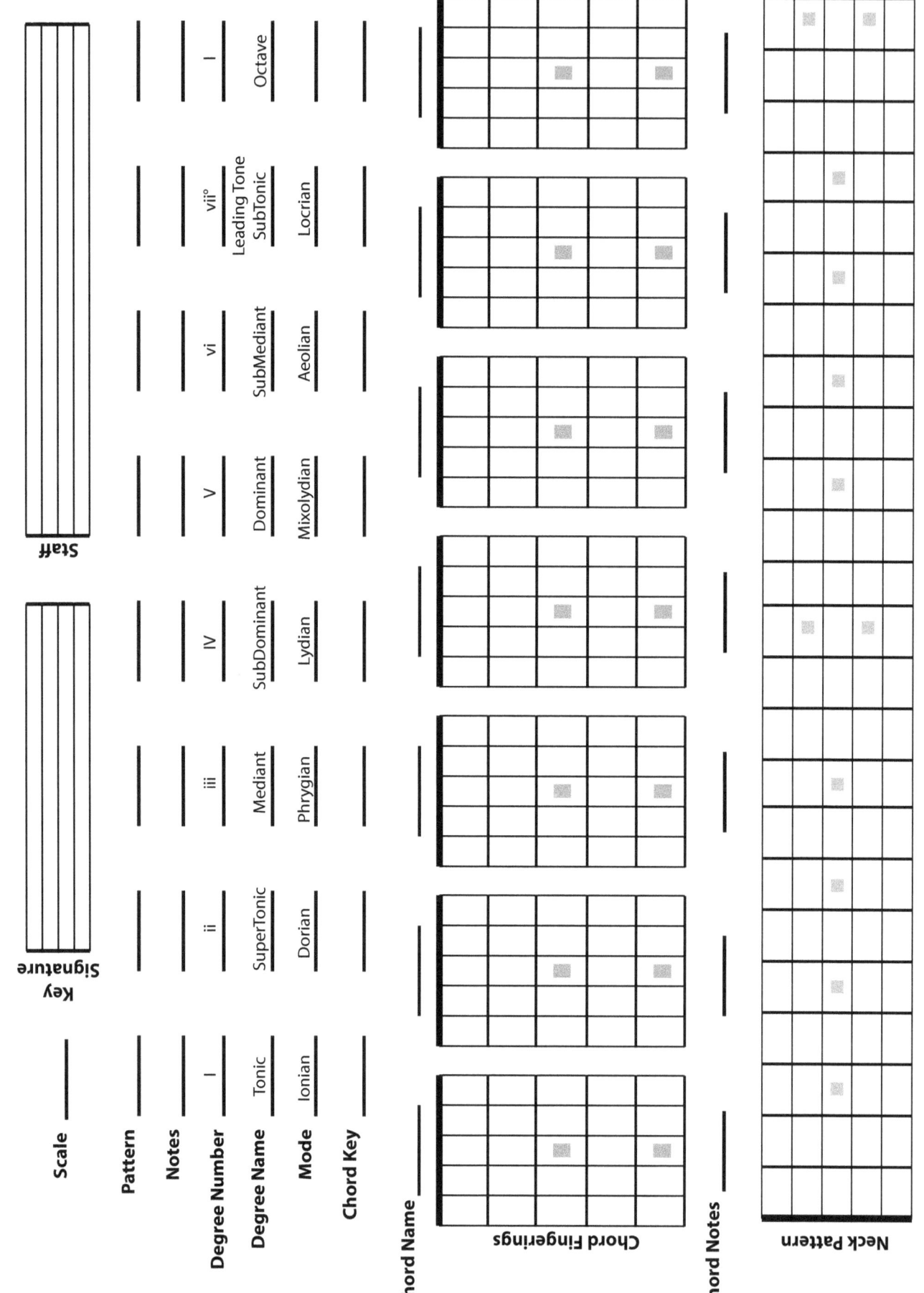

Staff

Key Signature

Scale _____

Pattern _____

Notes _____

Degree Number	I	ii	iii	IV	V	vi	vii°
Degree Name	Tonic	SuperTonic	Mediant	SubDominant	Dominant	SubMediant	Leading Tone / SubTonic	Octave
Mode	Ionian	Dorian	Phrygian	Lydian	Mixolydian	Aeolian	Locrian	

Chord Key _____

Chord Name _____

Chord Fingerings

Chord Notes _____

Neck Pattern

Scale/Chord Worksheet

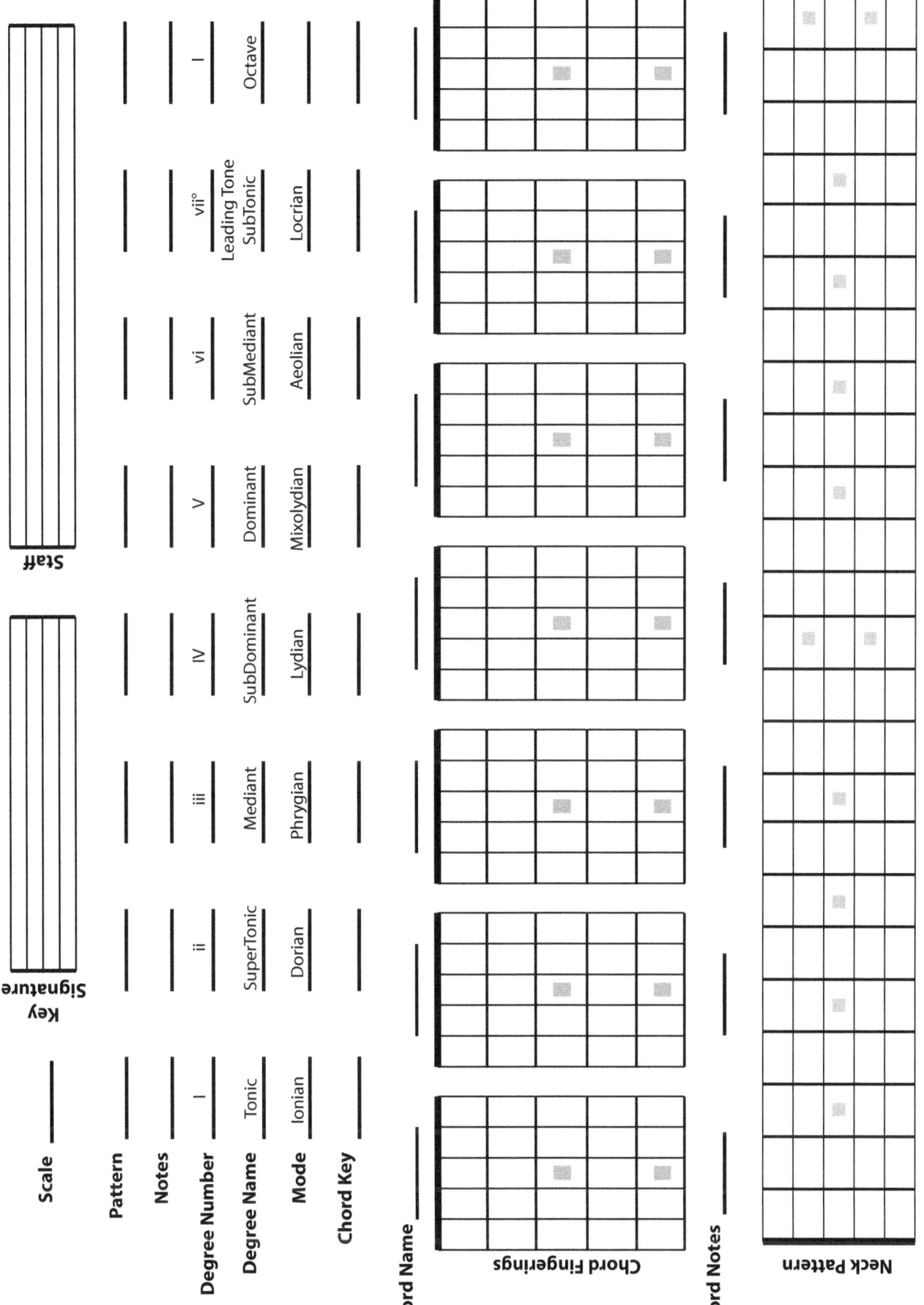

Staff

Key Signature

Scale _____

Pattern _____

Notes _____

Degree Number	I	ii	iii	IV	V	vi	vii°	I
Degree Name	Tonic	SuperTonic	Mediant	SubDominant	Dominant	SubMediant	Leading Tone / SubTonic	Octave
Mode	Ionian	Dorian	Phrygian	Lydian	Mixolydian	Aeolian	Locrian	

Chord Key _____

Chord Name _____

Chord Fingerings

Chord Notes _____

Neck Pattern

135

Scale/Chord Worksheet

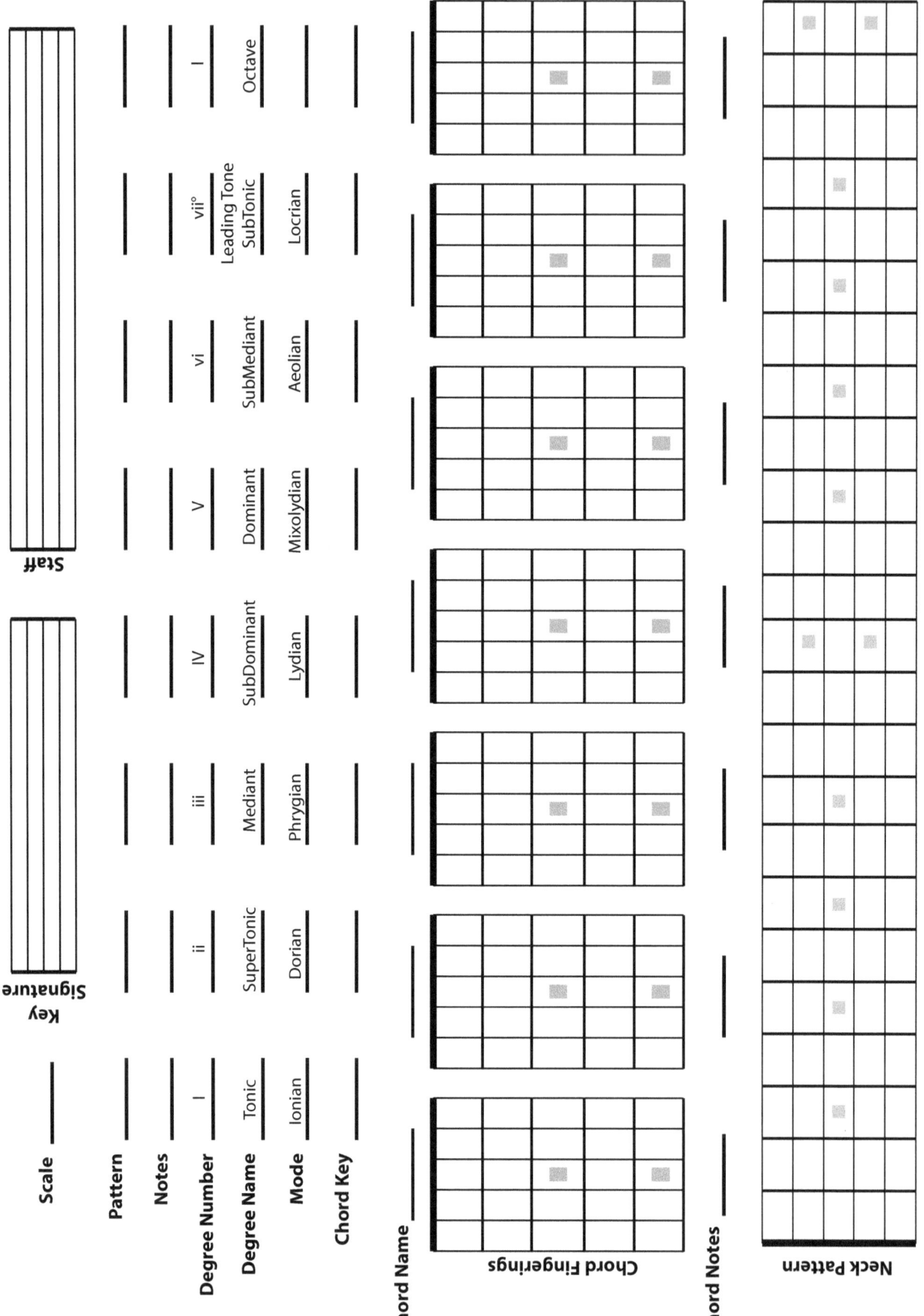

Staff

Key Signature

Scale ____

Pattern ____

Notes ____

Degree Number	I	ii	iii	IV	V	vi	vii°	I
							Leading Tone	
Degree Name	Tonic	SuperTonic	Mediant	SubDominant	Dominant	SubMediant	SubTonic	Octave
Mode	Ionian	Dorian	Phrygian	Lydian	Mixolydian	Aeolian	Locrian	

Chord Key ____

Chord Name ____

Chord Fingerings

Chord Notes ____

Neck Pattern

Scale/Chord Worksheet

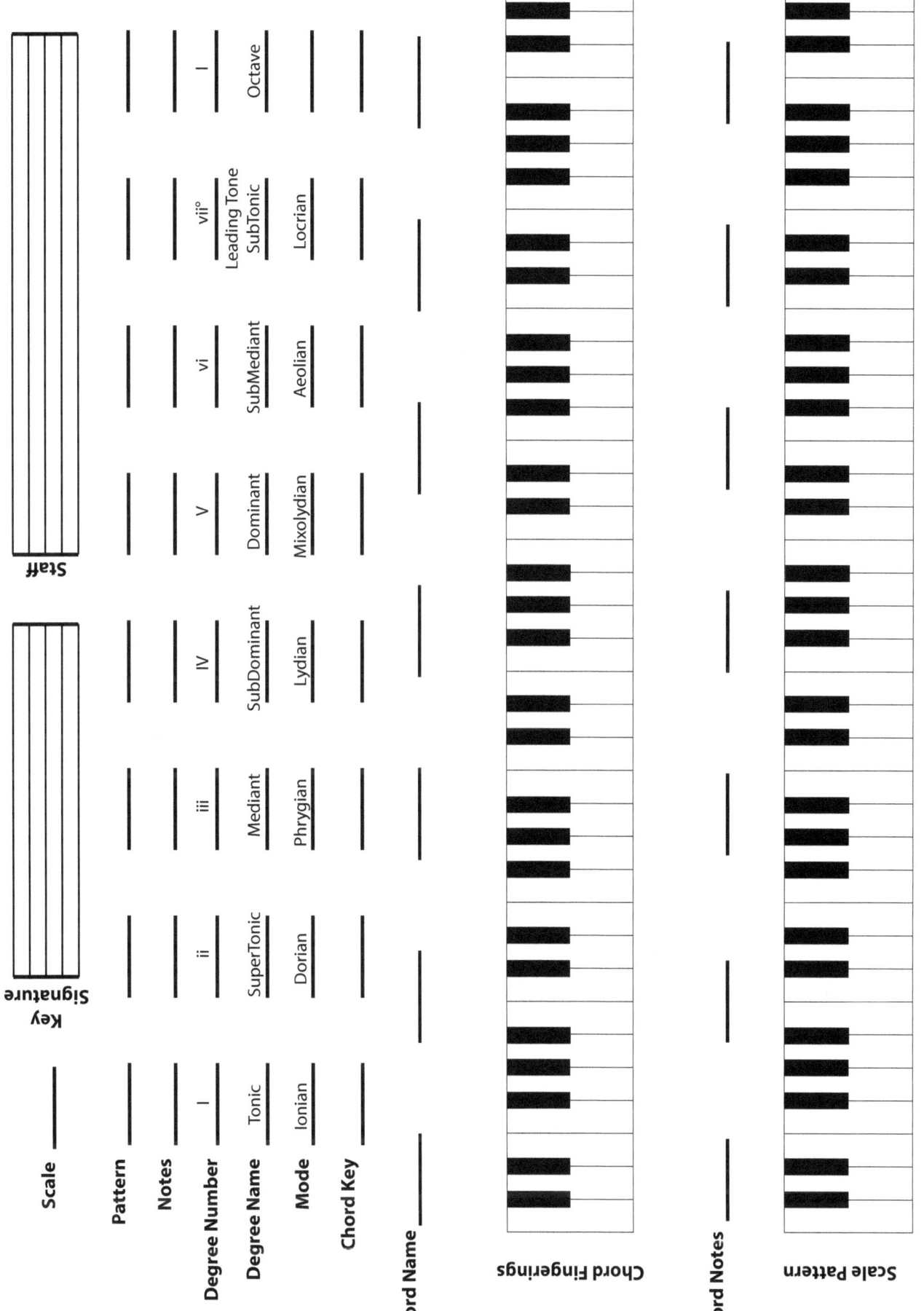

Scale _____

Pattern _____

Notes | | | | | | | |

Degree Number   I   ii   iii   IV   V   vi   vii°   —

Degree Name   Tonic   SuperTonic   Mediant   SubDominant   Dominant   SubMediant   Leading Tone / SubTonic   Octave

Mode   Ionian   Dorian   Phrygian   Lydian   Mixolydian   Aeolian   Locrian

Chord Key _____

Key Signature   Staff

Chord Name _____

Chord Fingerings

Chord Notes _____

Scale Pattern

137

Scale/Chord Worksheet

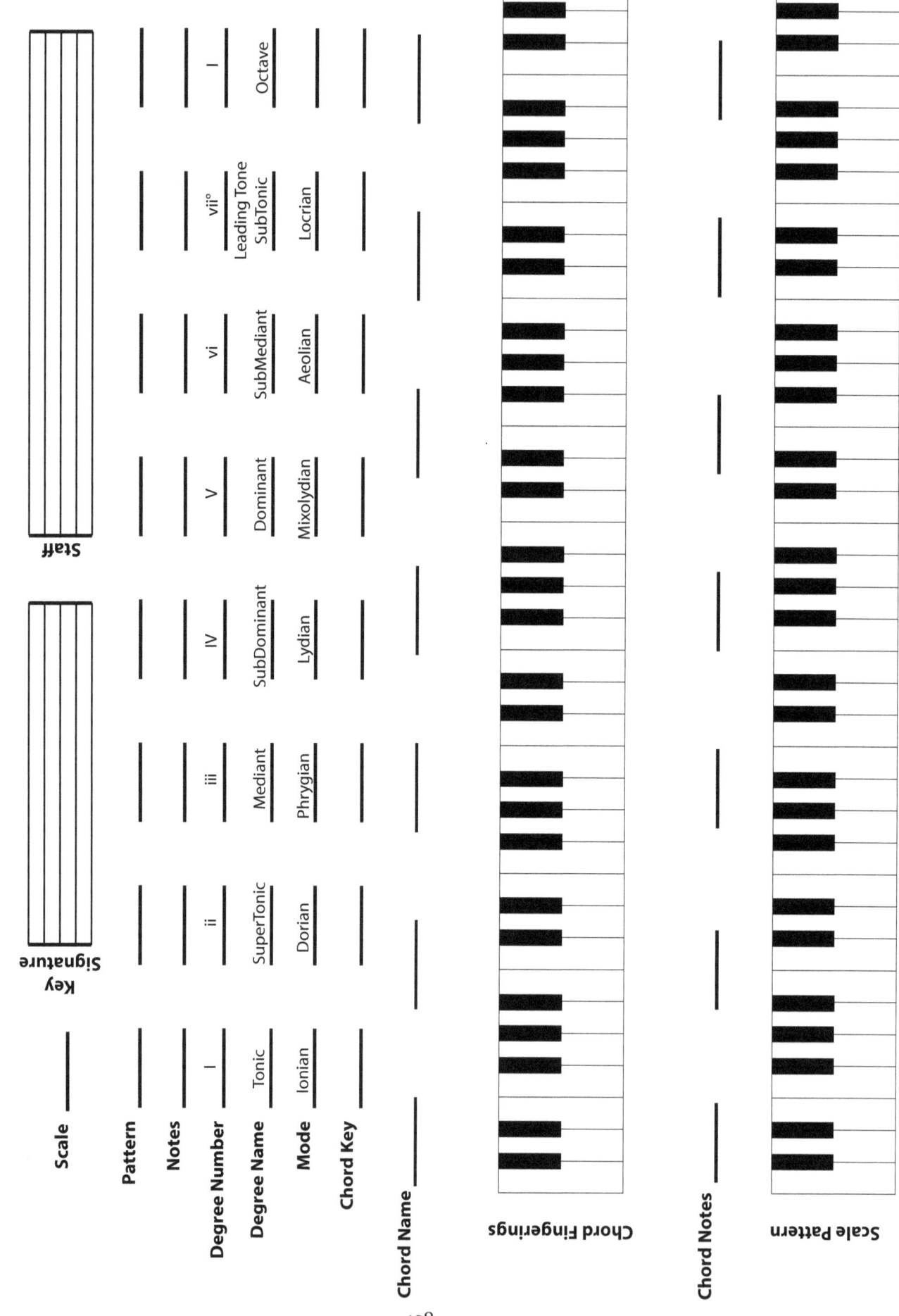

Scale _____

Pattern _____

Notes _____

Degree Number
I   ii   iii   IV   V   vi   vii°   I

Degree Name
Tonic   SuperTonic   Mediant   SubDominant   Dominant   SubMediant   Leading Tone / SubTonic   Octave

Mode
Ionian   Dorian   Phrygian   Lydian   Mixolydian   Aeolian   Locrian

Chord Key _____

Chord Name _____

Key Signature

Staff

Chord Fingerings

Chord Notes _____

Scale Pattern

Scale/Chord Worksheet

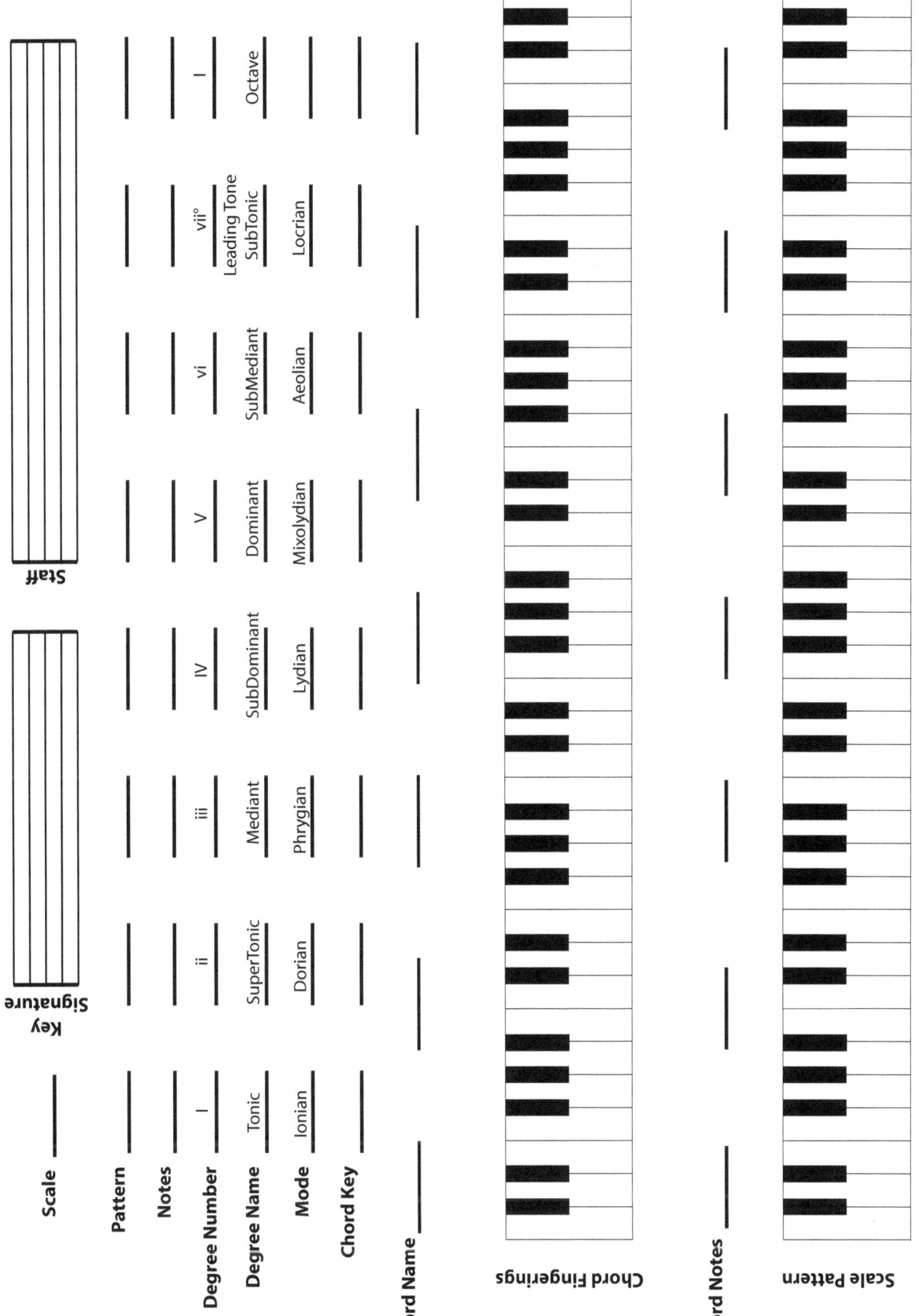

Scale _____

Key Signature

Staff

Pattern _____ _____ _____ _____ _____ _____ _____ _____

Notes _____ _____ _____ _____ _____ _____ _____ _____

Degree Number I ii iii IV V vi vii° I

Degree Name Tonic SuperTonic Mediant SubDominant Dominant SubMediant Leading Tone / SubTonic Octave

Mode Ionian Dorian Phrygian Lydian Mixolydian Aeolian Locrian

Chord Key _____ _____ _____ _____ _____ _____ _____ _____

Chord Name _____

Chord Fingerings

Chord Notes _____ _____ _____ _____ _____

Scale Pattern

139

Scale/Chord Worksheet

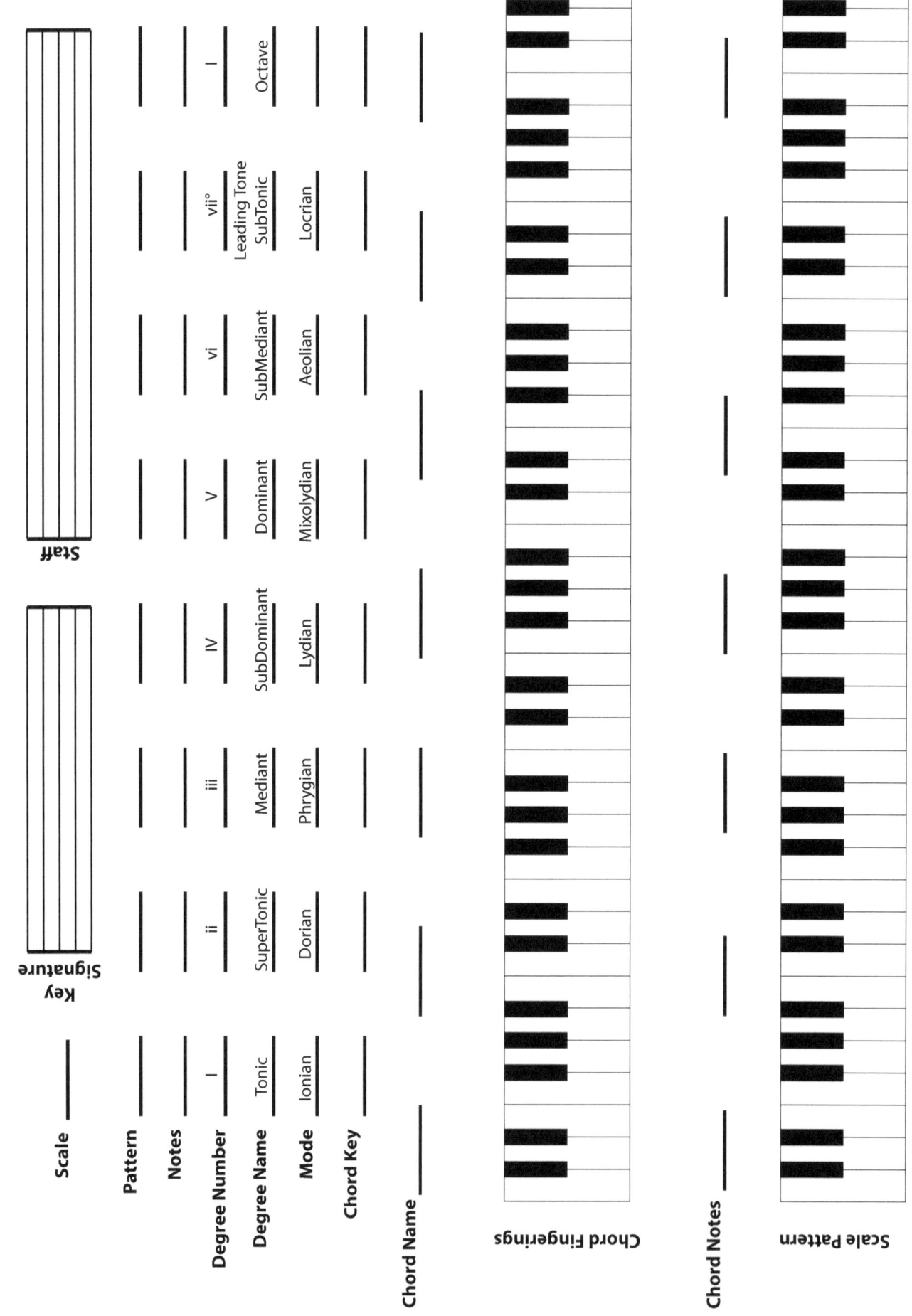

Staff

Key Signature

Scale ____

Pattern ____

Notes ____

Degree Number I ii iii IV V vi vii°

Degree Name Tonic SuperTonic Mediant SubDominant Dominant SubMediant Leading Tone / SubTonic Octave

Mode Ionian Dorian Phrygian Lydian Mixolydian Aeolian Locrian

Chord Key ____

Chord Name ____

Chord Fingerings

Chord Notes ____

Scale Pattern

140

Scale/Chord Worksheet

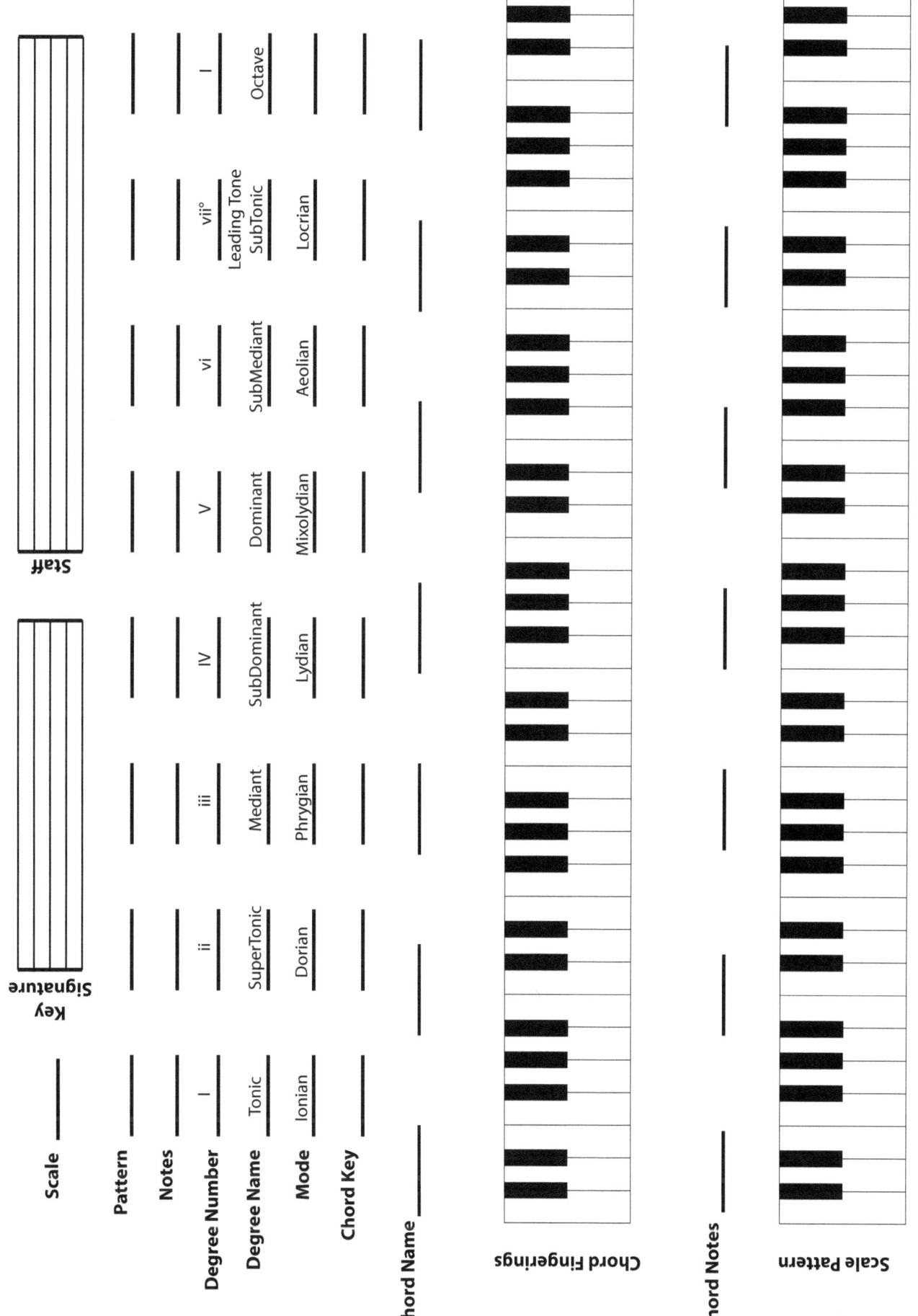

Key Signature

Staff

Scale _____

Pattern _____

Notes _____

Degree Number _____ I   ii   iii   IV   V   vi   vii°

Degree Name _____ Tonic   SuperTonic   Mediant   SubDominant   Dominant   SubMediant   Leading Tone   Octave
                                                                                                SubTonic

Mode _____ Ionian   Dorian   Phrygian   Lydian   Mixolydian   Aeolian   Locrian

Chord Key _____

Chord Name _____

Chord Fingerings

Chord Notes _____

Scale Pattern

141

Scale/Chord Worksheet

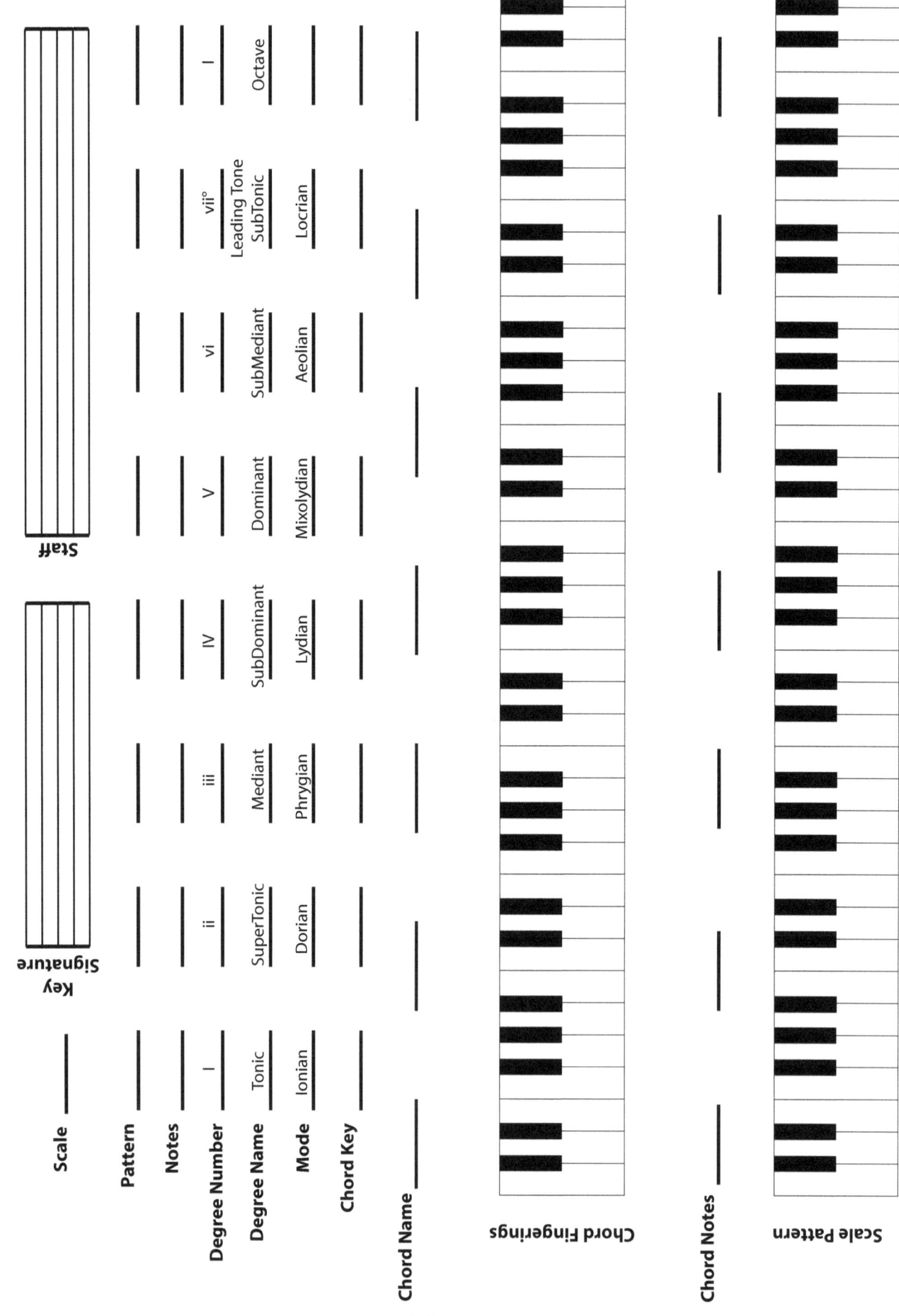

Scale _____

Pattern _____

Notes _____

Key Signature / **Staff**

Degree Number	I	ii	iii	IV	V	vi	vii°	I
Degree Name	Tonic	SuperTonic	Mediant	SubDominant	Dominant	SubMediant	Leading Tone / SubTonic	Octave
Mode	Ionian	Dorian	Phrygian	Lydian	Mixolydian	Aeolian	Locrian	

Chord Key _____ _____ _____ _____ _____ _____ _____ _____

Chord Name _____

Chord Fingerings

Chord Notes _____

Scale Pattern

142

Scale/Chord Worksheet

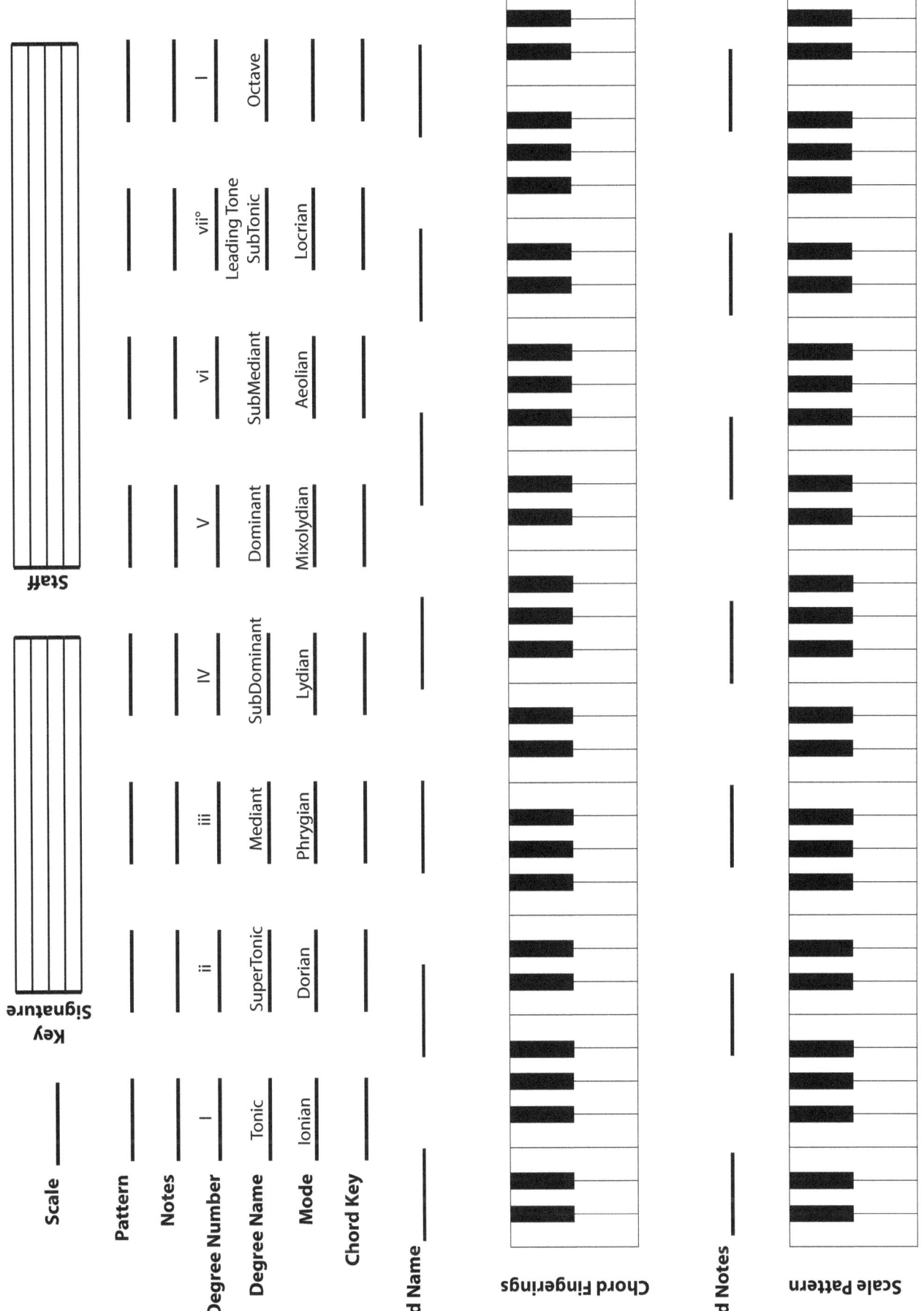

Scale _____

Pattern _____

Notes _____

Degree Number | I | ii | iii | IV | V | vi | vii° | I
Degree Name | Tonic | SuperTonic | Mediant | SubDominant | Dominant | SubMediant | Leading Tone / SubTonic | Octave
Mode | Ionian | Dorian | Phrygian | Lydian | Mixolydian | Aeolian | Locrian |

Chord Key _____

Chord Name _____

Key Signature

Staff

Chord Fingerings

Chord Notes _____

Scale Pattern

143

Scale/Chord Worksheet

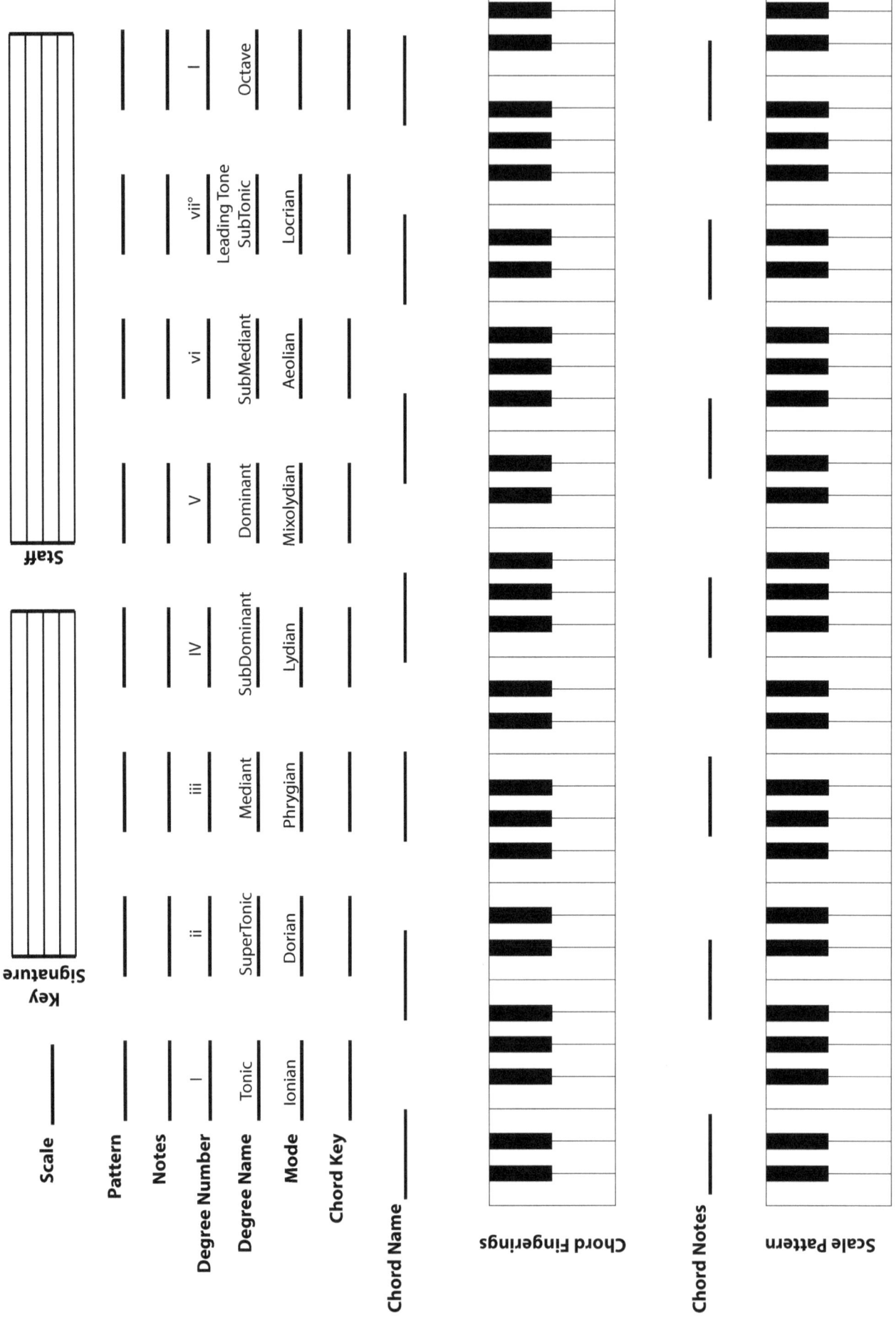

Scale _____

Key Signature

Staff

Pattern _____

Notes _____

Degree Number	I	ii	iii	IV	V	vi	vii°	
Degree Name	Tonic	SuperTonic	Mediant	SubDominant	Dominant	SubMediant	Leading Tone / SubTonic	Octave
Mode	Ionian	Dorian	Phrygian	Lydian	Mixolydian	Aeolian	Locrian	

Chord Key _____

Chord Name _____

Chord Fingerings

Chord Notes _____

Scale Pattern

Scale/Chord Worksheet

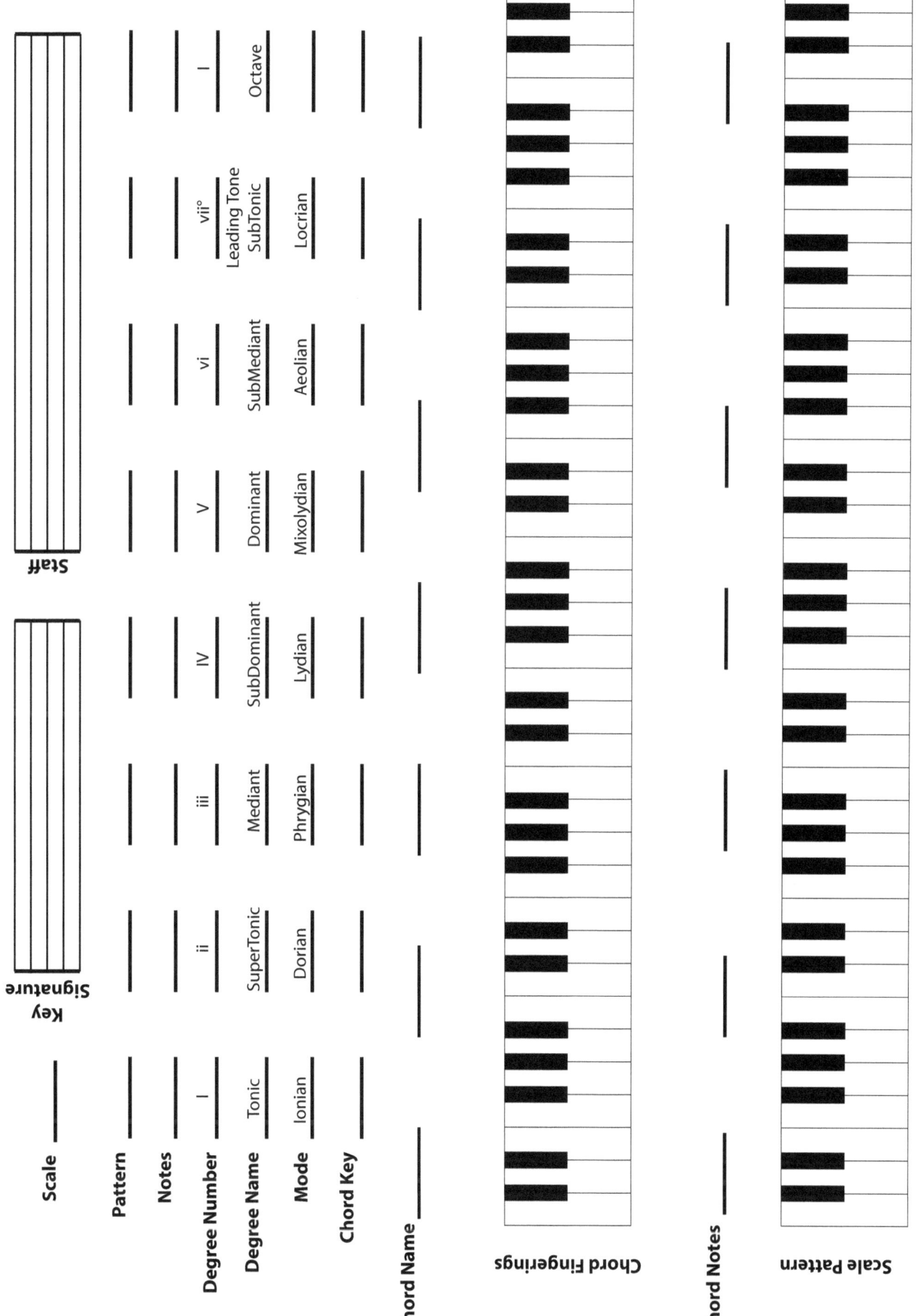

Key Signature

Staff

Scale ____

Pattern ____

Notes ____

Degree Number	I	ii	iii	IV	V	vi	vii°	
Degree Name	Tonic	SuperTonic	Mediant	SubDominant	Dominant	SubMediant	Leading Tone / SubTonic	Octave
Mode	Ionian	Dorian	Phrygian	Lydian	Mixolydian	Aeolian	Locrian	

Chord Key ____

Chord Name ____

Chord Fingerings

Chord Notes ____

Scale Pattern

145

Scale/Chord Worksheet

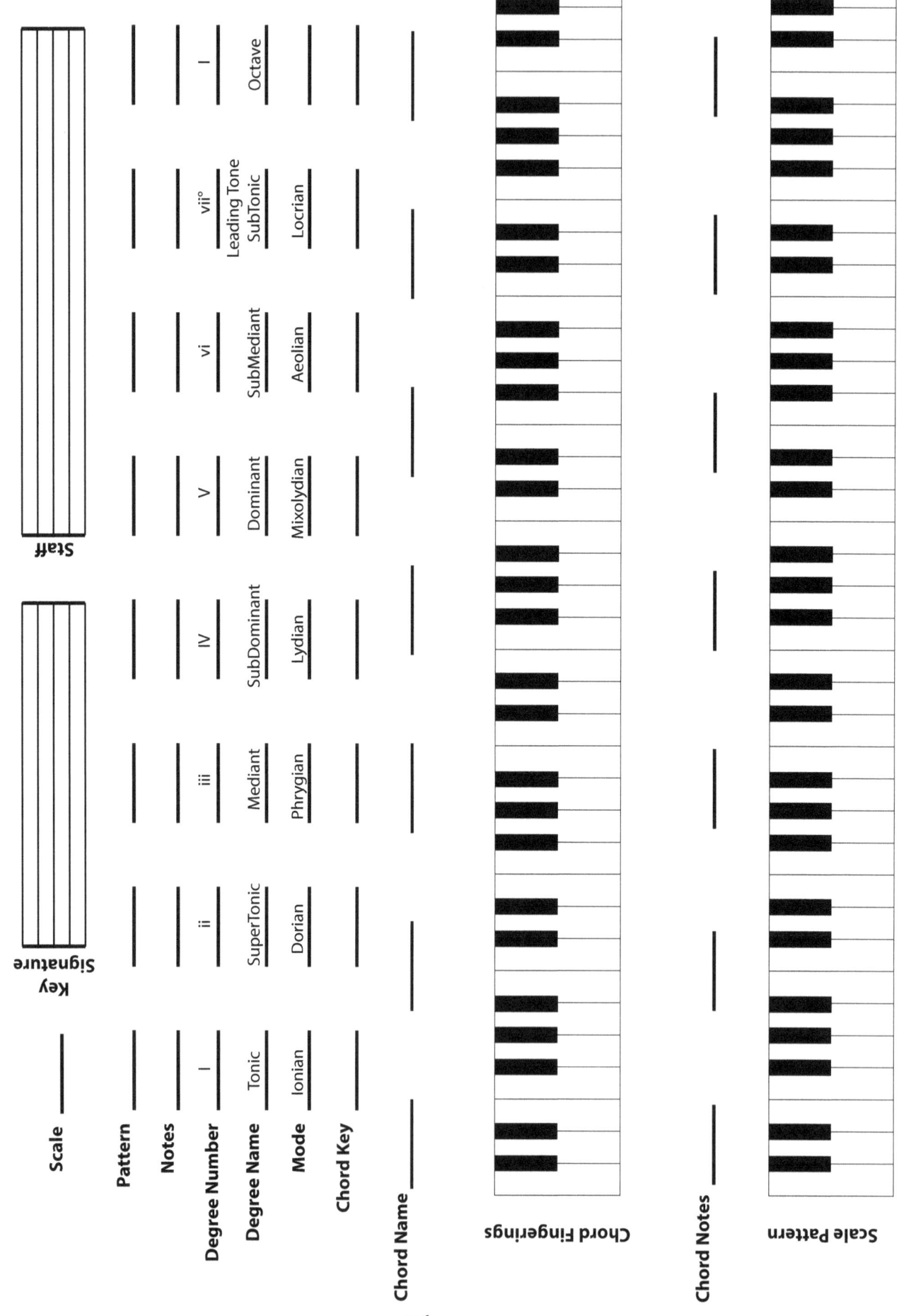

Scale _____

Key Signature

Staff

Pattern _____

Notes _____

Degree Number | I | ii | iii | IV | V | vi | vii° | I

Degree Name | Tonic | SuperTonic | Mediant | SubDominant | Dominant | SubMediant | Leading Tone / SubTonic | Octave

Mode | Ionian | Dorian | Phrygian | Lydian | Mixolydian | Aeolian | Locrian

Chord Key _____

Chord Name _____

Chord Fingerings

Chord Notes _____

Scale Pattern

Section 5: Timing & Rythm Practice

SECTION 5: Timing & Rhythm Practice

Timing is the foundation of musical performance. These worksheets help you internalize rhythm through metronome-based exercises. Start at a comfortable tempo and increase gradually. Focus on accuracy before speed. Record your BPM progression weekly in the provided chart to visualize growth.

Goal: To develop precise timing, rhythmic confidence, and internal pulse awareness.

Why Use a Metronome?
Music is built on rhythm. You can hit all the right notes, but if your timing is off, everything falls apart. The metronome is like your personal timekeeper. It helps:

> Lock in your tempo
> Identify weak spots in your technique
> Build speed the right way (slow and steady)
> Develop internal timing and groove

Even the most expressive musicians have spent countless hours with a metronome. It's not just for beginners, it's for anyone serious about improving.

Start Slow
Choose a tempo (BPM, beats per minute) that is comfortably slow, even if it feels too easy. You want to be able to play cleanly and in time with the click. If you can't play it slow, you can't play it fast. Speed comes from control, not moving faster.

Focus on Subdivisions
Most metronomes click once per beat. That's great for general timing, but many practice sessions benefit from subdividing the beat into smaller parts.

> Examples:
> Quarter Notes (1 click per beat)
> Eighth Notes (2 notes per beat: "1 & 2 & 3 & 4 &")
> Triplets (3 notes per beat: "1-trip-let, 2-trip-let...")
> Sixteenth Notes (4 notes per beat: "1-e-&-a, 2-e-&-a...")

Practicing your scales, riffs, or arpeggios to different subdivisions will give you a deeper sense of rhythm and improve your precision.

Use the "Less is More" Trick
Try this exercise: Set the metronome to half the speed you normally play. Let it click only on beats 2 and 4 (like a snare drum in a groove). This forces you to feel the groove internally and stay in time without being controlled by the metronome.

Gradually Increase the Tempo
Once you can play your exercise perfectly three times in a row at a certain tempo, bump it up by 2–4 BPM and repeat. Only increase the tempo when you're playing cleanly and in time.

Common Mistakes

Chasing the click: If you're constantly trying to "catch up" to the metronome, slow down and focus on staying centered in the beat.

Ignoring bad timing: If it sounds off, it is off. Don't settle for sloppy playing.
Going too fast too soon: Rushing progress leads to bad habits that are hard to brea

Memory Connection

Practicing with a metronome helps strengthen both: Procedural memory (muscle memory through repetition in time) and Internal rhythm awareness (developing an intuitive sense of groove)

Final Thoughts

The metronome isn't just a training tool, it's a mirror. It tells you exactly where your timing is strong and where it needs work. If you stick with it, your timing, confidence, and groove will improve dramatically.

Independent Hand Timing Exercise: Build Control. Strengthen Timing. Train Both Hands

When playing any instrument, especially piano, guitar, or drums. Developing the ability to use both hands independently and rhythmically is essential. Whether you're finger picking, chord switching, or playing melodies and bass lines together, both hands must stay in time, even when they're doing completely different things.

This exercise is simple and only requires:
A metronome
A sheet of paper (or use the chart provided)
Your left and right hands

Objective

To improve your ability to perform different rhythmic subdivisions with each hand, while keeping in time with a steady beat.

How It Works

Below is a simple timing grid. Each column represents one hand. Each row represents a number of hits (or taps) per beat.

Each number corresponds to how many taps per beat you'll perform. For example:

1 = one tap per beat (quarter notes)
2 = two taps per beat (eighth notes)
3 = triplets (three evenly spaced taps per beat)
4 = sixteenth notes (four taps per beat)

Left Hand	Right Hand
1	1
2	2
3	3
4	4

149

Step-by-Step Instructions
Set the metronome to a slow, comfortable tempo (around 60–70 BPM to start).

Start with both hands tapping once per beat (row 1). Tap your fingers or lightly drum on a table—just stay with the beat.

Once you're comfortable, keep your left hand tapping once per beat (still on row 1). Now, switch your right hand to row 2, tapping twice per beat while the left hand continues once per beat.

When that feels natural, switch your left hand to row 2 while the right hand stays.

Continue this process through all rows, practicing different combinations:

Left hand on 1, right hand on 3
Left hand on 2, right hand on 4
Left hand on 3, right hand on 1
And so on...

Why This Helps
This exercise works your procedural memory (muscle memory) and improves:
Hand independence
Subdivided rhythm awareness
Internal tempo control

It also helps you stay focused and calm under complexity, a skill that transfers directly into playing riffs, scales, and rhythms cleanly, especially when both hands are doing different things.

Left Hand	Right Hand
1	1
2	2
3	3
4	4

LEFT HAND	RIGHT HAND
1	1
2	2
3	3
4	4

LEFT HAND	RIGHT HAND
1	1
2	2
3	3
4	4

LEFT HAND	RIGHT HAND
1	1
2	2
3	3
4	4

153

LEFT HAND	RIGHT HAND
1	1
2	2
3	3
4	4

LEFT HAND	RIGHT HAND
1	1
2	2
3	3
4	4

LEFT HAND	RIGHT HAND
1	1
2	2
3	3
4	4

LEFT HAND	RIGHT HAND
1	1
2	2
3	3
4	4

LEFT HAND	RIGHT HAND
1	1
2	2
3	3
4	4

LEFT HAND	RIGHT HAND
1	1
2	2
3	3
4	4

1	1
2	2
3	3
4	4

Section 6: Independent Practice

SECTION 6: Independent Practice Pages

This final section gives you blank templates, staff lines, scale/chord worksheets with guitar necks, and scale/chord worksheets with piano keys, for creative exploration and extended practice. Use them to write short compositions, test new chord progressions, or reinforce weak areas.

Goal: To encourage independent study, creativity, and long-term musical growth.

Blank Staves

Blank Staves

Blank Staves

Blank Staves

Blank Staves

Blank Staves

Blank Staves

Blank Staves

Blank Staves

Blank Staves

Scale/Chord Worksheet

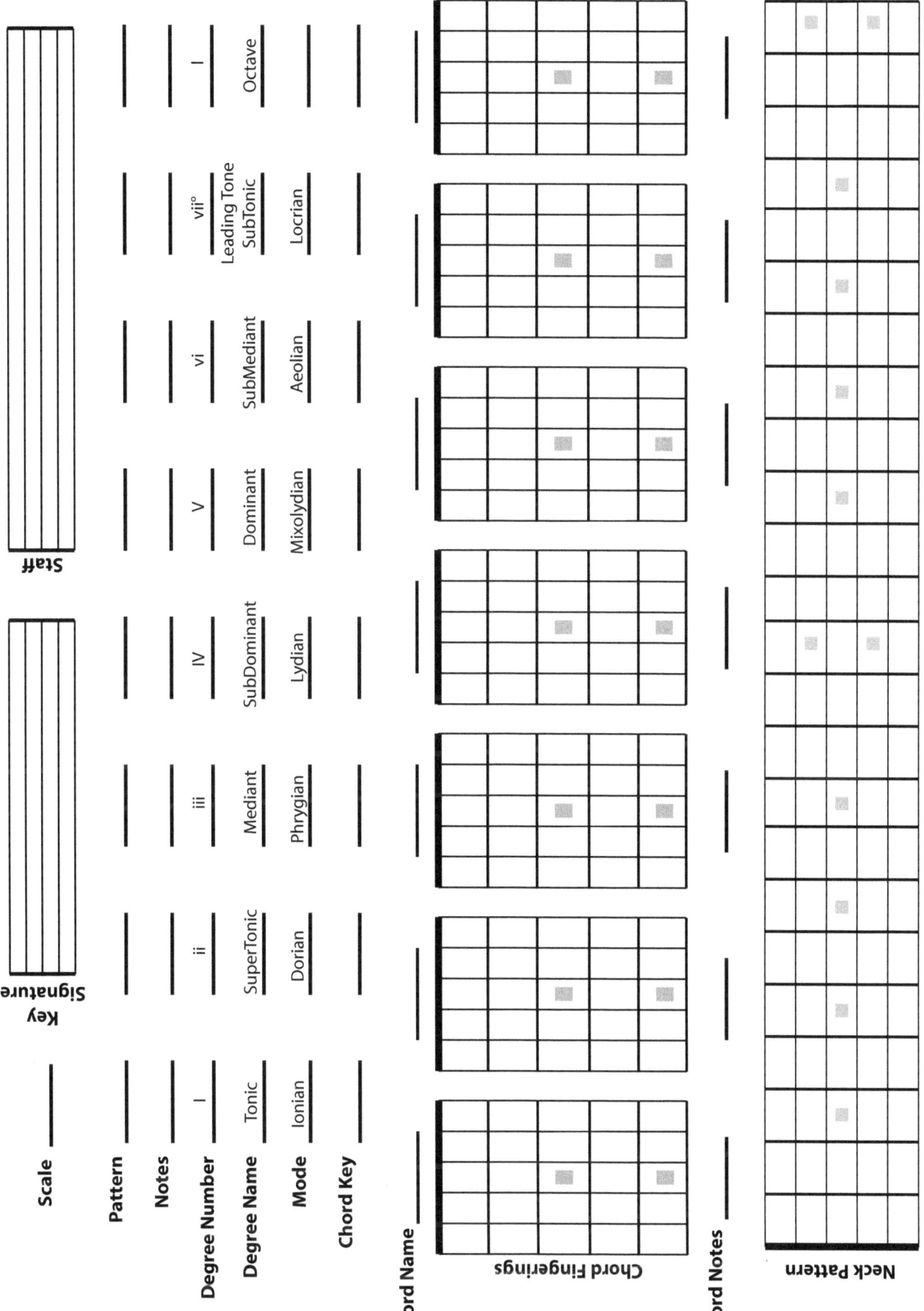

Staff

Key Signature

Scale _____

Pattern _____

Notes _____

Degree Number	I	ii	iii	IV	V	vi	vii°
							Leading Tone
Degree Name	Tonic	SuperTonic	Mediant	SubDominant	Dominant	SubMediant	SubTonic
Mode	Ionian	Dorian	Phrygian	Lydian	Mixolydian	Aeolian	Locrian

| | | | | | | | Octave |

Chord Key _____

Chord Name _____

Chord Fingerings

Chord Notes _____

Neck Pattern

Scale/Chord Worksheet

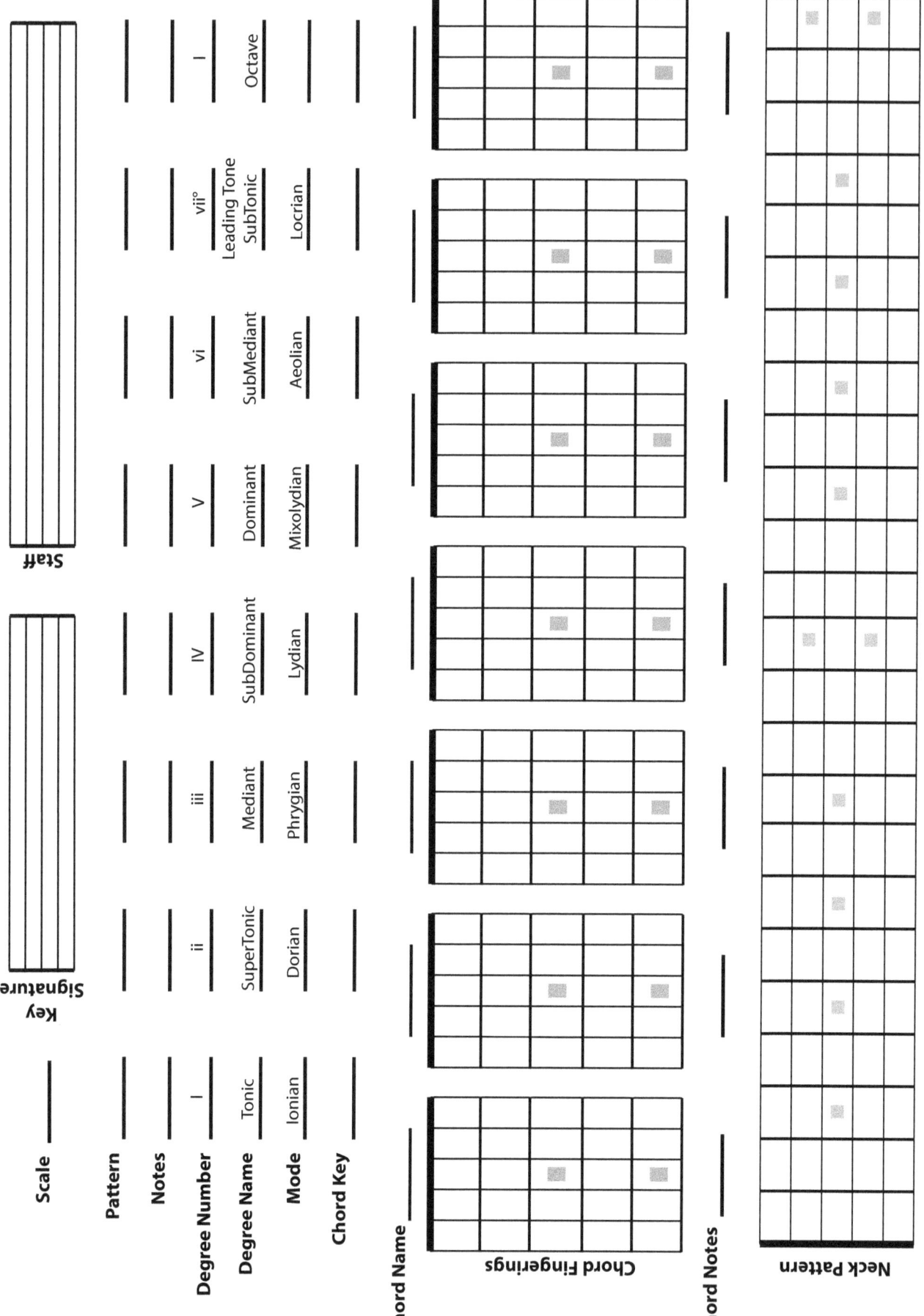

Scale _____

Key Signature

Pattern _____

Notes _____

Degree Number	I	ii	iii	IV	V	vi	vii°	I
Degree Name	Tonic	SuperTonic	Mediant	SubDominant	Dominant	SubMediant	Leading Tone / SubTonic	Octave
Mode	Ionian	Dorian	Phrygian	Lydian	Mixolydian	Aeolian	Locrian	

Chord Key _____

Chord Name _____

Chord Fingerings

Chord Notes _____

Neck Pattern

Scale/Chord Worksheet

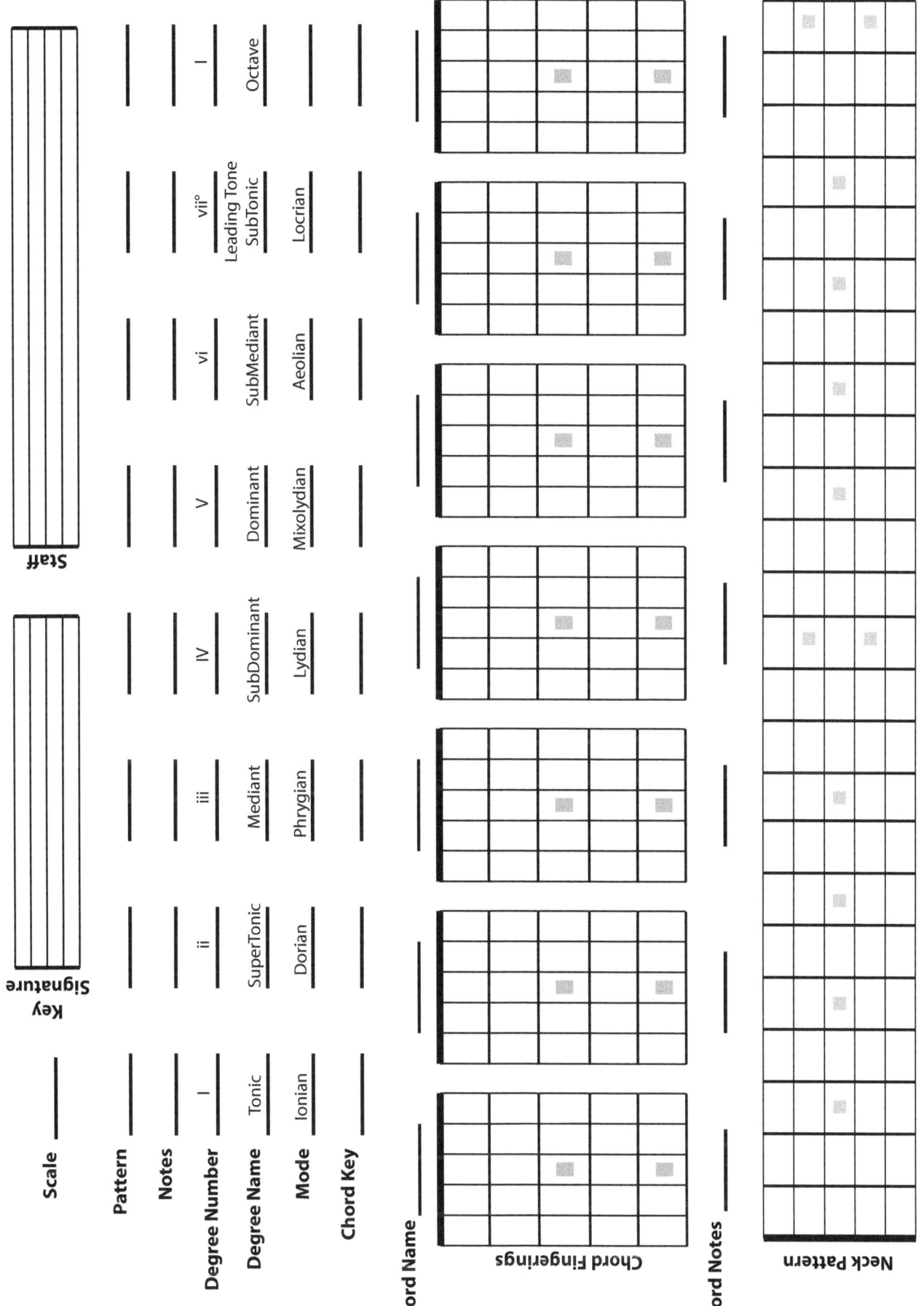

Staff

Key Signature

Scale _____

Pattern _____

Notes _____

Degree Number	I	ii	iii	IV	V	vi	vii°	I
Degree Name	Tonic	SuperTonic	Mediant	SubDominant	Dominant	SubMediant	Leading Tone / SubTonic	Octave
Mode	Ionian	Dorian	Phrygian	Lydian	Mixolydian	Aeolian	Locrian	

Chord Key _____

Chord Name _____

Chord Fingerings

Chord Notes _____

Neck Pattern

Scale/Chord Worksheet

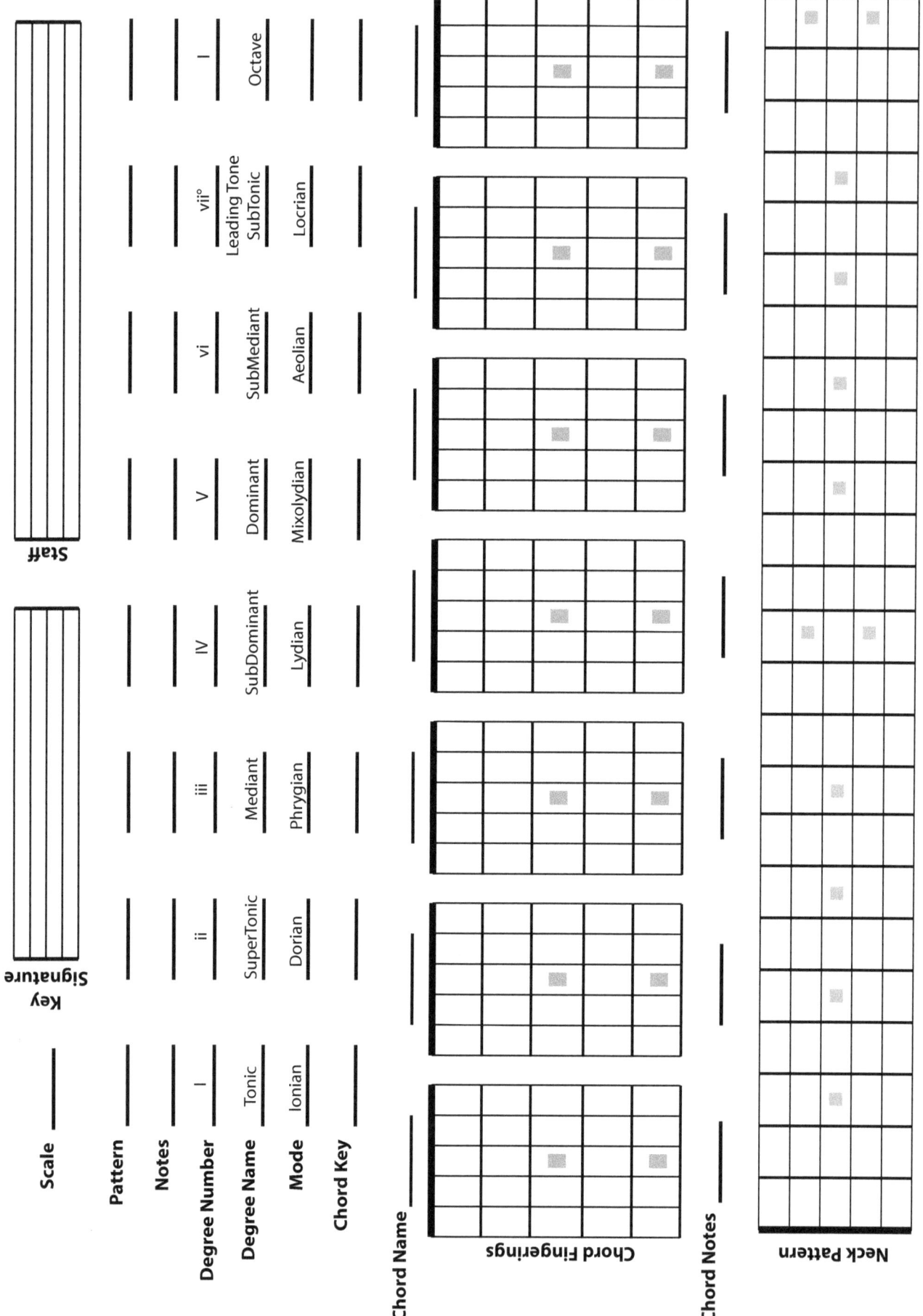

Staff

Key Signature

Scale _____

Pattern _____

Notes _____ | _____ | _____ | _____ | _____ | _____ | _____ | _____

Degree Number _____ | I | ii | iii | IV | V | vi | vii° | I

Degree Name _____ | Tonic | SuperTonic | Mediant | SubDominant | Dominant | SubMediant | Leading Tone / SubTonic | Octave

Mode _____ | Ionian | Dorian | Phrygian | Lydian | Mixolydian | Aeolian | Locrian

Chord Key _____

Chord Name _____

Chord Fingerings

Chord Notes _____

Neck Pattern

Scale/Chord Worksheet

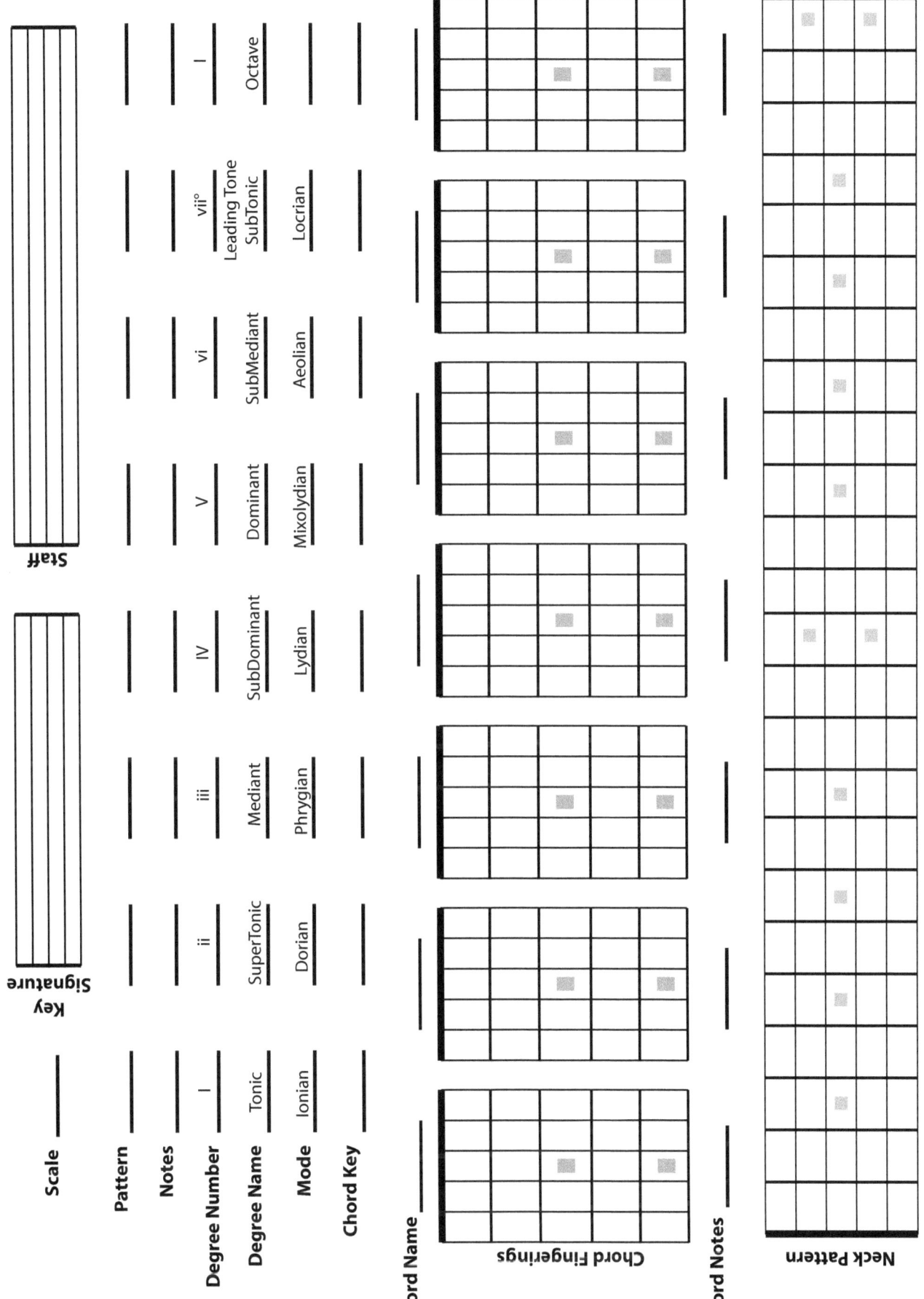

Staff

Key Signature

Scale _____

Pattern _____

Notes _____

Degree Number	I	ii	iii	IV	V	vi	vii°
							Leading Tone
Degree Name	Tonic	SuperTonic	Mediant	SubDominant	Dominant	SubMediant	SubTonic
Mode	Ionian	Dorian	Phrygian	Lydian	Mixolydian	Aeolian	Locrian

I — Octave

Chord Key _____

Chord Name _____

Chord Fingerings

Chord Notes _____

Neck Pattern

Scale/Chord Worksheet

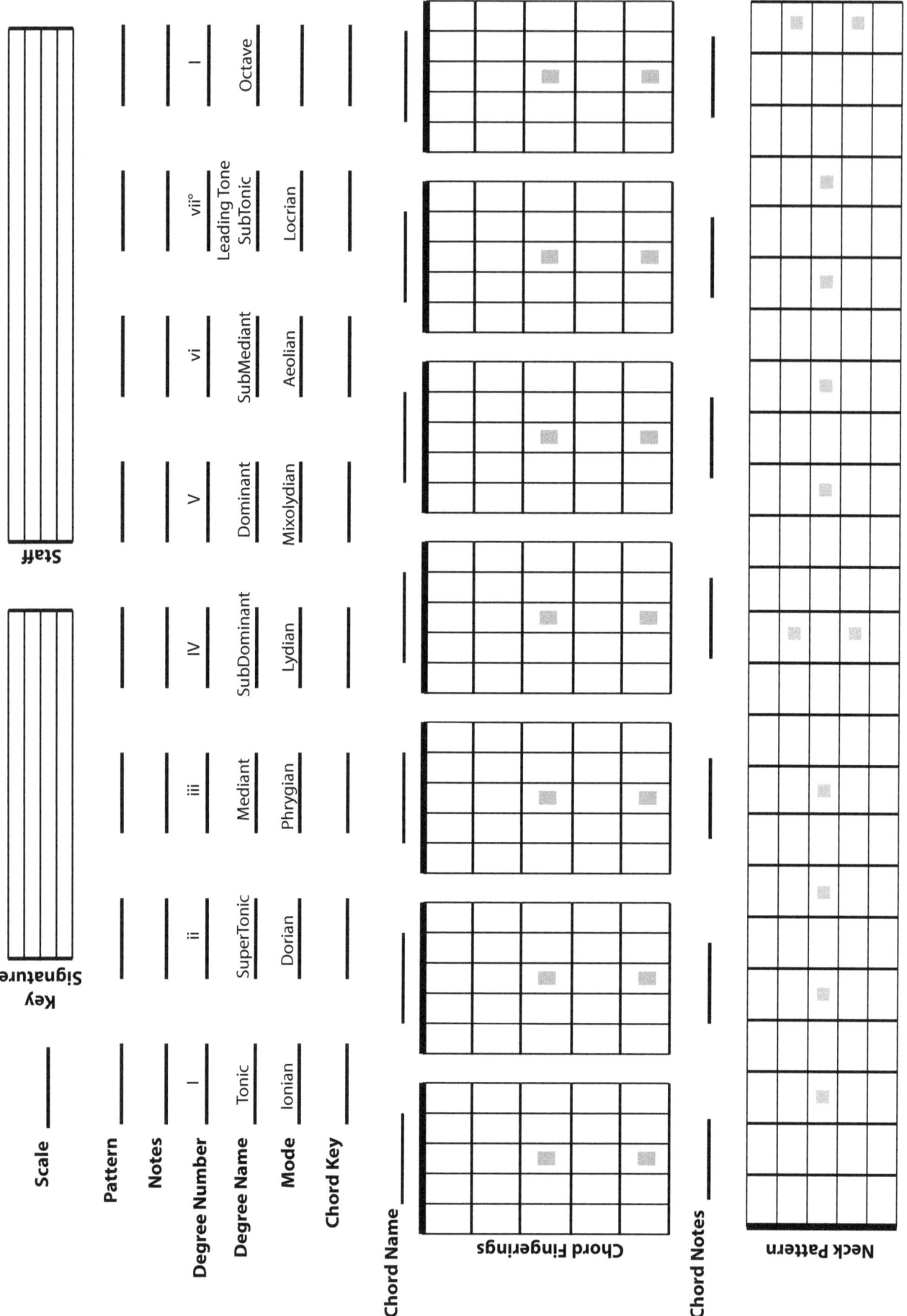

Staff

Key Signature

Scale ____

Pattern ____

Notes ____

Degree Number	I	ii	iii	IV	V	vi	vii°	I
Degree Name	Tonic	SuperTonic	Mediant	SubDominant	Dominant	SubMediant	Leading Tone / SubTonic	Octave
Mode	Ionian	Dorian	Phrygian	Lydian	Mixolydian	Aeolian	Locrian	

Chord Key ____

Chord Name ____

Chord Fingerings

Chord Notes ____

Neck Pattern

178

Scale/Chord Worksheet

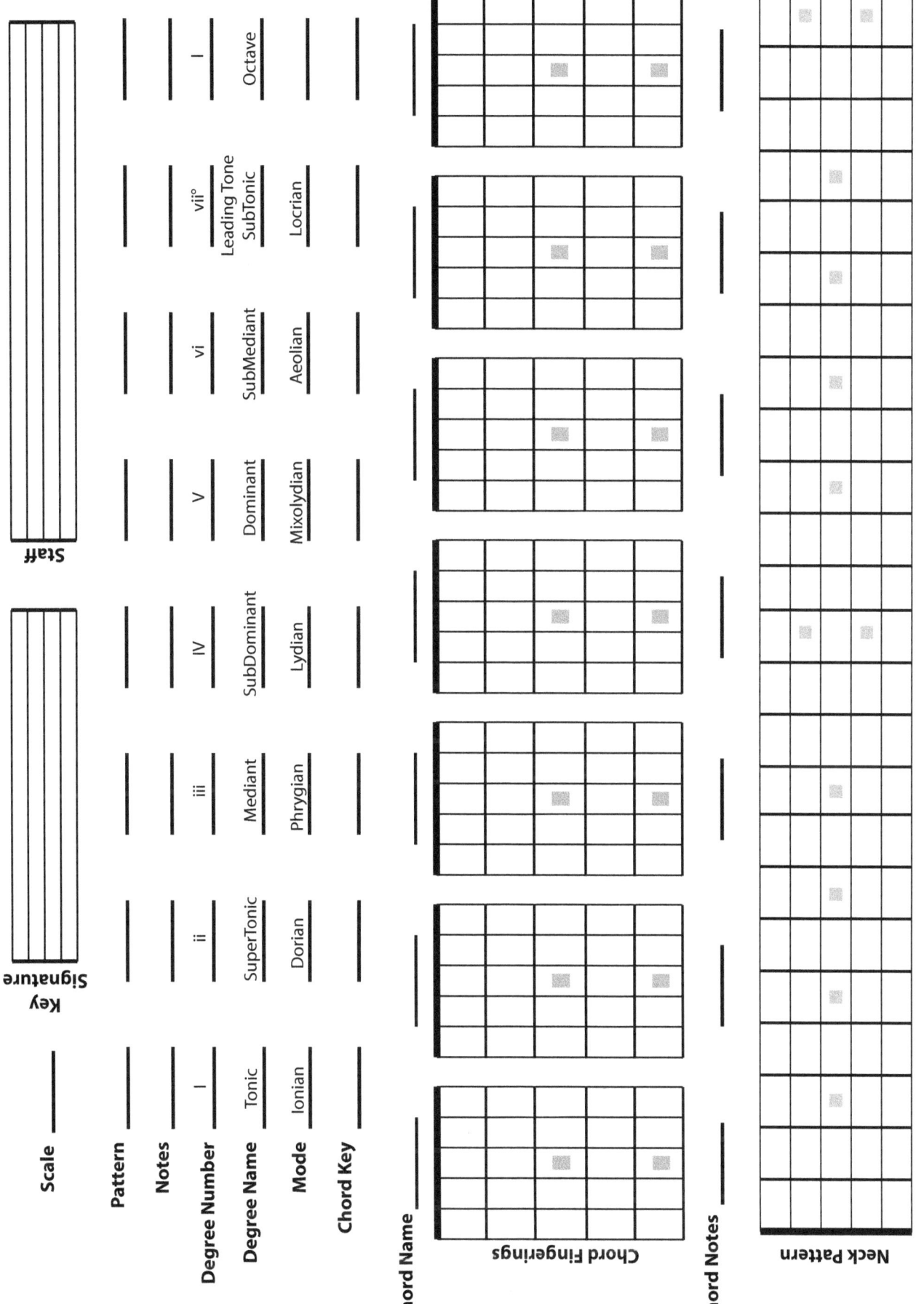

Staff

Key Signature

Scale _____

Pattern _____

Notes _____

Degree Number	I	ii	iii	IV	V	vi	vii°	I
							Leading Tone	
Degree Name	Tonic	SuperTonic	Mediant	SubDominant	Dominant	SubMediant	SubTonic	Octave
Mode	Ionian	Dorian	Phrygian	Lydian	Mixolydian	Aeolian	Locrian	

Chord Key _____

Chord Name _____

Chord Fingerings

Chord Notes _____

Neck Pattern

Scale/Chord Worksheet

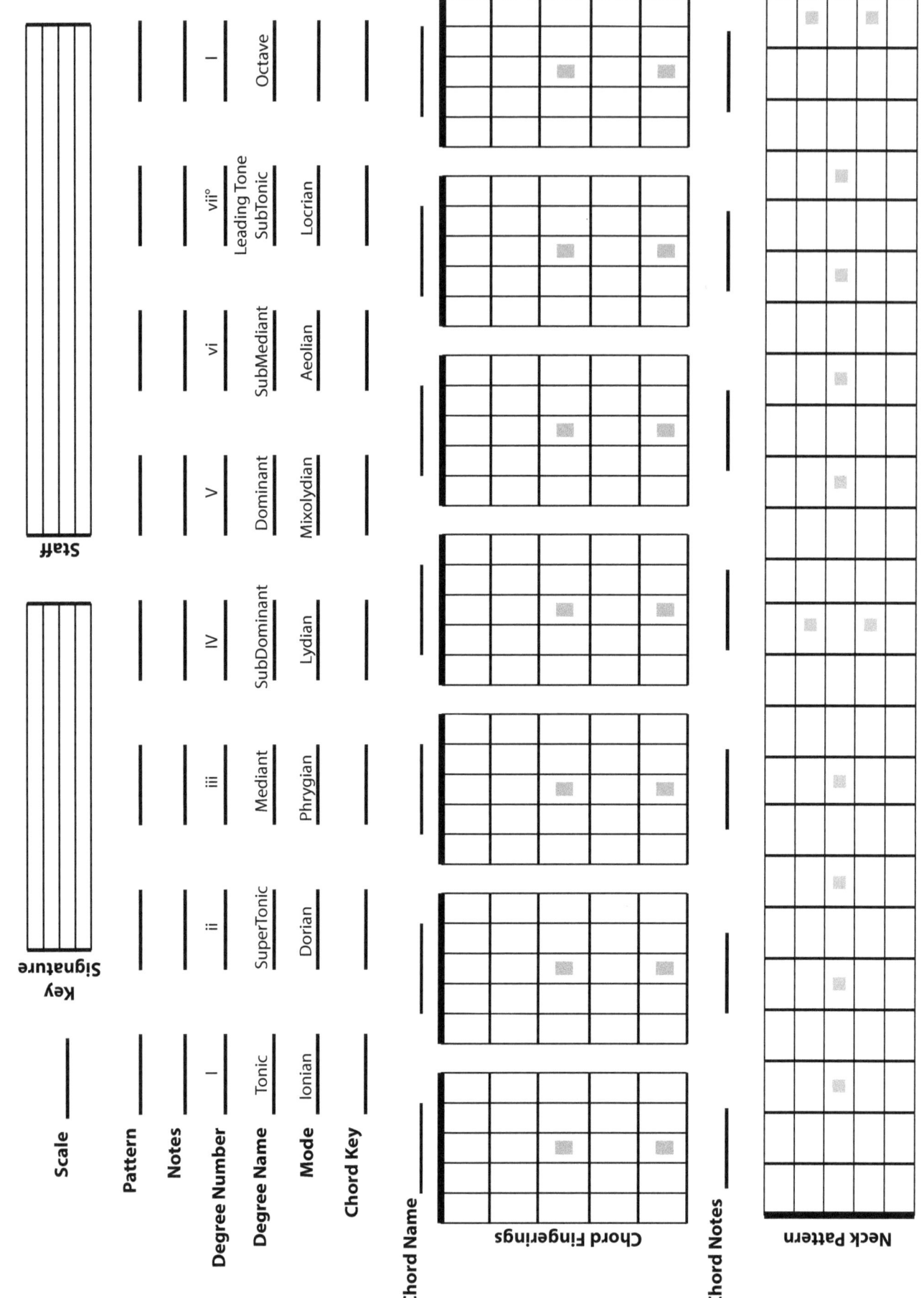

Staff

Key Signature

Scale _____

Pattern _____

Notes _____

Degree Number	I	ii	iii	IV	V	vi	vii°	I
Degree Name	Tonic	SuperTonic	Mediant	SubDominant	Dominant	SubMediant	Leading Tone / SubTonic	Octave
Mode	Ionian	Dorian	Phrygian	Lydian	Mixolydian	Aeolian	Locrian	

Chord Key _____

Chord Name _____

Chord Fingerings

Chord Notes _____

Neck Pattern

Scale/Chord Worksheet

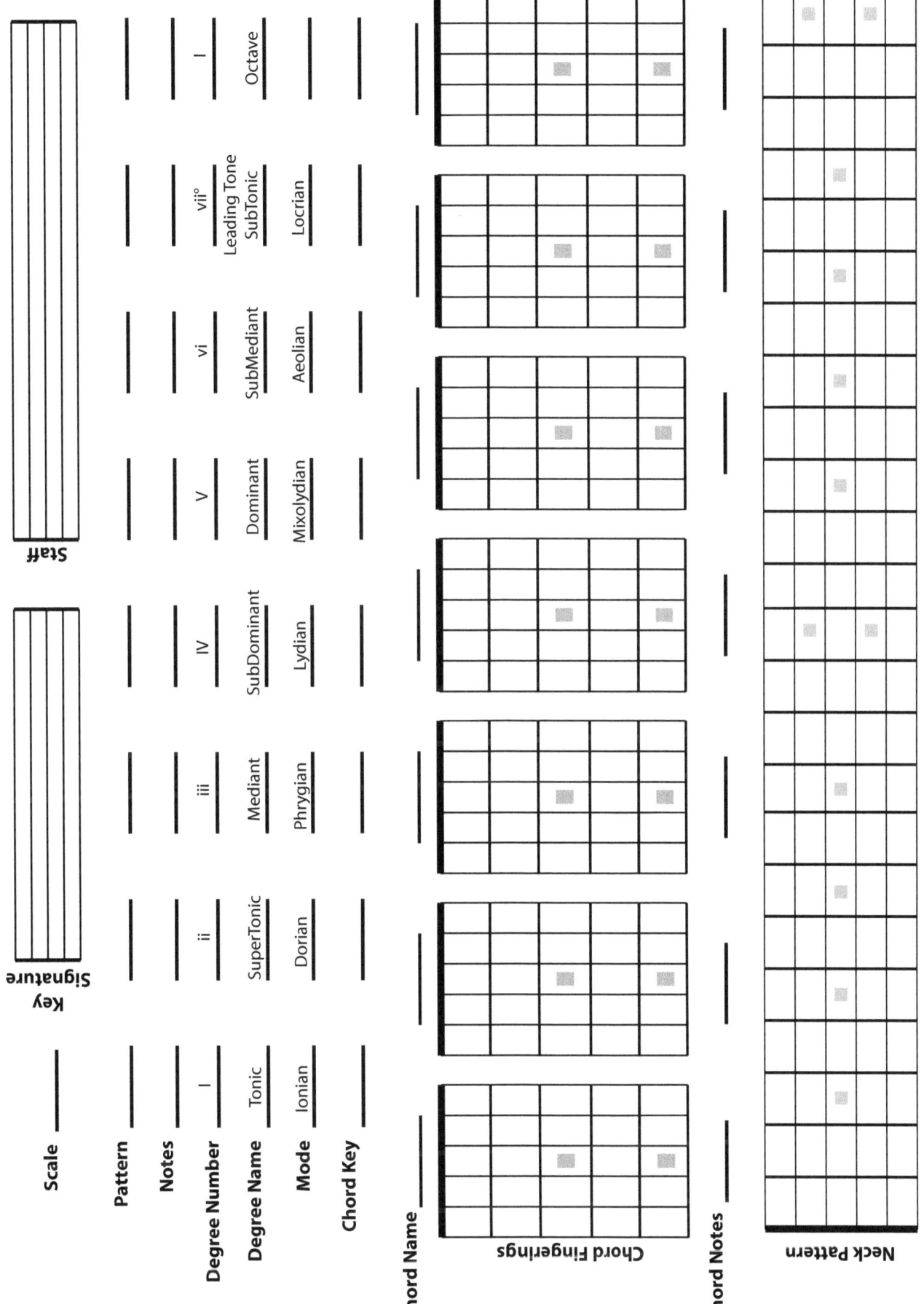

Staff

Key Signature

Scale ____

Pattern ____

Notes ____

Degree Number ____ I ii iii IV V vi $\frac{vii°}{Leading\ Tone}$ I

Degree Name ____ Tonic SuperTonic Mediant SubDominant Dominant SubMediant SubTonic Octave

Mode ____ Ionian Dorian Phrygian Lydian Mixolydian Aeolian Locrian

Chord Key ____

Chord Name ____

Chord Fingerings

Chord Notes ____

Neck Pattern

Scale/Chord Worksheet

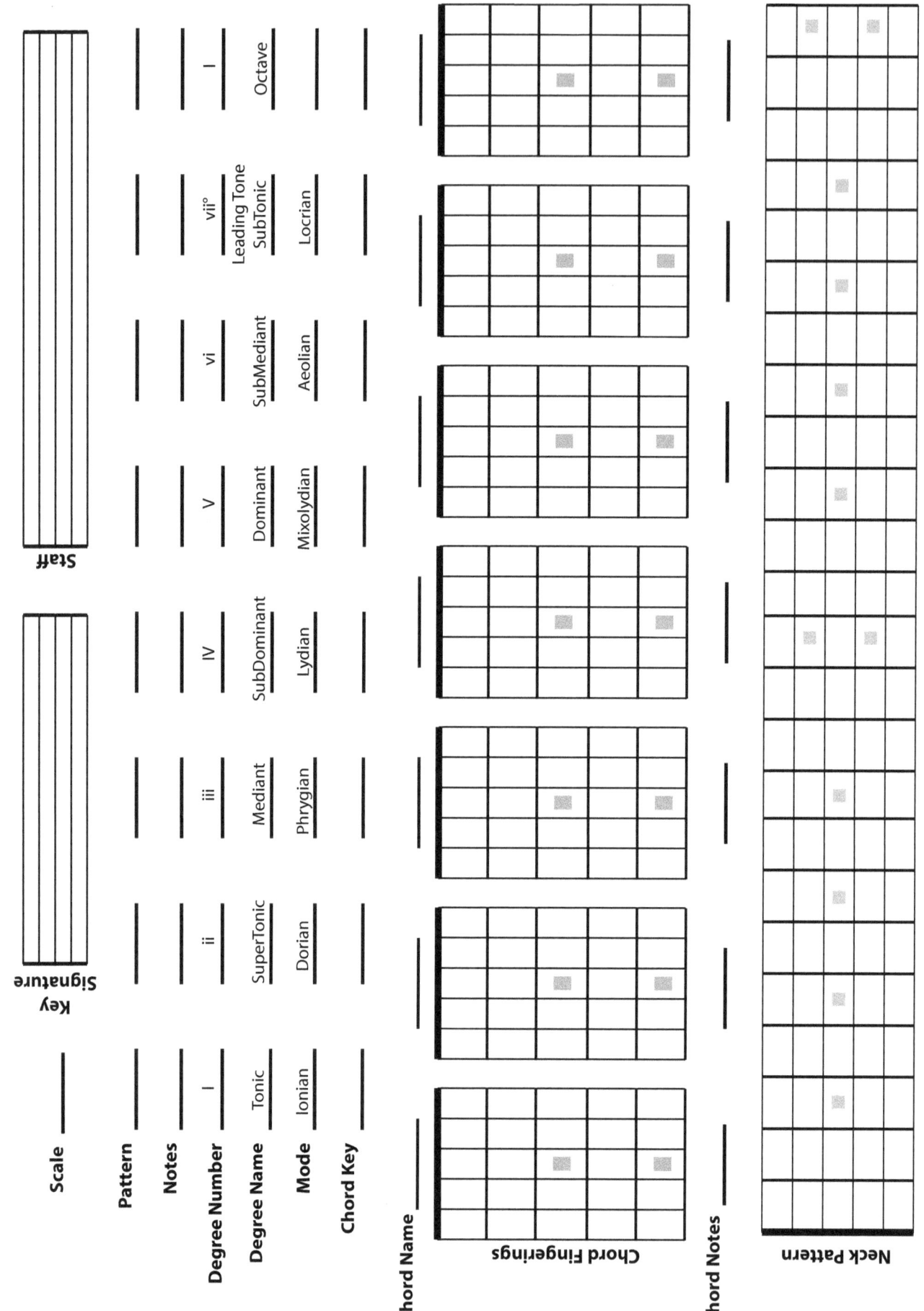

Staff

Key Signature

Scale _____

Pattern _____

Notes _____

Degree Number	I	ii	iii	IV	V	vi	vii°
Degree Name	Tonic	SuperTonic	Mediant	SubDominant	Dominant	SubMediant	Leading Tone SubTonic
Mode	Ionian	Dorian	Phrygian	Lydian	Mixolydian	Aeolian	Locrian

I
Octave

Chord Key _____

Chord Name _____

Chord Fingerings

Chord Notes _____

Neck Pattern

Scale/Chord Worksheet

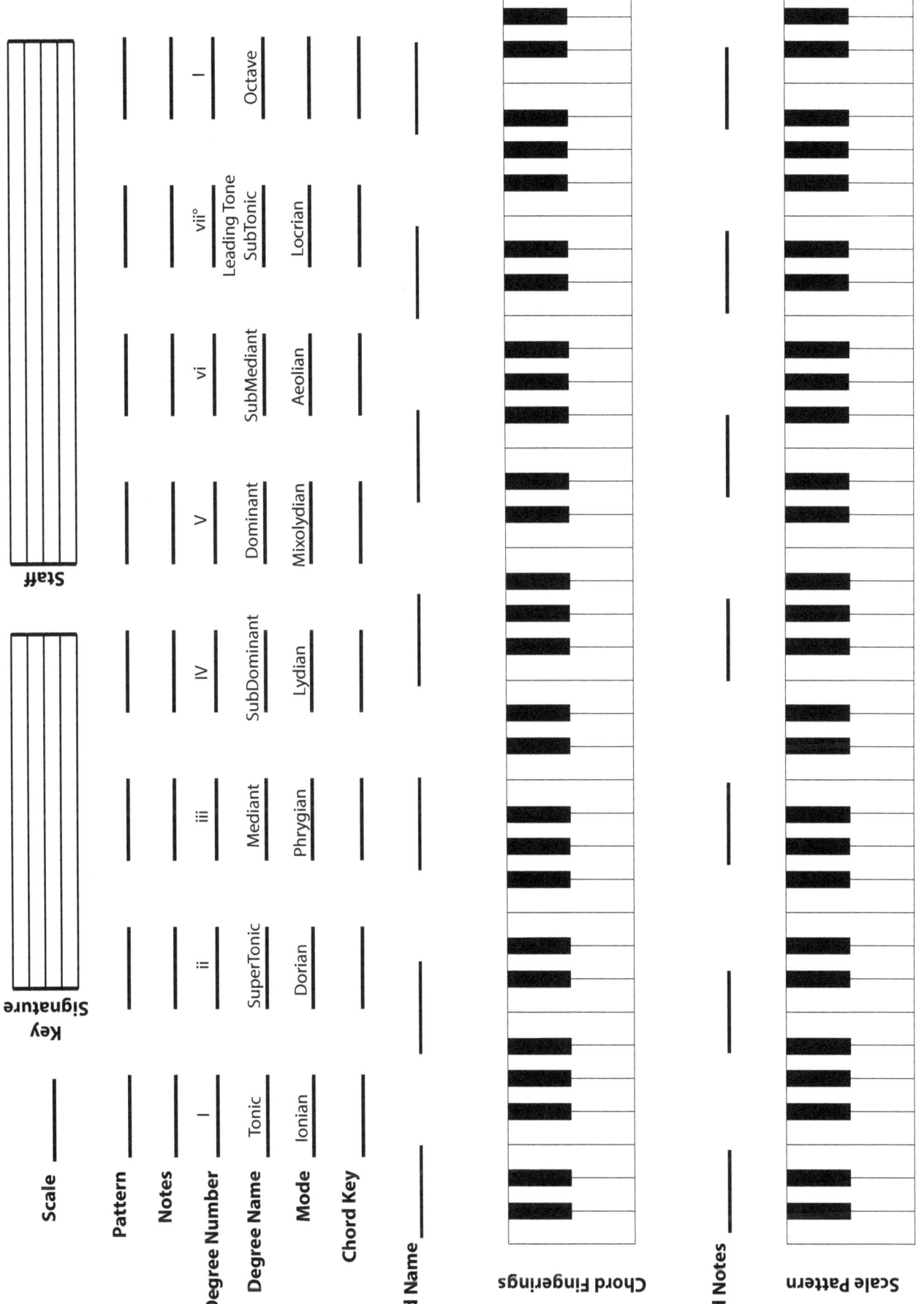

Scale _____

Key Signature

Staff

Pattern | ___ | ___ | ___ | ___ | ___ | ___ | ___

Notes | ___ | ___ | ___ | ___ | ___ | ___ | ___

Degree Number | I | ii | iii | IV | V | vi | vii° | I

Degree Name | Tonic | SuperTonic | Mediant | SubDominant | Dominant | SubMediant | Leading Tone / SubTonic | Octave

Mode | Ionian | Dorian | Phrygian | Lydian | Mixolydian | Aeolian | Locrian

Chord Key | ___ | ___ | ___ | ___ | ___ | ___ | ___

Chord Name _____

Chord Fingerings

Chord Notes _____

Scale Pattern

183

Scale/Chord Worksheet

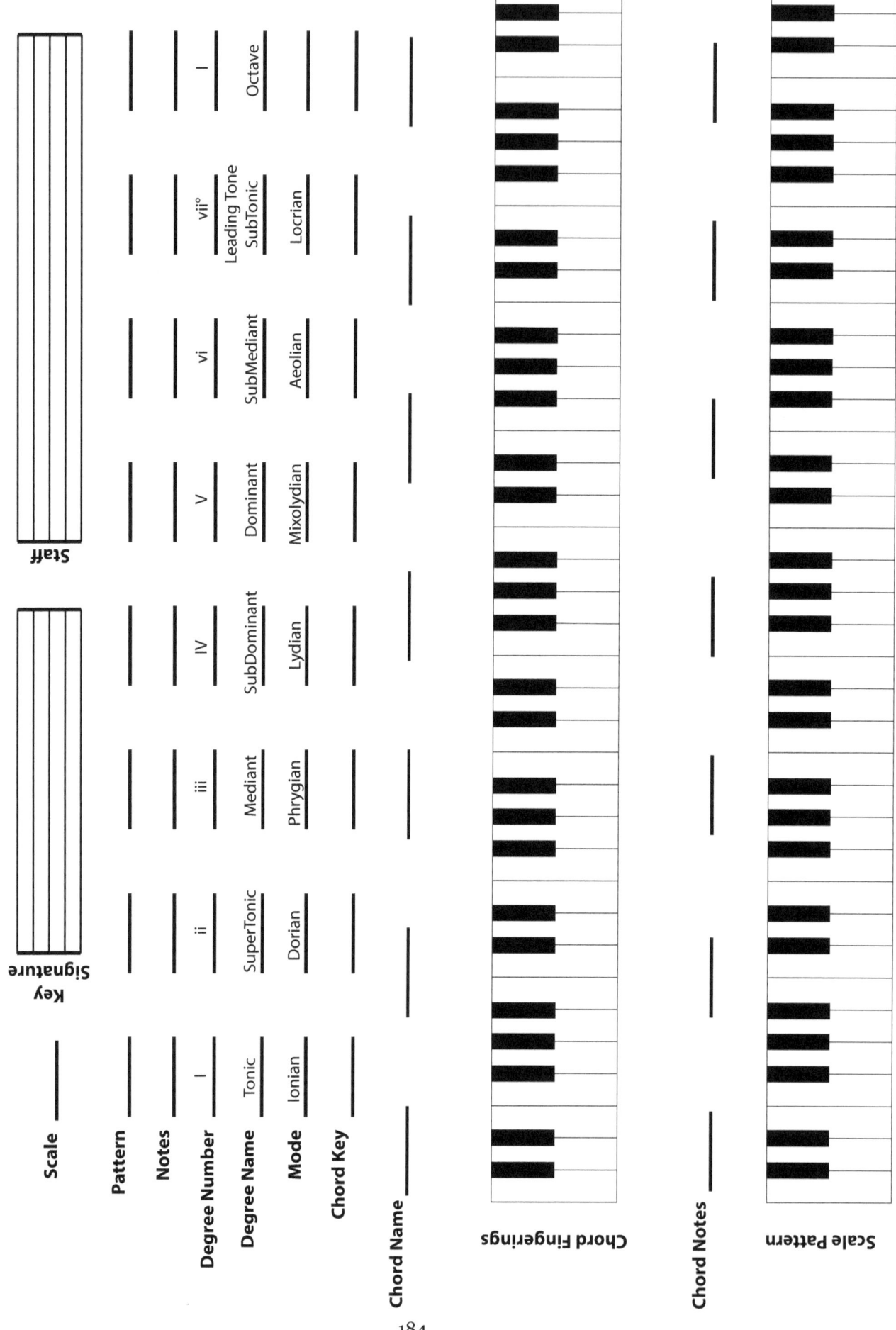

Staff

Key Signature

| Scale | ____ |

Pattern	____
Notes	____
Degree Number	I	ii	iii	IV	V	vi	vii°
Degree Name	Tonic	SuperTonic	Mediant	SubDominant	Dominant	SubMediant	Leading Tone / SubTonic	Octave
Mode	Ionian	Dorian	Phrygian	Lydian	Mixolydian	Aeolian	Locrian
Chord Key	____

Chord Name ____

Chord Fingerings

Chord Notes ____

Scale Pattern

Scale/Chord Worksheet

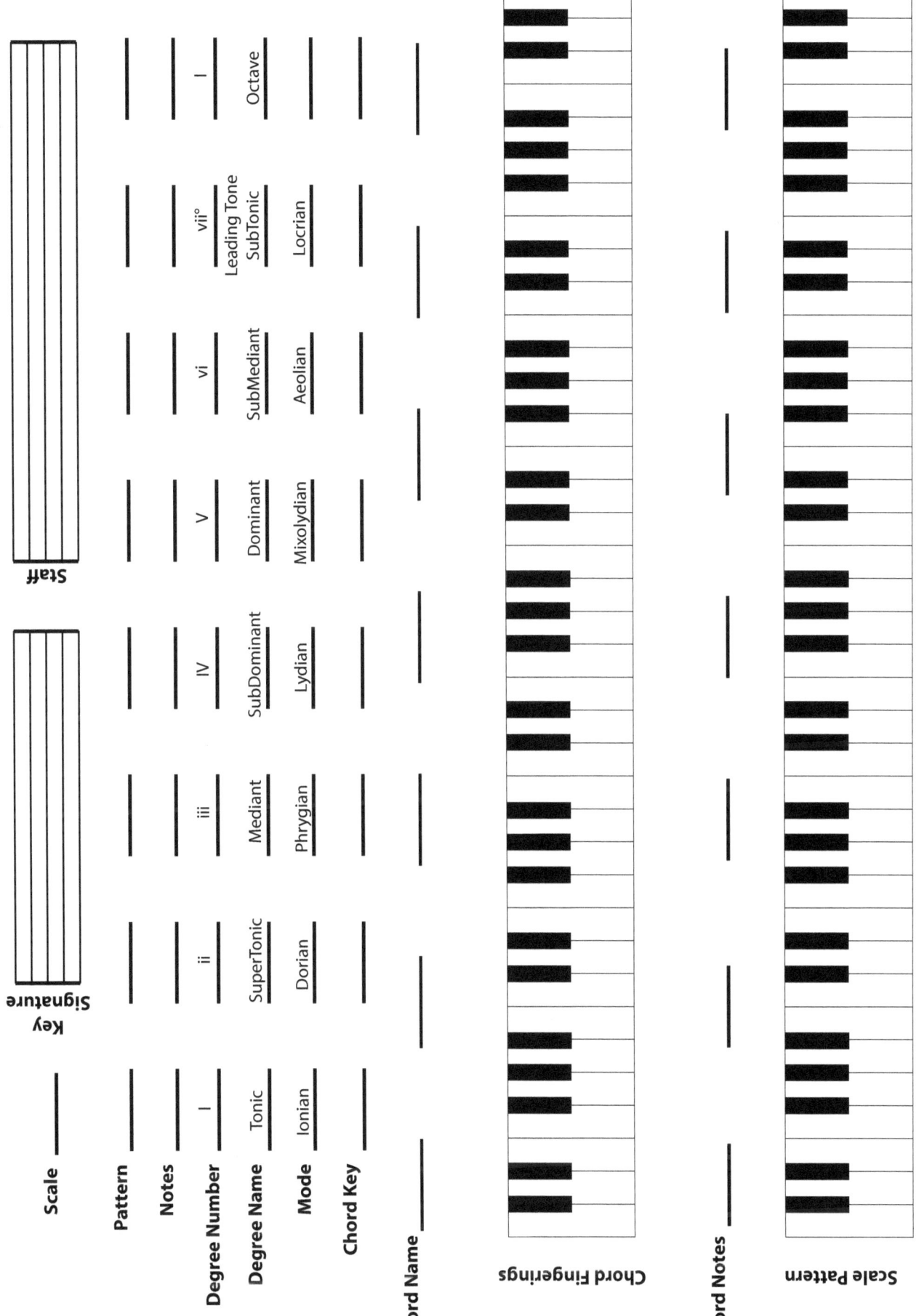

Staff

Key Signature

Scale ____

Pattern ____

Notes ____

Degree Number   I   ii   iii   IV   V   vi   vii°

Degree Name   Tonic   SuperTonic   Mediant   SubDominant   Dominant   SubMediant   Leading Tone / SubTonic   Octave

Mode   Ionian   Dorian   Phrygian   Lydian   Mixolydian   Aeolian   Locrian

Chord Key ____

Chord Name ____

Chord Fingerings

Chord Notes ____

Scale Pattern

185

Scale/Chord Worksheet

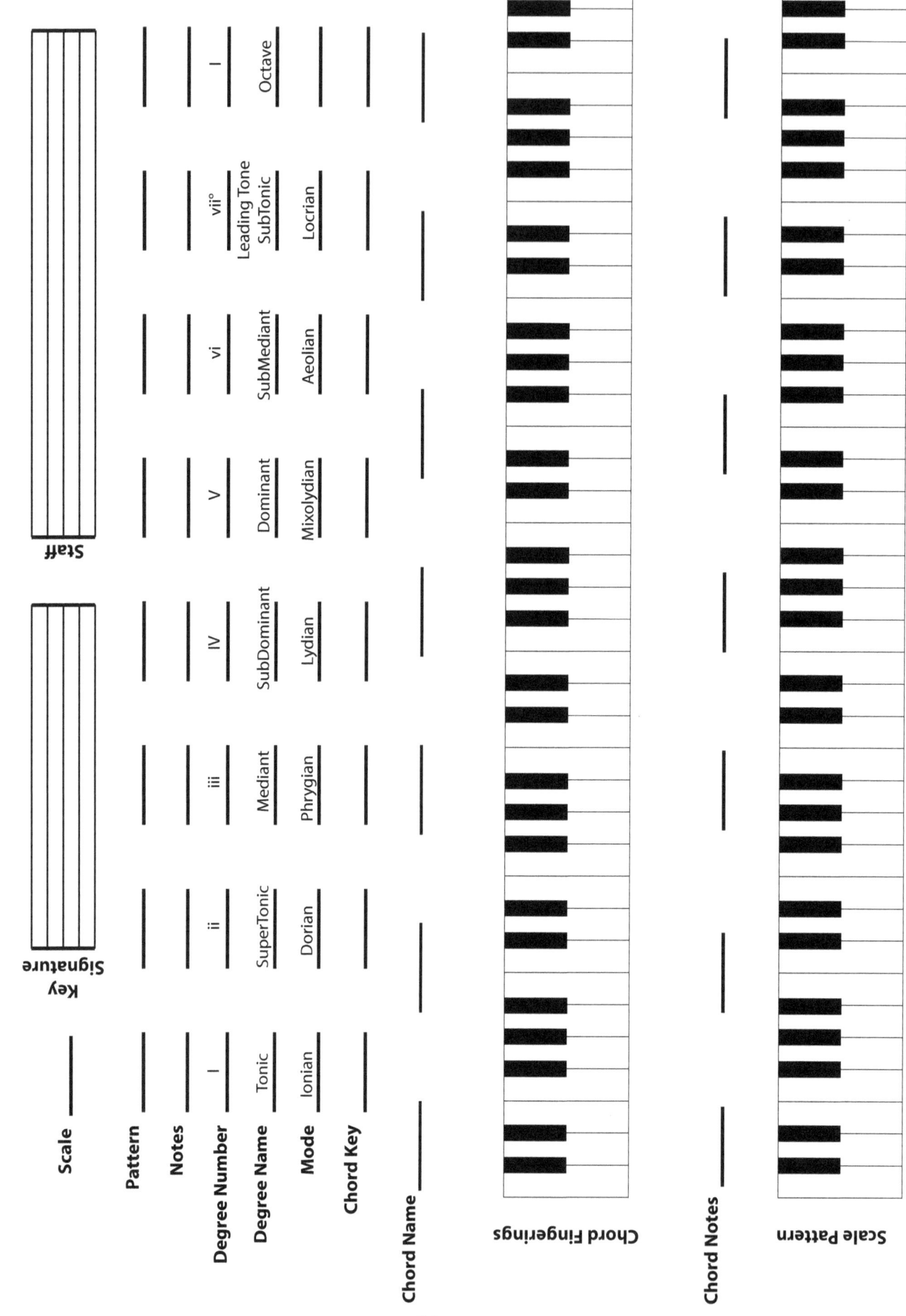

Scale _____

Key Signature

Staff

Pattern _____

Notes _____

Degree Number _____ I   ii   iii   IV   V   vi   vii°

Degree Name   Tonic   SuperTonic   Mediant   SubDominant   Dominant   SubMediant   Leading Tone / SubTonic   Octave

Mode   Ionian   Dorian   Phrygian   Lydian   Mixolydian   Aeolian   Locrian

Chord Key _____

Chord Name _____

Chord Fingerings

Chord Notes _____

Scale Pattern

186

Scale/Chord Worksheet

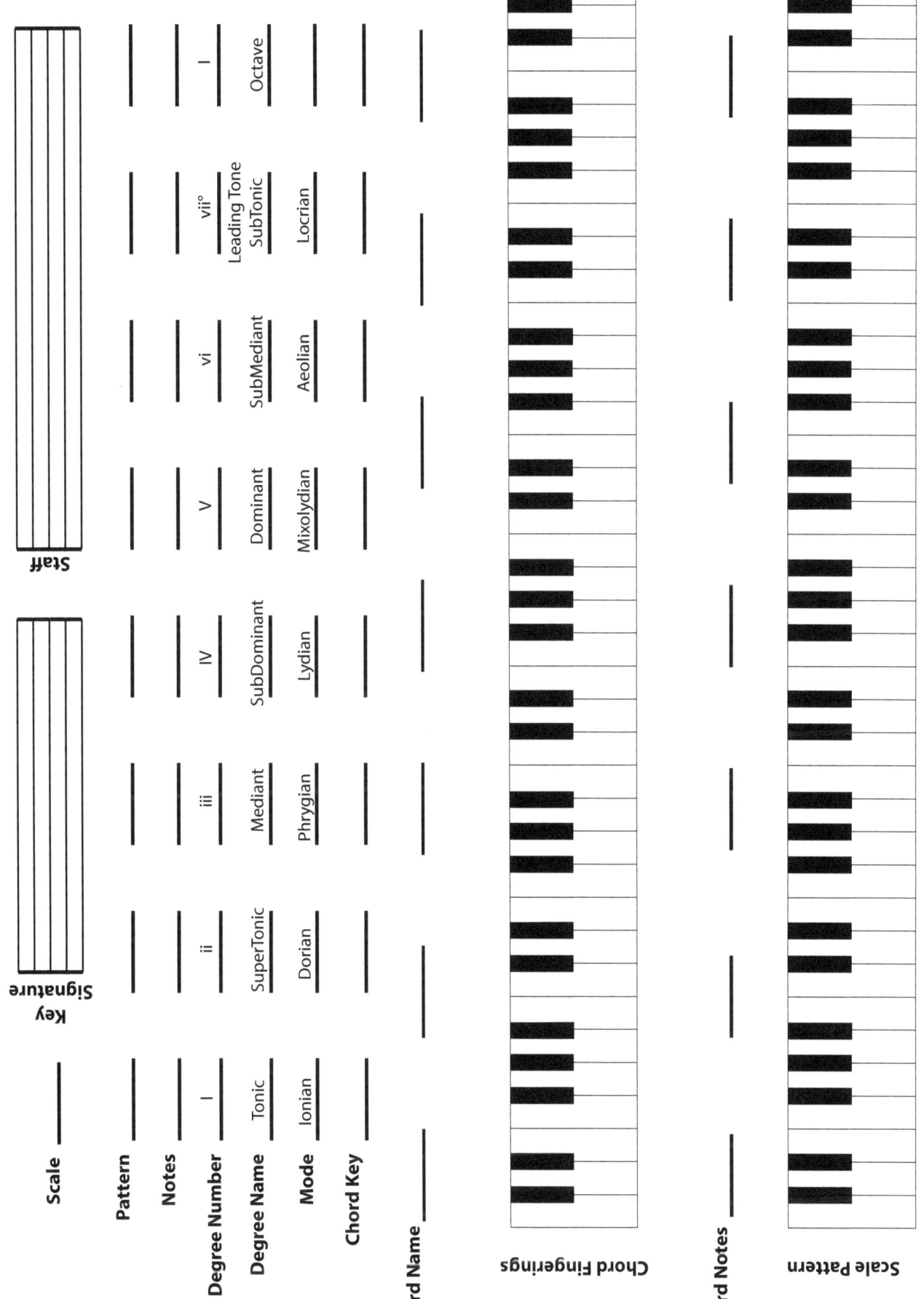

Staff

Key Signature

Scale ____

Pattern ____

Notes ____

Degree Number | I | ii | iii | IV | V | vi | vii°

Degree Name | Tonic | SuperTonic | Mediant | SubDominant | Dominant | SubMediant | Leading Tone / SubTonic

Mode | Ionian | Dorian | Phrygian | Lydian | Mixolydian | Aeolian | Locrian | Octave

Chord Key

Chord Name ____

Chord Fingerings

Chord Notes ____

Scale Pattern

187

Scale/Chord Worksheet

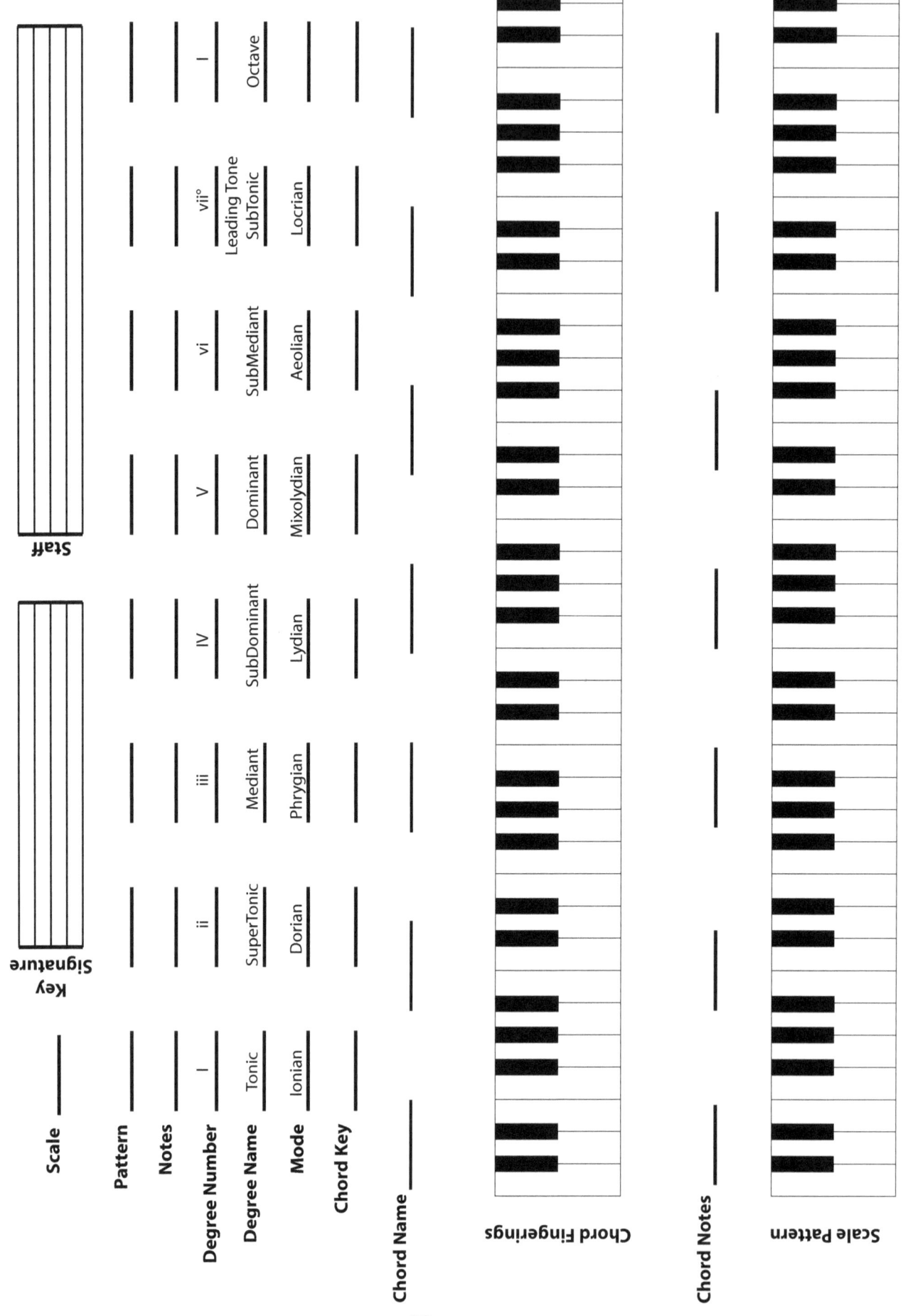

Scale _____

Key Signature

Staff

Pattern _____

Notes _____

Degree Number _____ I   ii   iii   IV   V   vi   vii°

Degree Name _____ Tonic SuperTonic Mediant SubDominant Dominant SubMediant Leading Tone / SubTonic Octave

Mode _____ Ionian Dorian Phrygian Lydian Mixolydian Aeolian Locrian

Chord Key _____

Chord Name _____

Chord Fingerings

Chord Notes _____

Scale Pattern

Scale/Chord Worksheet

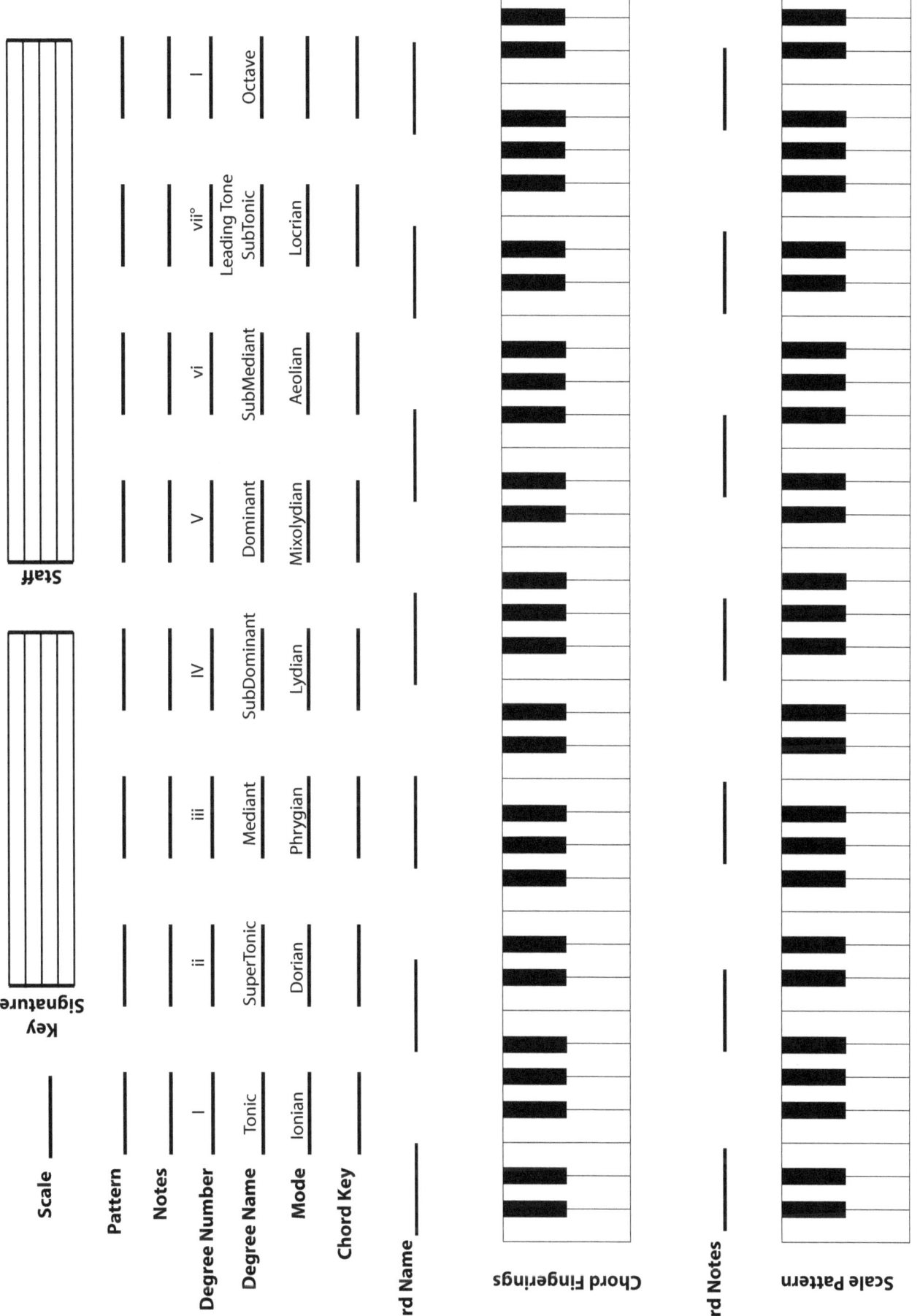

Scale _____

Pattern _____

Notes _____

Staff

Key Signature

Degree Number	I	ii	iii	IV	V	vi	vii°
Degree Name	Tonic	SuperTonic	Mediant	SubDominant	Dominant	SubMediant	Leading Tone / SubTonic	Octave
Mode	Ionian	Dorian	Phrygian	Lydian	Mixolydian	Aeolian	Locrian	

Chord Key _____

Chord Name _____

Chord Fingerings

Chord Notes _____

Scale Pattern

Scale/Chord Worksheet

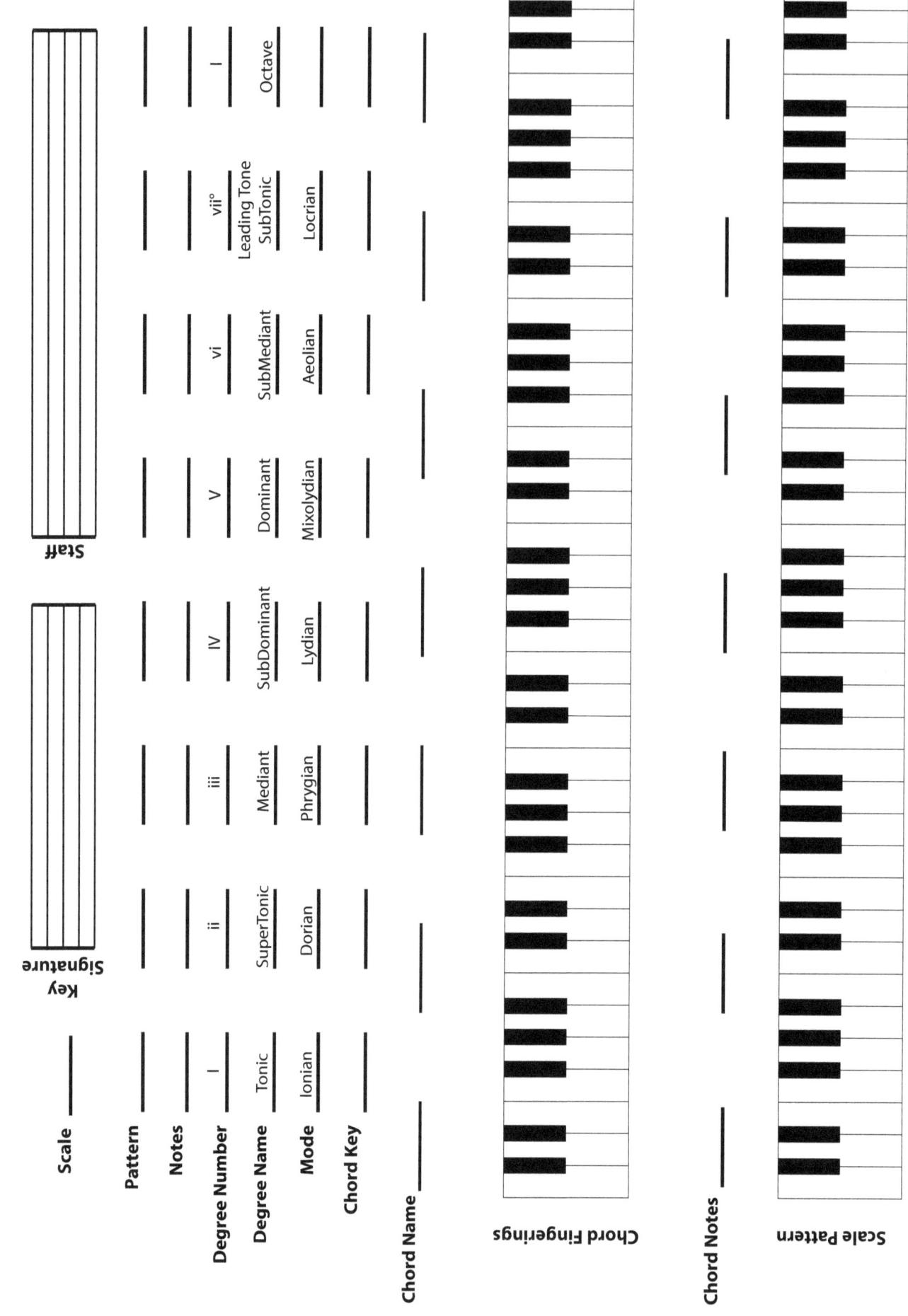

Scale _____

Pattern _____

Notes _____

Staff

Key Signature

Degree Number I   ii   iii   IV   V   vi   vii°

Degree Name Tonic SuperTonic Mediant SubDominant Dominant SubMediant Leading Tone / SubTonic Octave

Mode Ionian Dorian Phrygian Lydian Mixolydian Aeolian Locrian

Chord Key _____

Chord Name _____

Chord Fingerings

Chord Notes _____

Scale Pattern

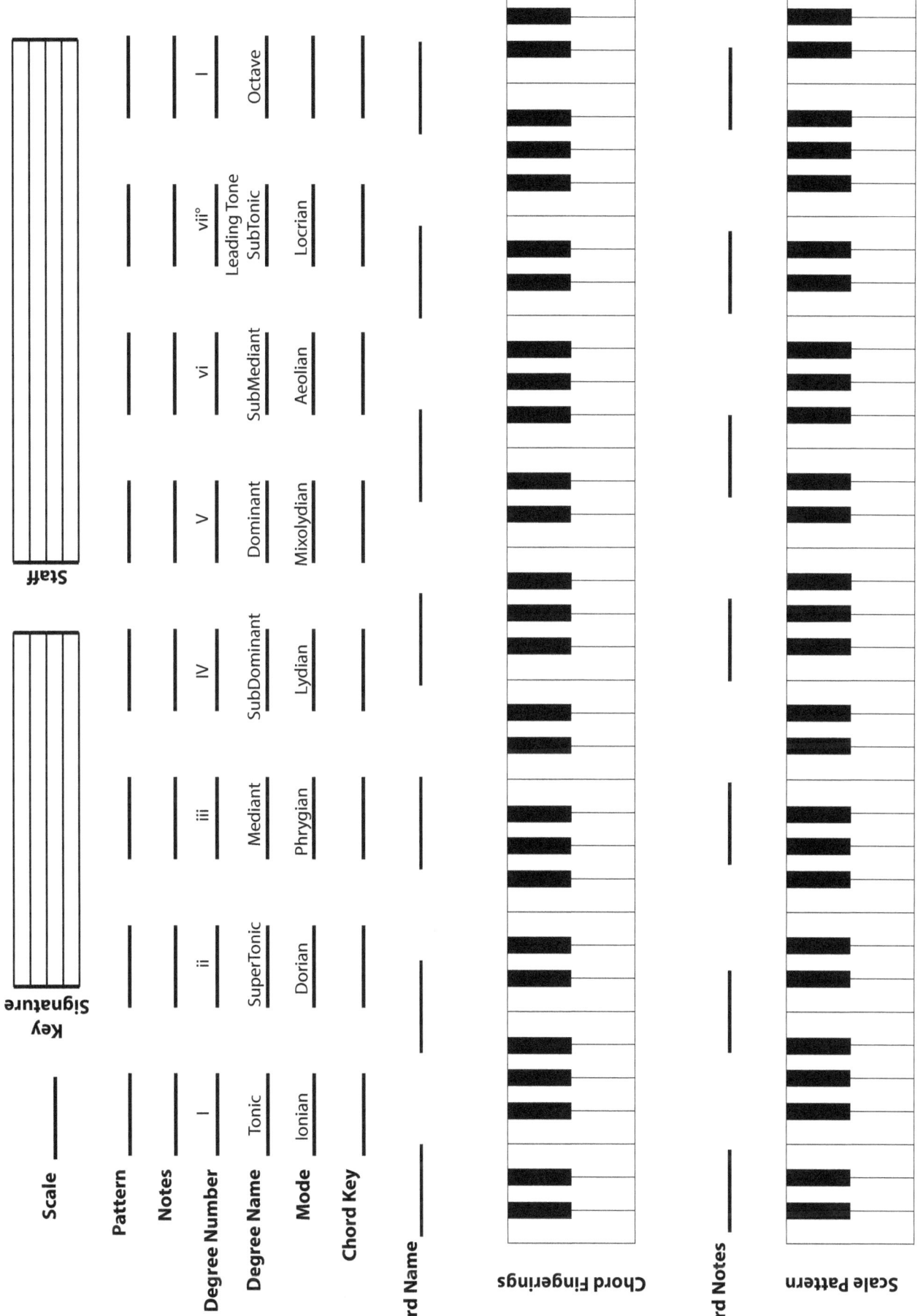

Scale/Chord Worksheet

Staff

Key Signature

Scale _____

Pattern _____

Notes _____

Degree Number	I	ii	iii	IV	V	vi	vii°	I
Degree Name	Tonic	SuperTonic	Mediant	SubDominant	Dominant	SubMediant	Leading Tone / SubTonic	Octave
Mode	Ionian	Dorian	Phrygian	Lydian	Mixolydian	Aeolian	Locrian	

Chord Key _____

Chord Name _____

Chord Fingerings

Chord Notes _____

Scale Pattern

191

Scale/Chord Worksheet

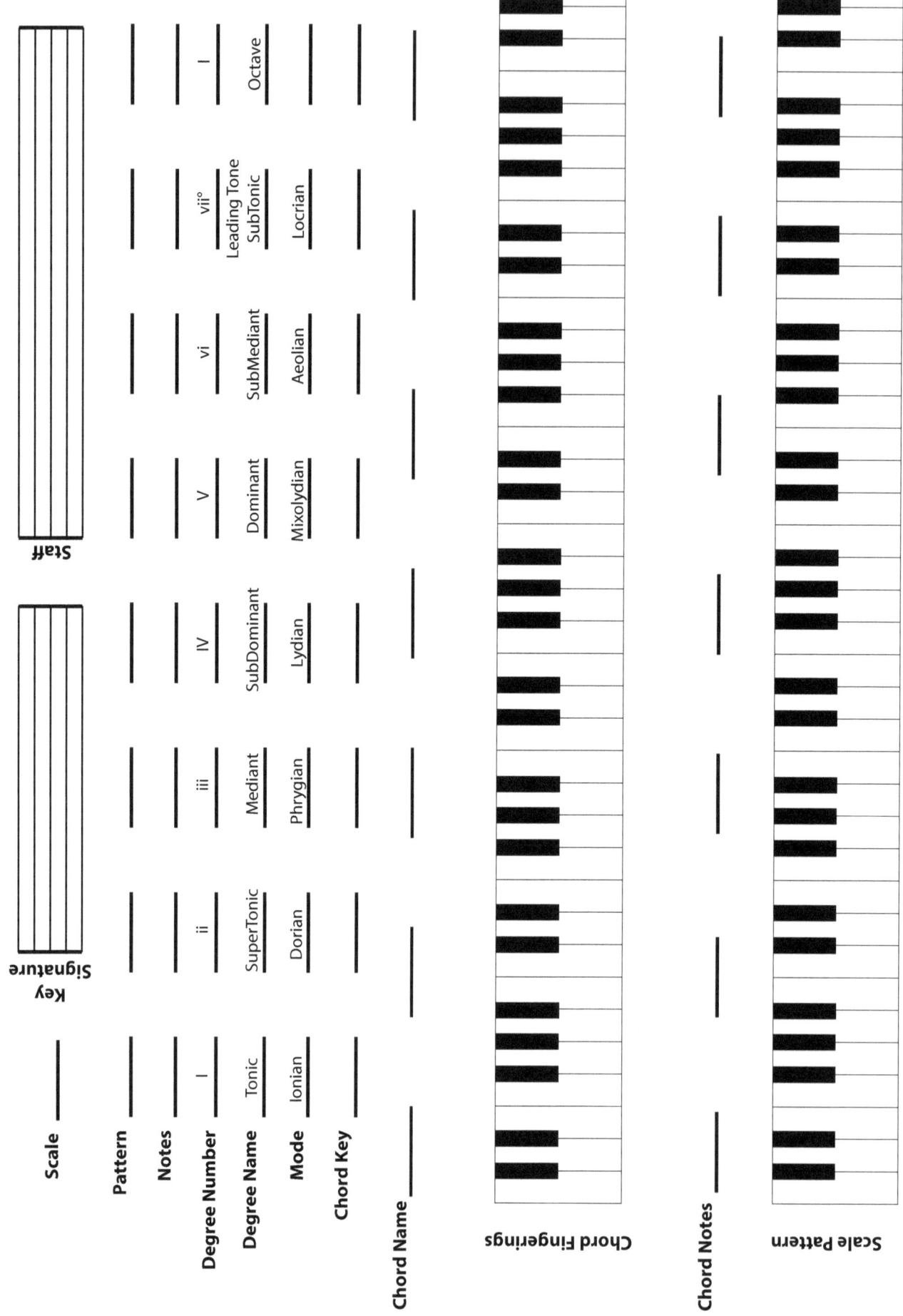

Key Signature

Staff

Scale ____

Pattern ____ ____ ____ ____ ____ ____ ____

Notes ____ ____ ____ ____ ____ ____ ____ ____

Degree Number I ii iii IV V vi vii° I

Degree Name Tonic SuperTonic Mediant SubDominant Dominant SubMediant Leading Tone / SubTonic Octave

Mode Ionian Dorian Phrygian Lydian Mixolydian Aeolian Locrian

Chord Key ____ ____ ____ ____ ____ ____ ____ ____

Chord Name ____

Chord Fingerings

Chord Notes ____ ____ ____ ____

Scale Pattern

192

Section 7: Reference Answer Key

Representative Solutions and Reference Answers

This Answer Key provides representative solutions and reference answers for the exercises in this book. For activities with multiple valid outcomes, such as scale and chord construction, one complete example is shown to demonstrate correct usage of each worksheet type. Exercises with fixed, limited answers, such as key signature identification and note or chord cross-reference, are presented in full.

Answer Key: Key Signature Memorization Worksheet

Major Key Signatures

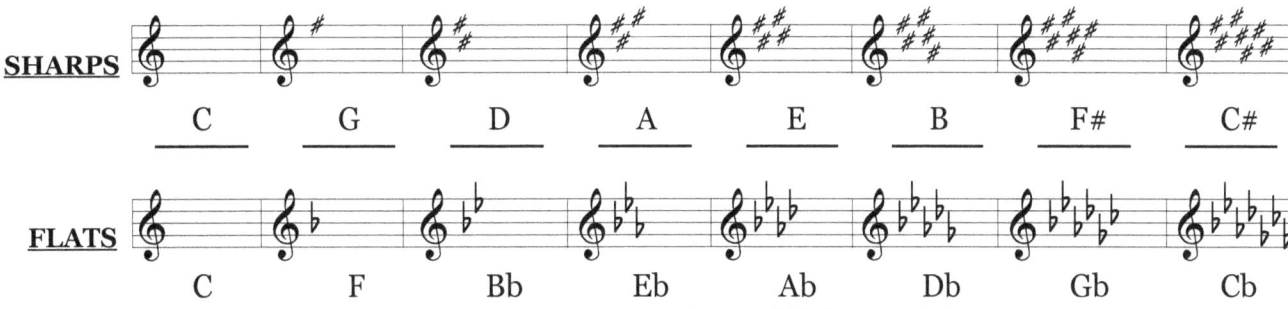

SHARPS   C   G   D   A   E   B   F#   C#

FLATS   C   F   Bb   Eb   Ab   Db   Gb   Cb

Relative Minor Key Signatures

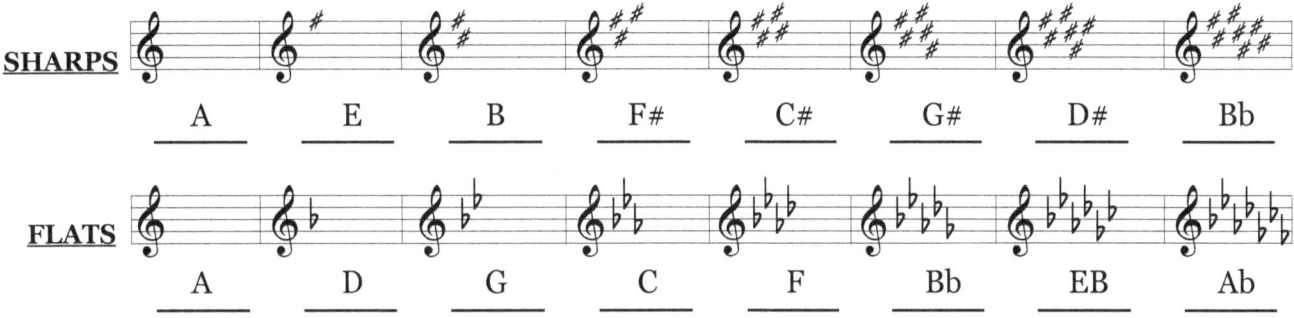

SHARPS   A   E   B   F#   C#   G#   D#   Bb

FLATS   A   D   G   C   F   Bb   EB   Ab

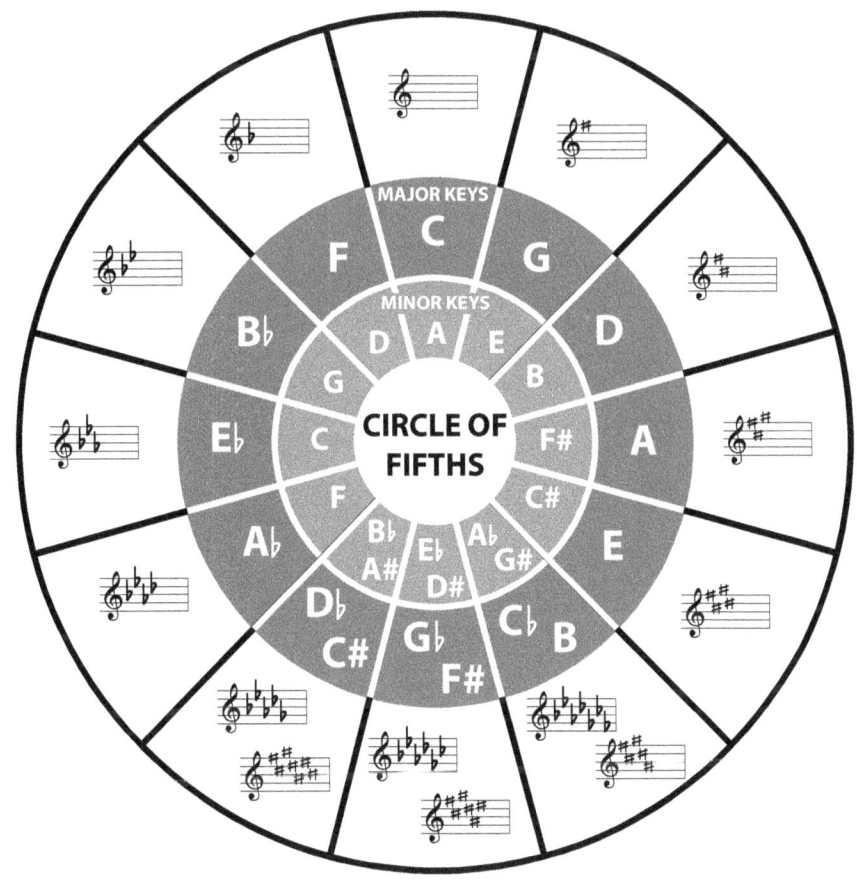

Write the number of sharps or flats
next to each Scale/Key

C	0	F	1b
G	1#	Bb	2b
D	2#	Eb	3b
A	3#	Ab	4b
E	4#	Db	5b
B	5#	Gb	6b
F#	6#	Cb	7b
C#	7#		

195

Key Signature Identification & Scale Practice

Key Signature   C

C	D	E	F	G	A	B
I	ii	iii	IV	V	vi	vii°

Key Signature   G

G	A	B	C	D	E	F#
I	ii	iii	IV	V	vi	vii°

Key Signature   D

D	E	F#	G	A	B	C#
I	ii	iii	IV	V	vi	vii°

Key Signature   A

A	B	C#	D	E	F#	G#
I	ii	iii	IV	V	vi	vii°

Key Signature   E

E	F#	G#	A	B	C#	D#
I	ii	iii	IV	V	vi	vii°

Key Signature   B

B	C#	D#	E	F#	G#	A#
I	ii	iii	IV	V	vi	vii°

Key Signature   F#

F#	G#	A#	B	C#	D#	E#
I	ii	iii	IV	V	vi	vii°

Key Signature   C#

C#	D#	E#	F#	G#	A#	B#
I	ii	iii	IV	V	vi	vii°

Answer Key (Flats)

Key Signature Identification & Scale Practice

Key Signature <u>C</u>

C	D	E	F	G	A	B
I	ii	iii	IV	V	vi	vii°

Key Signature <u>F</u>

F	G	A	Bb	C	D	E
I	ii	iii	IV	V	vi	vii°

Key Signature <u>Bb</u>

Bb	C	D	Eb	F	G	A
I	ii	iii	IV	V	vi	vii°

Key Signature <u>Eb</u>

Eb	F	G	Ab	Bb	C	D
I	ii	iii	IV	V	vi	vii°

Key Signature <u>Ab</u>

Ab	Bb	C	Db	Eb	F	G
I	ii	iii	IV	V	vi	vii°

Key Signature <u>Db</u>

Db	Eb	F	Gb	Ab	Bb	C
I	ii	iii	IV	V	vi	vii°

Key Signature <u>Gb</u>

Gb	Ab	Bb	Cb	Db	Eb	F
I	ii	iii	IV	V	vi	vii°

Key Signature <u>Cb</u>

Cb	Db	Eb	Fb	Gb	Ab	Bb
I	ii	iii	IV	V	vi	vii°

Answer Key (Sharps)

Key Signature Identification & Diatonic Chord Practice

Key Signature __C__

C	Dm	Em	F	G	Am	Bdim
I	ii	iii	IV	V	vi	vii°

Key Signature __G__

G	Am	Bm	C	D	Em	F#dim
I	ii	iii	IV	V	vi	vii°

Key Signature __D__

D	Em	F#m	G	A	Bm	C#dim
I	ii	iii	IV	V	vi	vii°

Key Signature __A__

A	Bm	C#m	D	E	F#m	G#dim
I	ii	iii	IV	V	vi	vii°

Key Signature __E__

E	F#m	G#m	A	B	C#m	D#dim
I	ii	iii	IV	V	vi	vii°

Key Signature __B__

B	C#m	D#m	E	F#	G#m	A#dim
I	ii	iii	IV	V	vi	vii°

Key Signature __F#__

F#	G#m	A#m	B	C#	D#m	E#dim
I	ii	iii	IV	V	vi	vii°

Key Signature __C#__

C#	D#m	E#m	F#	G#	A#m	B#dim
I	ii	iii	IV	V	vi	vii°

Answer Key (Flats)

Key Signature Identification & Diatonic Chord Practice

Key Signature   C

C	Dm	Em	F	G	Am	Bdim
I	**ii**	**iii**	**IV**	**V**	**vi**	**vii°**

Key Signature   F

F	Gm	Am	Bb	C	Dm	Edim
I	**ii**	**iii**	**IV**	**V**	**vi**	**vii°**

Key Signature   Bb

Bb	Cm	Dm	Eb	F	Gm	Adim
I	**ii**	**iii**	**IV**	**V**	**vi**	**vii°**

Key Signature   Eb

Eb	Fm	Gm	Ab	Bb	Cm	Ddim
I	**ii**	**iii**	**IV**	**V**	**vi**	**vii°**

Key Signature   Ab

Ab	Bbm	Cm	Db	Eb	Fm	Gdim
I	**ii**	**iii**	**IV**	**V**	**vi**	**vii°**

Key Signature   Db

Db	Ebm	Fm	Gb	Ab	Bbm	Cdim
I	**ii**	**iii**	**IV**	**V**	**vi**	**vii°**

Key Signature   Gb

Gb	Abm	Bbm	Cb	Db	Ebm	Fdim
I	**ii**	**iii**	**IV**	**V**	**vi**	**vii°**

Key Signature   Cb

Cb	Dbm	Ebm	Fb	Gb	Abm	Bbdim
I	**ii**	**iii**	**IV**	**V**	**vi**	**vii°**

Scale/Chord Worksheet

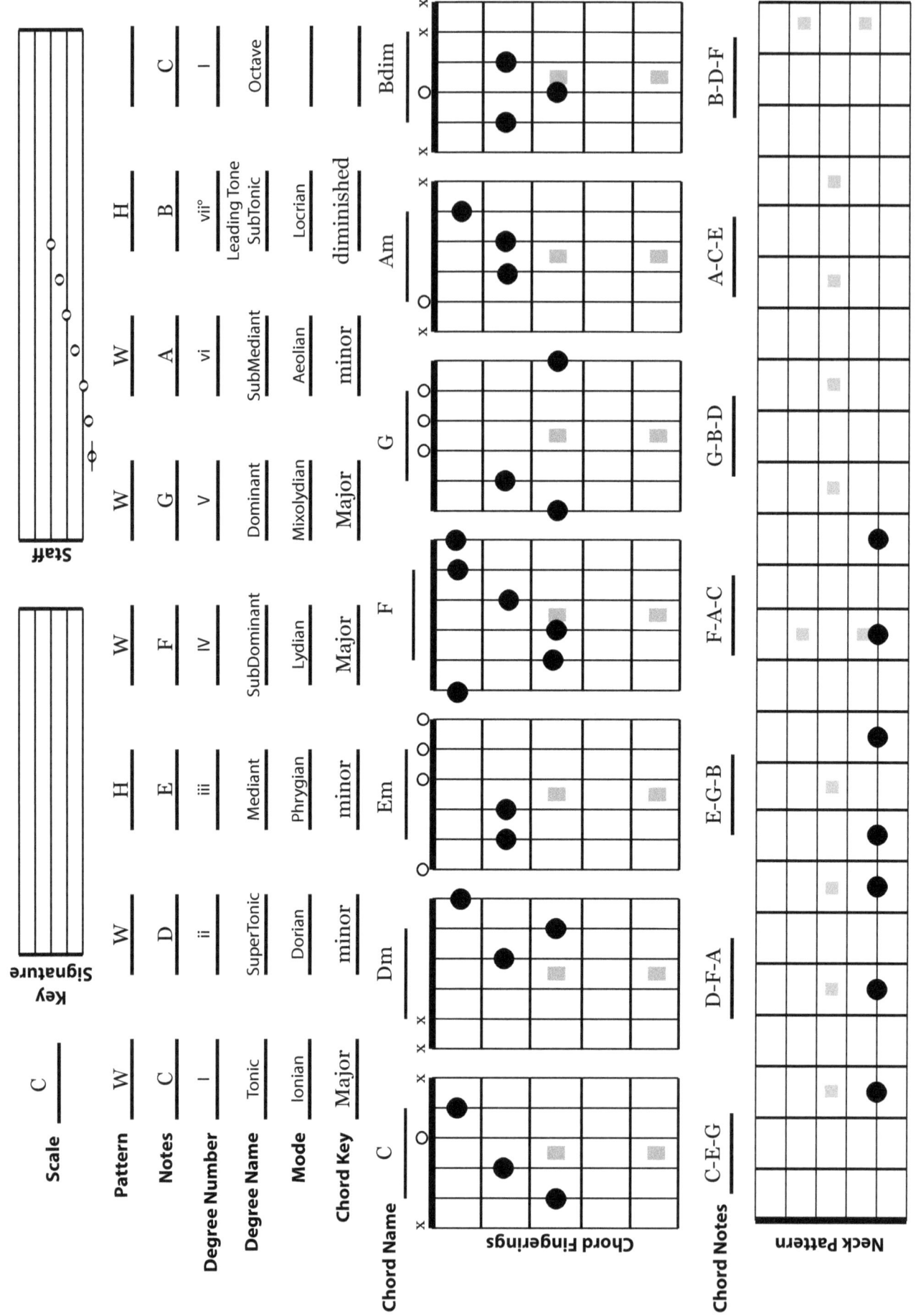

Scale/Chord Worksheet

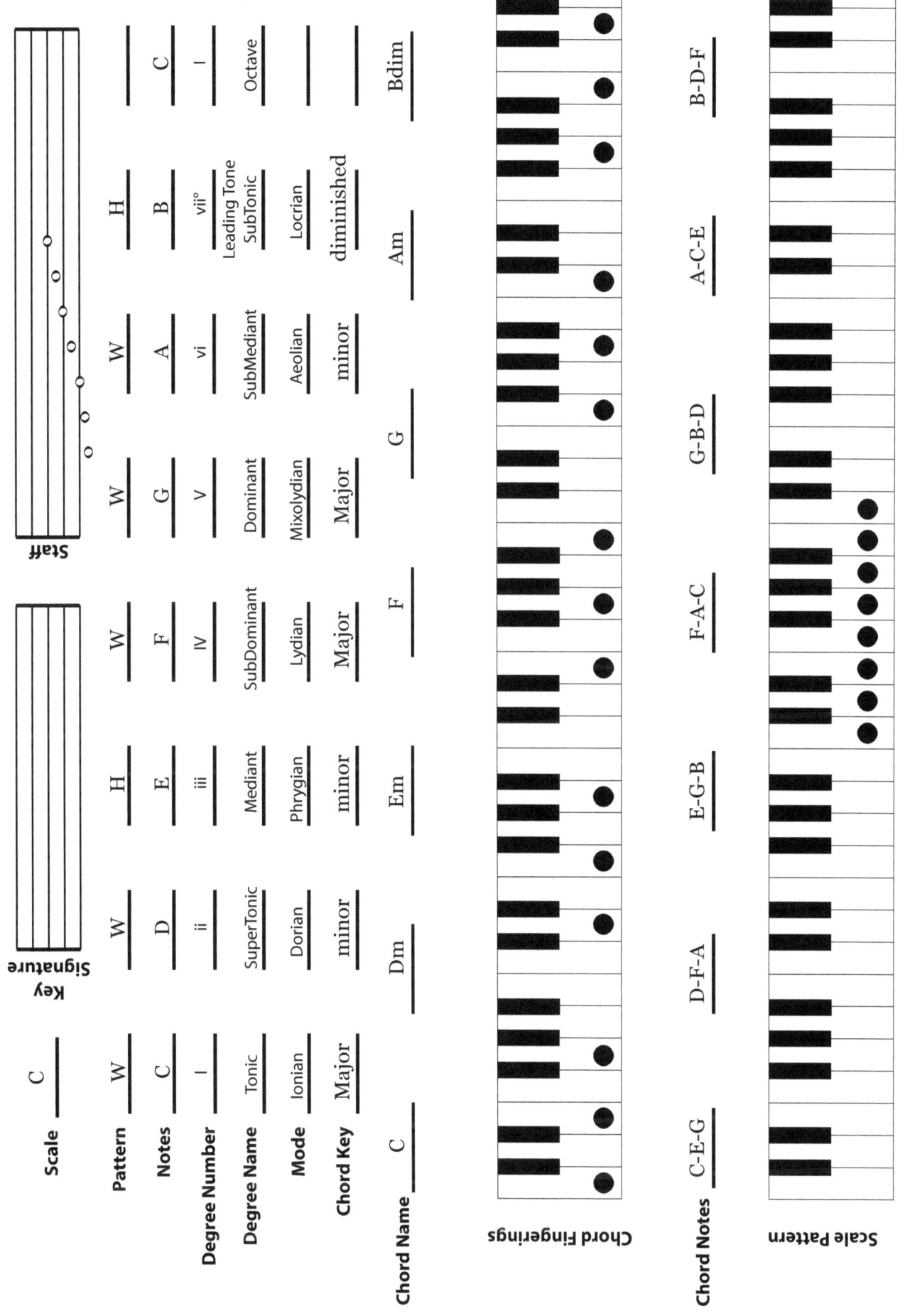

ABOUT THE PUBLISHER

3T Publishing is an independent publishing imprint focused on creating clear, practical learning resources for self-directed study.

Our publications emphasize structure, clarity, and usability, supporting learners as they apply concepts through focused practice and repetition.

Learn more at:
3TPublishing.com

ABOUT THE AUTHOR

Rick Alexander is an independent author and publisher focused on developing structured, application-based learning materials. Through 3T Publishing, his work supports self-directed learners by presenting foundational concepts in a clear, organized, and practical format.